Research on Urban Teacher Learning

Examining Contextual Factors Over Time

edited by

Andrea J. Stairs
University of Southern Maine

and

Kelly A. Donnell
Roger Williams University

Information Age Publishing, Inc.
Charlotte, North Carolina • www.infoagepub.com

Library of Congress Cataloging-in-Publication Data

Research on urban teaching learning examining contextual factors over time / edited by Andrea J. Stairs and Kelly A. Donnell.
   p. cm.
  Includes bibliographical references.
  ISBN 978-1-60752-401-4 (pbk.) — ISBN 978-1-60752-402-1 (hardcover) — ISBN 978-1-60752-403-8 (e-book)
  1. Education, Urban—United States—Research. 2. Teachers—Training of—United States. 3. Urban schools—United States. I. Stairs, Andrea J. II. Donnell, Kelly A.
  LC5119.8.R47 2010
  370.9173'2—dc22

                                     2009048051

Printed in the United States of America

Research on
Urban Teacher Learning

Examining Contextual Factors Over Time

DEDICATION

We dedicate this book to our parents,
Robert and Shirley Stairs,
and Charles and Zoe Donnell.

CONTENTS

PART III:
IMPACT OF POLICY ON URBAN TEACHER LEARNING

FOREWORD

J. Amos Hatch
University of Tennessee

I am happy to submit this Foreword to *Research on Urban Teacher Learning*. It brings together three dimensions of scholarly work that are very important to how I think about my professional responsibilities: urban teaching, teacher preparation, and qualitative research. A major portion of my life has been spent in urban schools. I attended urban elementary, middle, and high schools; I taught in urban elementary schools for the first 13 years of my professional life; and I have worked for several years preparing future teachers to work in urban settings. I believe urban teaching is difficult work that is undervalued and understudied. I like this collection because it brings the special contexts of learning to teach in urban schools into the foreground, making the unique circumstances that characterize urban teaching an integral part of the story of learning to teach.

It seems to me that research, theorizing, and policy related to teacher preparation are at a crossroads. Neoliberal forces pushing for the privatization of teacher licensure via a variety of alternative certification routes threaten traditional university-based teacher education programs in ways not seen in the past. While some of these alternatives may offer effective ways to get individuals ready to teach, many (especially those designed to prepare urban teachers) ignore research, theory, and policy that support

Research on Urban Teacher Learning: Examining Contextual Factors Over Time
pp. ix–x

rigorous pedagogical preparation as part of sound teacher education practices. Books like *Research on Urban Teacher Learning* provide much needed substance to arguments that favor teacher programs with depth and substance, especially programs designed specifically for future urban teachers.

When I began doing qualitative research in the middle 1980s, one of the arguments for accepting this "new" methodological approach as legitimate science was that by collecting a variety of qualitative studies, a rich and nuanced picture of particular educational phenomena could be painted. That rationale seems to have been lost along the way; while of late, meta-analyses of statistical studies have come to the fore. Another thing I like about this book is its portrayal of learning to teach in urban settings as a kind of tapestry that turns out to be much more than a sum of its parts. In the spirit of the best qualitative research, readers are taken into the real worlds of urban teaching and teacher preparation in ways that are simply impossible to duplicate in quantitative analyses, no matter how complex. More books of this type are needed, books that focus a variety of perspectives on a particular educational phenomenon.

In sum, this edited collection is a welcome addition to the scholarship on urban schooling, teacher education, and qualitative research. I congratulate the authors and editors for providing readers with an incisive look into the complexities of urban teacher preparation. The text provides value in and of itself. In addition, it generates a model of the kind of academic work that is desperately needed in a climate that valorizes simplistic solutions based on narrow research questions and questionable policy. In order to get better at preparing urban teachers, the field needs more scholarship like this.

ACKNOWLEDGMENTS

We would like to thank our contributing authors for their hard work on this book and their commitment to urban education. We also would like to thank our colleagues and our publisher, Mr. George Johnson, for their support and encouragement.

PART I

THEORIES OF URBAN TEACHER LEARNING

CHAPTER 1

WHY RESEARCH ON URBAN TEACHER LEARNING MATTERS

An Introduction

Andrea J. Stairs and Kelly A. Donnell

Research suggests that America's urban schools are facing serious challenges recruiting and, especially, retaining teachers (Ingersoll, 2002; Quartz et al., 2008). Advancing our understanding of how people learn to teach in the urban context, particularly with regard to how the urban context enables or constrains teacher learning, is critical in addressing the "revolving door" phenomenon (Ingersoll, 2001) in urban schools and in supporting both teacher and student learning.

A variety of factors affect the recruitment of urban teachers. For example, preservice teachers who self-select teacher education are predominantly White, middle-class women who want to teach in familiar school contexts. It has proven difficult to recruit students of color to teacher education, often for financial reasons. Additionally, bureaucratic hiring processes of urban school districts dissuade quality candidates who accept jobs in districts that hire earlier. Ingersoll (2002), though, cites the problem as one not of recruitment but retention. He has argued that "high

Research on Urban Teacher Learning: Examining Contextual Factors Over Time
pp. 3–9
Copyright © 2010 by Information Age Publishing
All rights of reproduction in any form reserved.

rates of teacher turnover are problematic not only because they may indicate underlying problems in how well schools are functioning but also because, in and of themselves, they can disrupt the quality of school cohesion and performance" (p. 19). With close to 40% of beginning teachers leaving the profession after five years, and urban and high poverty teachers leaving at a greater rate than suburban or rural teachers (Ingersoll, 2002), it is no wonder that urban schools are underperforming.

As Hirsch and Emerick (2007) have noted, "Teacher working conditions are student learning conditions" (p. 1). Research has demonstrated that addressing school conditions and contexts is vital to improving teacher retention and student learning. At least six factors appear critical in prompting teachers to leave their urban teaching jobs: (a) a lack of resources, support, and recognition from the school administration, (b) a lack of teacher influence over school and classroom decision-making, (c) too many intrusions on classroom teaching time, (d) inadequate time to prepare, (e) poor salaries, and (f) student discipline problems (Ingersoll, 2001). Similarly, in their reports to individual states on working conditions within their districts, Hirsch and Emerick (2007) have identified professional development, teacher empowerment, adequate time, appropriate facilities and resources, and effective leadership as working conditions that impact teacher retention and student learning.

Understanding the conditions and contexts that affect teacher retention is critical. Furthermore, it is also vital to determine what and how teachers learn about teaching within these conditions and contexts. Recently, teacher learning over time has been cited as a necessary research focus to address gaps in the research literature (Cochran-Smith & Zeichner, 2005), but few scholars have examined the contexts and conditions associated with learning across time, particularly in underserved, urban communities.[1] Many of the underlying interpretations and ideas that guide programs and initiatives intended to support teacher learning are tacit and underexamined (Cochran-Smith & Lytle, 1999). What Feiman-Nemser and Remillard (1996) noted more than a decade ago still remains true today:

> We do not have well-developed theories of learning to teach and the phrase itself covers many conceptual complexities. What does learning teaching entail? How is teacher learning similar to and different from other learning? What sort of teaching is being learned? What sort of teaching do we hope teachers will learn? As these questions imply, learning to teach raises both descriptive and normative issues that must be addressed in any serious effort to build a model of learning to teach. (p. 63)

Nonetheless, policymakers have responded to the crisis in education and in urban education, in particular, by calling for outcomes-based teacher education that focuses on prescriptive techniques and competencies that work to delimit rather than expand the scope of what teaching and learning to teach encompass (Weiner, 2002; Zeichner, 1999). Given the urgent state of urban education, we especially need research and practice that recognize and utilize complexity in teaching as a way to shed "more rather than less light" on the situation (Florio-Ruane, 2002). Despite its potentially messy nature, a willingness to explore the complexity of learning to teach helps us develop more accurate and more useful understandings. Valenzuela (2002) comes to a similar conclusion: "A complex view of teaching and learning is not only desirable but necessary given the conditions created by a predominantly Anglo teaching force in increasingly poor and minority inner-city schools throughout our nation" (p. 235). She reminds us that the study of urban teaching, in particular, must embrace multiple perspectives and resist subtractive tendencies.

Cohen, Raudenbush, and Loewenberg Ball (2002) have recently noted the traditional view within policy reform assumes that control over the flow of conventional resources such as money, materials, and facilities will directly influence pupil learning outcomes. The authors question this assumption and argue that, rather than having direct effects on pupil learning, the effects of resources are dependent on their use by educators:

> Researchers report that schools and teachers with the same resources do different things, with different results for students' learning. Resources are not self-enacting, and differences in their effects depend on differences in their use. That makes school improvement a difficult enterprise, one that depends as much on what is done with resources as what resources are available. (Cohen, et al., 2002, p. 80, 81)

Many "resources" that are critical to teacher and student learning are not conventional resources—assignment of appropriate responsibilities and a collegial community, for example. These are not generally viewed as resources that require thoughtful planning and funding. Nor are these kinds of conditions "the sort of resources that could be captured well in measures of teachers' formal qualifications, their schools' expenditures, or other such things" (Cohen et al., 2002, p. 83). Cohen et al.'s argument suggests greater attention must be paid to the conditions of teachers' work and learning experiences as valuable resources.

Much of the current literature frames teacher learning within a cognitive psychological perspective where learning is an active, constructive process that is contextually situated (Putnam & Borko, 2000). As teachers learn and experience new knowledge, such as pedagogical content knowledge, that knowledge and learning must be situated in the contexts in which they will be used. The complexity and unpredictable nature of learning to teach require research and teacher education that is flexible, sustained over time, and open-ended. In the research literature to this point, the challenges of urban teacher recruitment and retention have been addressed, but the connection has not been sufficiently made between the retention literature and what, why, and how teachers learn to teach in urban schools. The purpose of this book is to trouble the retention literature and illuminate the issue by examining research studies focused on urban teacher learning within, around, and beyond the conditions and contexts of urban schools.

Some scholars are publishing relevant books that consider promising recruitment and retention practices to ensure that urban students have qualified, competent, professional teachers (e.g., Howey, Post, & Zimpher, 2006; Peterman, 2008; Solomon & Sekayi, 2007). As scholars committed to understanding the urban context and urban teacher learning, we have gained much from these accounts, and we believe these works make significant contributions to theory and practice. However, these publications primarily focus on stories from the field and lessons learned—accounts that may derive from systematically collected and analyzed empirical evidence supporting these practices, but that often omit research methodologies. We contend that in this age of accountability urban scholars must be publishing articles and books that put research at the center of discussions of the preparation and professional lives of urban teachers in order to have a voice in the policy arena. Of teacher education research, Wilson, Floden, and Ferrini-Mundy (2002) have argued the following:

> To move our collective understanding forward, and to give those outside our field reasons to accept our claims, our research reports—in journals, reports, or books—need to devote more space to descriptions of research design, as well as data collection and analysis, so that the basis for our conclusions is open to scrutiny. (p. 201)

We believe this book addresses the call for more systematic and transparent research practices not often evident in similar publications.

In the chapters that follow, the current gap in the literature is addressed as the reader explores a range of evidence-based analyses focused on the role of contextual factors on urban teacher learning. The first section of the book, Part I: Theories of Teacher Learning, introduces the reader to the conceptual and empirical literature on urban teacher learning. Dunn, Donnell, and Stairs organize the abundance of research in chapter 2 into four subsections: the current state of urban teacher recruitment and retention; the theories and concepts of learning to teach; the goals and outcomes of preservice teacher education programs; and the multiple avenues to teacher preparation, including traditional, alternative certification, multicultural/urban, and professional development schools.

Part II: Research on Urban Teacher Learning shares eight research studies that examine how, what, and why urban teachers learn in the form of rich longitudinal studies. Chapter 3 begins this section with an urban teacher's voice, a true emic perspective from an insider who acknowledges the strengths and weaknesses of urban teacher preparation on teacher learning. Here, Dunn reports on a five-year self-study of her progression through an urban teacher preparation program to teaching high school in a large, urban school district in the southeastern United States.

Chapters 4 through 7 present four different avenues to learning about and becoming prepared for urban teaching. In chapter 4, Stairs reports on a 5-year qualitative study of four White, middle-class urban high school teachers prepared in the same northeastern teacher education program in an urban professional development school. In Chapter 5, Tricarico and Yendol-Hoppey's year-long phenomenological study focuses on two alternatively licensed first-year teachers in urban, high-poverty elementary schools in the southeastern United States. In chapter 6, Ross, Dodman, and Vescio compare elementary teachers who completed a high-needs internship in an urban area with those who completed the same southeastern teacher education program but completed a traditional internship in a 3-year survey and interview study. Finally, in chapter 7, Mueller, Wineski, and File report on a year-long qualitative study of eight first- and second-year early childhood teachers in a midwestern, urban school district who were prepared in an urban-focused early childhood teacher education program.

In chapters 8 through 10, researchers explore the tensions that result when contextual factors work against implementation of pedagogy and curriculum in urban schools. In chapter 8, Meller's two-year qualitative case study focuses on a White, middle-class woman as she implemented a critical literacy curriculum in a first-grade urban classroom during preservice and inservice teaching. In chapter 9, Pardo reports on a year-long, ethnographic case study of a second-year urban teacher in a fourth-grade classroom struggling to enact meaningful writing pedagogies in the face of test pressure. Chapter 10, Donnell's grounded theory study, concludes Part II with a theoretical framework for the role of contextual factors in learning about urban teaching based on a longitudinal, qualitative study of 26 teachers as they move from two different preparation programs into their first years of teaching.

The book concludes with two chapters in Part III: Impact of Policy on Urban Teacher Learning. In chapter 11, Friedman and Daniello analyze the ways federal, state, and local policies affect urban teacher learning and highlight the role of urban teacher professionalism in accommodating and compensating for the lapses of politics, policy, and pedagogy. In chapter 12, Donnell and Stairs look across all the chapters and discuss the synergistic relationship between urban teacher learning and context.

What makes this collection powerful is not only that it moves research front and center in discussions of urban teacher learning, but also that it recognizes the importance of learning over time. Longitudinal studies, either quantitative or qualitative, are lacking in teacher education research (Cochran-Smith & Zeichner, 2005). It is our hope that this collection of qualitative, longitudinal studies will contribute to the research literature in meaningful ways and allow for a clearer understanding of how urban schools' contexts and conditions enable and constrain teacher learning over time.

NOTE

1.   Some scholars who have examined the influence of urban contexts and conditions on teacher learning across time include Costigan (2008), Donnell (2007), Hagiwara and Way (2009), Pardo (2006), and Roth, Tobin, Carambo, and Dalland (2004).

REFERENCES

Cochran-Smith, M., & Lytle, S. L. (1999). Relationships of knowledge and practice: Teacher learning in communities. In A. Iran-Nejad & C. Pearson (Eds.), *Review of research in education* (Vol. 24, pp. 249-306). Washington, DC: American Educational Research Association.

Cochran-Smith, M., & Zeichner, K. M. (Eds.). (2005). *Studying teacher education: The report of the AERA Panel on Research and Teacher Education*. Washington, DC: American Educational Research Association and Lawrence Erlbaum Associates.

Cohen, D., Raudenbush, S., & Loewenberg Ball, D. (2002). Resources, instruction, and research. In F. Mosteller & R. Boruch (Eds.), *Evidence matters: Randomized trials in education research* (pp. 80-119). Washington, DC: Brookings Institute Press.

Costigan, A. T. (2008). Canaries in the coal mine: Urban rookies learning to teach language arts in "high priorty" schools. *Teacher Education Quarterly, 35*(2), 85-103.

Donnell, K. (2007). Getting to we: Developing a transformative urban teaching practice. *Urban Education, 42*(3), 223-249.

Feiman-Nemser, S., & Remillard, J. (1996). Perspectives on learning to teach. In F. B. Murray (Ed.), *The teacher educator's handbook: Building a knowledge base for the preparation of teachers* (pp. 63-91). San Francisco, CA: Jossey-Bass.

Florio-Ruane, S. (2002). More light: An argument for complexity in studies of teaching and teacher education. *Journal of Teacher Education, 53*(3), 205-215.

Hagiwara, S., & Wray, S. (2009). Transformation in reverse: Naive assumptions of an urban educator. *Education and Urban Society, 41*(3), 338-363.

Hirsch, E., & Emerick, S. (2007). *Teacher working conditions are student learning conditions: A report on the 2006 North Carolina Working Conditions Survey.* Retrieved from www.teachingquality.org

Howey, K. R., Post, L. M., & Zimpher, N. L. (Eds.). (2006). *Recruiting, preparing, and retaining teachers for urban schools.* Washington, DC: American Association of Colleges for Teacher Education.

Ingersoll, R. M. (2001). Teacher turnover and teacher shortages: An organizational analysis. *American Educational Research Journal, 38*(3), 499-534.

Ingersoll, R. M. (2002). The teacher shortage: A case of wrong diagnosis and wrong prescription. *NASSP Bulletin, 86*(631), 16-31.

Pardo, L. (2006). The role of context in learning to teach writing: What teacher educators need to know to support beginning urban teachers. *Journal of Teacher Education, 57*(4), 378-394.

Peterman, F. P. (Ed.). (2008). *Partnering to prepare urban teachers: A call to activism.* New York: Peter Lang.

Putnam, R. T., & Borko, H. (2000). What do new views of knowledge and thinking have to say about research on teacher learning? *Educational Researcher, 29*(1), 4-15.

Quartz, K. H., Thomas, A., Anderson, L., Masyn, K., Lyons, K. B., & Olsen, B. (2008). Careers in motion: A longitudinal retention study of role changing among early-career urban educators. *Teachers College Record, 110*(1), 218-250.

Roth, W. -M., Tobin, K., Carambo, C., & Dalland, C. (2004). Coteaching: Creating resources for learning and learning to teach chemistry in urban high schools. *Journal of Research in Science Teaching, 41*(9), 882-904.

Solomon, R. P., & Sekayi, D. N. R. (Eds.). (2007). *Urban teacher education and teaching: Innovative practices for diversity and social justice.* Mahwah, NJ: Erlbaum.

Valenzuela, A. (2002). Reflections on the subtractive underpinnings of education research and policy. *Journal of Teacher Education, 53*(3), 235-241.

Weiner, L. (2002). Book reviews. *Educational Researcher, 31*(9), 29-33.

Wilson, S. M., Floden, R. E., & Ferrini-Mundy, J. (2002). Teacher preparation research: An insider's view from the outside. *Journal of Teacher Education, 53*(3), 190-204.

Zeichner, K. M. (1999). The new scholarship in teacher education. *Educational Leadership, 28*(9), 4-15.

CHAPTER 2

URBAN TEACHER LEARNING

A Review of Related Literature

Alyssa Hadley Dunn, Kelly A. Donnell, and Andrea J. Stairs

Ask any teacher her how he or she was prepared to teach, and anticipate a multitude of responses. Teachers may say they learned to teach by watching others, either as students or as student teachers. Others may cite a preservice teacher preparation program, a field experience, or even a particular course that shaped their philosophy. Their experiences could range from traditional preparation to alternative certification to programs specifically targeted to a particular setting, such as multicultural or urban schools.

The variety of responses should come as no surprise because the academic literature on learning how to teach is as wide-ranging. Some scholars believe the process of learning how to teach starts as early as one's own childhood experiences; others believe it is a lifelong process of transformation (Cochran-Smith, 1999). Examining the existing research on teacher learning is particularly vital when considering how to prepare teachers for urban environments. Indeed, these programs must encompass the best components of all aspects of learning to teach, in addition to

Research on Urban Teacher Learning: Examining Contextual Factors Over Time
pp. 11–25
Copyright © 2010 by Information Age Publishing

instilling in future teachers the knowledge and desire to work in urban schools.

This chapter is organized so that readers might come to a better understanding of the broad range of scholarship on teacher learning. First, we must gauge the current state of the teaching force to contextualize the environment into which new teachers are entering. Who is teaching in our schools now? How are they recruited and retained? This section will present empirical evidence that contradicts the supposed teacher shortage and counters that enough teachers are being prepared, but they are not staying in the profession or are not choosing to be employed in urban settings.

Then, we turn our attention to *how* teachers are being prepared. The second section of this chapter deals with the theories and concepts of learning how to teach. That is, how do preservice teachers understand their new profession, and how do they learn what it means to be a teacher? Because researchers define "learning to teach" in diverse forms, the section will deal primarily with theoretical research rather than empirical.

Empirical research will be foregrounded in the next section on the goals and outcomes of preservice teacher education programs, one way in which "learning to teach" occurs. Are the programs intended to balance knowledge of content and pedagogy? Importantly, do the goals and outcomes of preservice programs align?

Finally, the fourth section of the chapter will narrow the focus of teacher learning even further and examine the different avenues to teacher preparation. Traditional preparation, alternative certification, programs focused on multicultural and urban communities, and school-university partnerships will all be discussed. This extensive range of literature should help situate this text on urban teacher learning within the broader context of scholarship on teacher education.

CURRENT STATE OF THE TEACHING FORCE[1]

According to the National Center for Education Statistics (2005), 2.2 million teachers will be needed in the next ten years, and the majority of those teachers will be needed in urban areas that are traditionally hard to staff. This perennial "teacher shortage" is better defined as one of teacher misdistribution, since the greatest number and the most highly qualified teachers are hired in suburban, well-paying districts, while urban centers are left behind (Ingersoll, 2002). In fact, in the latest report of The National Center of Education Statistics (2005), researchers stated that the U.S. *would* have enough teachers to staff public schools in 2014. However, these teachers would not be evenly distributed into the areas that need them most. Some areas in the northwest, northeast, and mid-Atlantic, in fact, have surpluses of teachers; wealthy areas within these states have even more of a surplus (Darling-Hammond, 2001). The National Teacher Recruitment Clearinghouse (2003) agreed that "the teacher shortage problem does not affect all areas equally" (p. 1) and claimed that teacher shortages are most acute in urban and rural areas; in border states with immigration increases; and in specific subject areas like math, science, bilingual education, and special education.

What is the cause of this shortage then? In 1999, Merrow conducted a television special for the Public Broadcasting System (PBS) entitled, "The Teacher Shortage: False Alarm?" and, like Ingersoll (2002, 2003), concluded that experts were "diagnosing the problem incorrectly and then proposing inappropriate cures." Merrow believed that no recruitment strategies or "quick fixes" would work unless the country addressed the bigger problem of "mediocrity at all levels of education." However, the general public remained misinformed about the realities of the teacher shortage, perhaps because of government and media attention on the problem.

In fact, the teacher shortage in the United States today can be better described as one of both teacher turnover and teacher misdistribution (Ingersoll, 2002; National Commission on Teaching and America's Future, 2002). Because urban students need the most support and guidance from teachers, the teacher shortage is thus exacerbated when these students receive unqualified and fewer teachers. Additionally, many teachers in urban districts tend to leave within their first 3 years of teaching; within 5 years, teacher attrition was close to 40% thus turning schools into "revolving doors" (Ingersoll, 1999; 2002).

The National Commission on Teaching and America's Future (NCTAF) contended that the U.S. appeared to have teacher shortages because there was a lack of teachers willing to work in inner-cities and under poor conditions, the same type of schools that get the most national attention because of President Bush's No Child Left Behind (NCLB) legislation in 2001. NCLB has had a tremendous impact on the teacher shortage problem because, as one of many tenets of the law, public schools are required to have "highly qualified" teachers in every classroom. For typically hard-to-staff schools, this is a large burden because they already have difficulty recruiting *any* teachers. Thus, the field of teacher education must reform itself and better prepare its teachers for urban schools instead of focusing on recruiting a new work force.

CONCEPTS OF LEARNING HOW TO TEACH

Conceptualizations of learning how to teach form the theoretical basis for urban teacher learning. How do teachers learn what it means to be a teacher? How do their own beliefs inform their practice? And how do they understand their role in the classroom? One method in which teachers learn, their preservice teacher education programs, will be discussed in detail in the next section; but as this is only *one* framework in which teachers learn (Feiman-Nemser & Remillard, 1996), other contexts for learning formation will be focused on here. These other contexts can be categorized as knowledge acquisition; developments of attitudes and beliefs; and inquiry (Donnell, 2004).

In general, the scholarship concurs that teachers learn by undergoing some form of change or growth (Kagan, 1992; Richardson & Placier, 2001). How teachers *acquire* this change and *utilize* this growth is where the literature diverges. The literature on learning to teach encompasses how teachers change, why they change, and what is or could be the focus of the change. The first impetus for this change is the acquisition of both formal and practical knowledge. During teacher preparation, students are exposed to formal and academic concepts about education, including educational policies, the psychology of teaching and learning, and history of schooling. Teachers then apply this formal knowledge through their practice (Carter, 1990; Wideen et al., 1998).

Complimentary to formal academic knowledge is the acquisition of practical knowledge. Though the two do not have to be dichotomous, some researchers believe that practical knowledge should be highlighted. Borko and Putnam's (1996) model for understanding learning to teach as a construct of pedagogy, content, and content pedagogy is an informative and skilled melding of the two theories. In this framework, the scholars are able to outline the importance of what teachers know about their subject, what they know about teaching, and what they know about how to teach their subject.

Another dimension of learning to teach is the development of beliefs and attitudes about teaching and a teacher's role. Because teaching is a "deeply personal activity," new teachers must first examine their own background and schooling experiences before conceptualizing their new place in the classroom hierarchy (Wideen, Mayer-Smith, & Moon, 1998, p. 161). Indeed, some educational psychologists, such as Pajares (1992), believe that a teacher's beliefs are the best predictor of his/her actions in the classroom. However, though a teacher's beliefs do not always translate into classroom practice, it is also imperative that beginning teachers not overlook the ways in which their prior beliefs and attitudes inform their practice. For example, how do their views about student behavior and student participation translate into how they, as teachers, manage their classrooms?

Examining attitudes is closely linked to inquiring and reflecting on teaching. Reflection can lead to a form of teacher research, action research, collaborative inquiry, or inquiry as stance (Cochran-Smith & Lytle, 1999). Teaching as inquiry is a construct that allows change to occur over a teacher's career; one is constantly learning and continuously forming ideas about how to improve practice. Because this model enables teachers to have voice in how they respond to challenges, it is a particularly useful model for preparing teachers to work in large, multicultural, or urban communities in which top-down bureaucracy can often seem stifling (Auger & Wideman, 2000).

GOALS AND OUTCOMES OF PRESERVICE TEACHER EDUCATION PROGRAMS

Preservice teachers also learn through experience. While it should not be assumed that preservice teachers learn all they need to know about teaching from being in a school setting, when implemented correctly and paired with a model for reflection and socialization, this model offers some unique ways to learn about the profession (Feiman-Nemser & Buchmann, 1991; Britzman, 1991). Cochran-Smith & Lytle (1999) refer to this combination of experience and reflection as "knowledge-in-practice;" for many teacher education programs, the use of "knowledge-in-practice" is a primary goal.

Some goals of teacher education have been established by professional organizations. The National Council for the Accreditation of Teacher Education (NCATE) believes that effective teacher education programs are run by qualified, competent faculty; promote university and school partnerships; focus on specific outcomes for teacher candidates and their pupils; and promote diversity (2002). If teacher education programs meet these standards, NCATE accredits the program. The Interstate New Teacher Assessment and Support Consortium (INTASC) is also committed to increasing preservice teachers' knowledge around 10 standards, including integrating content and pedagogical knowledge; working with diverse learners; varying assessments and instructional strategies; reflecting on practice; and collaborating with the school community (INTASC, 1992).

Research outlines similar goals for preservice teacher education. Reynolds (1992) synthesized these goals: develop in teachers a focus on subject matter; model teaching strategies; increase pedagogical content knowledge; encourage teachers to consider school culture when teaching; and enhance reflective practice. However, because of the many different approaches to teacher education and to evaluation of those programs, the research literature is difficult to synthesize and remains fragmented. Yet, research points to a positive trend toward a more reflective approach to teacher education; schools are moving away from formal, propositional knowledge as the only goal and moving toward understanding teacher learning on a continuum across the professional lifespan. Because researching goals of teacher education is a complicated maneuver, highlighting outcomes of teacher education is also problematic.

Teacher education programs that remain attached to the outdated methods of using behavioristic training models are consistently discovered to be weak interventions (Wideen, Mayer-Smith, & Moon, 1998). While some research on learning to teach has been applied by adding individual courses to licensure programs, overall, the changes in these prescriptive programs have been minimal. Comprehensive reviews by Wideen, Mayer-Smith, and Moon (1998) and Wilson, Floden, and Ferrini-Mundy (2001) both concluded that research is lacking about what preservice teachers actually learn in their preservice programs. Zeichner and Conklin (2005) stated that a full understanding of how teacher education programs' goals and outcomes match is necessary, but is not possible without a concrete focus on "the characteristics teachers bring to their programs, the complexities of programs as they are actually implemented, what students learn in their programs, and the schools in which they teach" (p. 697). Overall, major reforms to teacher education have not been implemented, despite research showing their necessity, and because the effectiveness of teacher education programs in supporting learning to teach is regarded as inconclusive at best, most programs are considered out of touch with the needs of teachers as learners.

In recent years, however, programs that focus on a particular avenue of learning to teach have been increasing in popularity and success. Below, these multiple avenues to teacher preparation, including alternative certification, urban and multiculturally-focused programs, and professional development schools, are discussed.

TWO ROADS DIVERGED:
MULTIPLE AVENUES TO TEACHER PREPARATION

Teachers enter the classroom after various types of preparatory experiences. Traditional teacher preparation was mentioned in the previous section. Here, we review the literature that focuses on newer methods of teacher preparation. First, there is alternative certification, whereby, instead of training through a traditional 4-year undergraduate teacher preparation program, many teachers have been able to enter the classroom after enrolling in an alternative program. Alternative certification requirements vary by state and program, but the majority of them seek to compress the amount of time preservice teachers (who have their bachelor's degree in a content area) must spend in coursework and student teaching before entering their own classrooms. Some programs, called "fast-track" certification, allow teachers to enter the classroom *before* they receive state certification. Though such teachers are supposed to take required education classes and become certified at a later date, Hansen (2001) stated that "in states with severe teacher shortages, uncertified teachers with fast-track training often teach for years with 'emergency' or 'provisional' licenses" (p. 5). From the outset, the federal government has supported alternative preparation of teachers in many states.

During his tenure as Secretary of Education under President George W. Bush, Paige championed the development of alternative certification programs. In his 2002 report on teacher quality, Paige advocated a dismantling of certification systems that imposed "burdensome requirements" instead focusing on high verbal ability and content knowledge, the two skills Paige viewed as most important for teacher success (pp. 8-14). In a later report, Paige (2004) explained that "many wonderful candidates with families and mortgages will have no choice but to say no" to teaching as a profession if they were required to undergo traditional preparation (p. v), and alternative programs held the promise of bringing "thousands of talented soldiers of democracy into our schools" (p. vi).

Despite the federal and state push for alternative programs, research continued to show that alternative certification was not as rigorous or effective as traditional teacher preparation programs. Though there was no guarantee that traditionally prepared teachers would fare well once they enter into a classroom, many critics still preferred traditional over alternative preparation. Jean Miller, director of INTASC, quoted in Hansen (2001), stated that allowing teachers to enter the classroom after only a few weeks of training was "tantamount to treating kids like guinea pigs" (p. 6).

The strongest critic of alternative certification has been Darling-Hammond. In a review of scholarship on staffing schools for the teacher shortage, she opposed "abbreviated" programs because their graduates lacked both pedagogical knowledge and stability in urban schools (2001). Citing Gomez and Grobe (1990), the author contended that "students of teachers with little or no preparation for teaching learn less than students who have fully prepared teachers" (p. 14). In her review, Darling-Hammond also showed alternatively prepared teachers had difficulty developing curriculum, varying teaching methods, managing the classroom, and motivating students.

In another critique of alternative certification, Zeichner (2003) wrote about the "deregulation agenda" of school reform and advocates who wanted to establish alternative certification programs to break the "monopoly" of teacher education colleges. Such advocates, Zeichner noted, argued that "teachers' subject matter knowledge and verbal ability are the main determinants of teaching success" and that many teacher training classes' themes and methods could be better learned through on-the-job training (p. 503). Zeichner disagreed with the deregulation agenda:

> Majoring in a subject or passing a subject matter test, even if the bar is set high, is no guarantee that teachers understand the central concepts in their discipline and have the pedagogical content knowledge needed to transform content to promote understanding by diverse learners. (pp. 505-506)

Urban and Multiculturally-Focused Programs

As the demographics of American classrooms change, so must the preparation programs for teachers who are to enter those schools. Programs that focus on working in urban, multicultural environments have grown in the last few decades, and while Ladson-Billings (1999) feels that there should be no difference between "teacher preparation" and "teacher preparation for diverse learners" (p. 242), the majority of teacher education programs are offering courses that focus on working with this unique group. These programs emphasize race as the most salient aspect of diversity. Weiner (1993) argued that effective urban teacher preparation must encourage preservice teachers to understand the lives of poor, racially diverse groups and must "accommodate the differences among teacher-candidates so that they can learn how to deal with students who differ from each other and the teacher" (p. 134). Other goals for these types of programs include developing positive teacher attributes for those working with African-American children (Irvine & Collison, 1999; Ladson-Billings, 1994, 2000) and addressing racism directly (Cochran-Smith, 1995, 2000; Kailin, 1998; Marx, 2004; Sleeter, 2001; Solomona, Portelli, Daniel, & Campbell, 2005). Further, urban programs need to address preservice teachers' negativity and resistance toward student diversity (Cockrell, Placier, Cockrell, & Middleton, 1999; McAllister & Irvine, 2000; Schultz, Neyhart, & Reck, 1996) by asking teachers, especially White teachers, to examine their previous beliefs and determine appropriate ways to respond to those beliefs (Garmon, 2004; Olmedo, 1997; McIntyre, 1997). Finally, these programs should advance the use of culturally relevant pedagogy (Garibaldi, 1992; Gay, 2002; Howard, 2003; Ladson-Billings, 1994; Mason, 1999; Phuntsog, 1999).

In addition to discussing race, urban teacher preparation programs also need to consider the sociopolitical context of urban schools, including underfunding, bureaucracy, and prescriptive curriculum (Haberman,

1993; Quartz, 2003; Weiner, 1993; Yeo, 1997). Haberman and Post (1998) believe that teachers need to be additionally informed about the urban community, relationship skills, empathy, an understanding of cultural conflicts, skills for coping with violence, and the ability to function in chaos (pp. 98-99). Field experiences in urban schools were seen as vital to preservice teacher education (Burant & Kirby, 2002; Fry & McKinney, 1997; Sleeter, 2001), but the literature was divided on whether field experiences increased motivation to work in urban schools (Pagano, Weiner, Obi, & Swearingen, 1995) or decreased teachers' interest (Cross, 2003; Luft, Bragg, & Peters, 1999; Weiner, 1990).

School-University Partnerships and Professional Development Schools

Though the terms are used interchangeably, there is a difference between school-university partnerships (SUPs), as required by the NCATE standards discussed above, and professional development schools (PDSs). SUPs are symbiotic partnerships between school-based and university-based personnel who come together to educate educators (Goodlad, 1993). SUPs have existed longer than PDSs (Sirotnik & Goodlad, 1988; Abdal-Haqq, 1998), while PDSs were conceptualized in the mid-1980's and expected to be more systematic about meeting the four stated goals: preparing new teachers, providing professional development for inservice teachers, improving school achievement, and creating inquiry communities (Holmes Group, 1990). The empirical research base on SUPs and PDSs is still developing, but some recent evidence points to the success of PDSs in preparing teachers for instruction and reflection (Abdal-Haqq, 1998; Book, 1996; Teitel, 2001). In particular, Adbal-Haqq's synthesis reports that graduates of PDSs are more varied in their pedagogical practice, are more reflective, are knowledgeable about school routines and procedures, are confident, are less prone to "culture shock," and are more likely to seek employment in urban schools than teachers prepared in non-PDSs (p. 15).

Other empirical research studied individual SUPs or PDSs (Cristol & Gimbert, 2002; Freese, 1999; Groulx, 2001; Reynolds, 2000; Rock & Levin, 2002; Thompson & Ross, 2000). Sample size was small, and generalizability was limited because there was often only one self-reported data source. The common link among these studies was that participants reported positive results from the partnership, including a feeling of community with the school, satisfaction with preparation, more effective instruction, and increased reflection. Other studies, like Duquette and Cook (1999) and Ridley, Hurowitz, Hackett, and Miller (2005), showed little or no difference between PDSs and traditional preparation programs. Some of the most recent studies point to positive results in SUP and PDS teacher preparation in general (Castle, Fox, & Souder, 2006), and in urban schools in particular (Beardsley & Teitel, 2004; Wong & Glass, 2005).

CONCLUSION

As in many reviews of scholarly literature, the most important conclusion that can be drawn is that there is no emphatic conclusion. While there is an increased need for teachers, in particular teachers who are willing to work in urban schools, retention of these teachers remains a problem. There are many ways to conceptualize how preservice teachers learn to teach, including knowledge acquisition; development of attitudes and beliefs; and most prominent in the literature, the role of field experiences and student teaching. Also varied are the goals for preservice teacher preparation. Outcomes, too, fluctuate based on the reviewer: some scholars believe that traditional programs succeed in fulfilling their goals, while other researchers do not believe that traditional programs prepare teachers for the realities of public education today. Finally, the avenues to teacher preparation are multitudinous. In addition to traditional preparation, there exist alterative certification, urban and multiculturally-focused programs, and professional development schools and university partnerships. It is the authors' hope that the chapters that follow will add to the extensive body of literature on these valuable topics of inquiry.

ACKNOWLEDGMENT

Portions of this chapter were taken, with permission of the authors, from Donnell (2004) and Stairs (2006).

NOTE

1.   The majority of this section was taken, with permission of the author, from Hadley, A. (2006).

REFERENCES

Abdal-Haqq, I. (1998). *Professional development schools: Weighing the evidence*. Thousands Oaks, CA: Corwin Press.

Auger, W., & Wideman, R. (2000). Using action research to open the door to life long professional learning. *Education, 121*(1), 120-127.

Beardsley, L. V., & Teitel, L. (2004). Learning to see color in teacher education: An example framed by the professional development school standard for diversity and equity. *The Teacher Educator, 40*(2), 91-115.

Book, C. L. (1996). Professional development schools. In J. Sikula, T. J. Buttery & E. Guyton (Eds.), *Handbook of research on teacher education* (2nd ed., pp. 194-210). New York: Simon & Schuster Macmillan.

Borko, H., & Putnam, R. T. (1996). Learning to teach. In D. C. Berliner & R. C. Calfee (Eds.), *Handbook of educational psychology* (pp. 673-708). New York: Macmillan.

Britzman, D. (1991). *Practice makes practice.* Albany, NY: State University of New York Press.

Burant, T, & Kirby, D. (2002). Beyond classroom-based early field experiences: Understanding an "educative practicum" in an urban school and community. *Teaching and Teacher Education, 18*(5), 561-575.

Carter, K. (1990). Teachers' knowledge and learning to teach. In W. R. Houston (Ed.), *Handbook of research on teacher education: A project of the Association of Teacher Educators* (pp. 212-233). New York: Macmillan.

Castle, S., Fox, R. K., & Souder, K. O. H. (2006). Do professional development schools (PDSs) make a difference? *Journal of Teacher Education, 57*(1), 65-80.

Cochran-Smith, M. (1995). Color blindness and basket making are not the answers: Confronting the dilemmas of race, culture, and language diversity in teacher education. *American Education Research Journal, 32*(3), 493-522.

Cochran-Smith, M. (1999). Learning to teach for social justice. In G. Griffin (Ed.), *The education of teachers: Ninety-eighth yearbook of the National Society for the Study of Education.* (pp. 114-144). Chicago, IL: University of Chicago Press.

Cochran-Smith, M. (2000). Blind vision: Unlearning racism in teacher education. *Harvard Educational Review, 70*(2), 157-190.

Cochran-Smith, M., & Lytle, S. (1999). Relationship of knowledge and practice: Teacher learning in communities. In A. Iran-Nejad & C. D. Pearson (Eds.), *Review of research in education* (Vol. 24, pp. 249-306). Washington, DC: American Educational Research Association.

Cockrell, K., Placier, P., Cockrell, D., & Middleton, J. (1999). Coming to terms with "diversity" and "multiculturalism" in teacher education: Learning about our students, changing our practice. *Teaching and Teacher Education, 15*, 351-366.

Cristol, D. S., & Gimbert, B. G. (2002). A case study of an urban school-university partnership: Designing and implementing curriculum for contextual teaching and learning. *Professional Educator, 25*(1), 43-54.

Cross, B. (2003). Learning and unlearning racism: Transferring teacher education curriculum to classroom practices. *Theory into Practice, 42*(3), 203-209.

Darling-Hammond, L. (2001). The challenge of staffing our schools. *Educational Leadership 58*(8), 12-17.

Donnell, K.A. (2004) *Learning to teach in an urban setting: The struggle to develop transformative practice.* Unpublished doctoral dissertation, Boston College, Chestnut Hill, MA.

Duquette, C., & Cook, S. A. (1999). Professional development schools: Preservice candidates' learning and sources of knowledge. *Alberta Journal of Educational Research, 45*(2), 198-207.

Feiman-Nemser, S., & Buchmann, M. (1987). When is student teaching teacher education? *Teacher and Teacher Education, 3*(4), 255-273.

Feiman-Nemser, S., & Remillard, J. (1996). Perspectives on learning to teach. In F. B. Murray (Ed.), *The teacher educator's handbook: Building a knowledge base for the preparation of teachers* (pp. 63-91). San Francisco, CA: Jossey-Bass.

Freese, A. R. (1999). The role of reflection on preservice teachers' development in the context of a professional development school. *Teaching and Teacher Education, 15*(8), 895-909.

Fry, P., & McKinney, L. (1997). A qualitative study of preservice teachers' early field experiences in an urban, culturally different school. *Urban Education, 32*(2), 184-201.

Garibaldi, A. (1992). Preparing teachers for culturally diverse classrooms. In M. Dilworth (Ed.), *Diversity in teacher education: New expectations* (pp. 22-39). San Francisco, CA: Jossey-Bass.

Garmon, M.A. (2004). Changing preservice teachers' beliefs/attitudes about diversity. *Journal of Teacher Education, 55*(3), 201-213.

Gay, G. (2002). Preparing for culturally responsive teaching. *Journal of Teacher Education, 53*(2), 106-116.

Gomez, D.L., & Grobe, R.P. (1990, April). *Three years of alternative certification in Dallas: Where are we?* Paper presented at the meeting of the American Educational Research Association, Boston, MA.

Goodlad, J. (1993). School-university partnerships and partner schools. *Educational Policy, 7*(1), 24-39.

Groulx, J. G. (2001). Changing preservice teacher perceptions of minority schools. *Urban Education, 36*(1), 60-92.

Haberman, M. (1993). Predicting the success of urban teachers (The Milwaukee trials). *Action in Teacher Education, 15*(3), 1-5.

Haberman, M., & Post, L. (1998). Teachers for multicultural schools: The power of selection. *Theory into Practice, 37*(2), 96-104.

Hadley, A. (2006). *Foreign teacher recruitment: A comprehensive literature review.* Unpublished master's thesis, Emory University, Atlanta, GA.

Hansen, B. (2001). Teacher shortages [Electronic Version]. *The CQ Researcher, 11.* Retrieved from http://library.cqpress.com/cqresearcher

Holmes Group. (1990). *Tomorrow's schools: Principles for the design of professional development schools.* East Lansing, MI: Author.

Howard, T.C. (2003). Culturally relevant pedagogy: Ingredients for critical teacher reflection. *Theory into Practice, (42)*3, 195-202.

Ingersoll, R. (1999). The problem of underqualified teachers in American secondary schools. *Educational Researcher, 28*(2), 26-37.

Ingersoll, R. (2002). The teacher shortage: A case of wrong diagnosis and wrong prescription. *NASSP Bulletin, 86*(361), 16-31.

Ingersoll, R. (2003). Teacher shortage: Myth or reality? *Education Horizons,* 147-152.

INTASC. (1992). *Model standards for beginning teacher licensing, assessment and development: A resource for state dialogue*. Washington, DC: Council of Chief State School Officers.

Irvine, J., & Collison, M. (1999). Preparing teachers for urban classrooms. *Black Issues in Higher Education*, pp. 30-32.

Kagan, D. M. (1992). Professional growth among preservice and beginning teachers. *Review of Educational Research, 62*(2), 129-169.

Kailin, J. (1998). Preparing urban teachers for schools and communities: An antiracist perspective. *High School Journal, 82*(2), 80-81.

Ladson-Billings, G. (1994). *The dreamkeepers*. San Francisco: Jossey-Bass.

Ladson-Billings, G. (1999). Preparing teachers for diverse student populations: A critical race theory perspective. In A. Iran-Nejad & P. D. Pearson (Eds.), *Review of Research in Education* (Vol. 24, pp. 211-248). Washington, DC: American Educational Research Association.

Ladson-Billings, G. (2000). Fighting for our lives: Preparing teachers to teach African American students. *Journal of Teacher Education, 51*(3), 206-214.

Luft, J., Bragg, J., & Peters, C. (1999). Learning to teach in a diverse setting: A case study of a multicultural science education enthusiast. *Science Education, 83*(5), 527-543.

Marx, S. (2004). Regarding whiteness: Exploring and intervening in the effects of White racism in teacher education. *Equity & Excellence in Education, 37*(1), 31 43.

Mason, T. (1999). Prospective teachers' attitudes toward urban schools: Can they be changed? *Multicultural Education, 6*(4), 9-13.

McAllister, G., & Irvine, J. J. (2000). Cross cultural competency and multicultural teacher education. *Review of Educational Research, 70*(1), 3-24.

McIntyre, A. (1997). *Making meaning of whiteness: Exploring racial identity with White teachers*. Albany, NY: State University of New York Press.

NCATE. (2002). *Professional standards for the accreditation of schools, colleges, and departments of education*. Retrieved from www.ncate.org

National Center for Education Statistics. (2005). *Projections of Education Statistics to 2014*. Retrieved from http://nces.gov/pubs2005/2005074.pdf

National Commission on Teaching and America's Future. (2002). *Unraveling the "teacher shortage" problem: Teacher retention is the key*. New York, NY: National Commission on Teaching and America's Future.

National Teacher Recruitment Clearinghouse. (2003). *Recruiting new teachers: Teacher shortage areas*. Retrieved from http://recruitingteachers.org

Olmedo, I. (1997). Challenging old assumptions: Preparing teachers for inner schools. *Teaching & Teacher Education, 13*, 245-258.

Pagano, A., Weiner, L., Obi, R., & Swearingen, J. (1995). How student teaching in an urban setting affects teacher candidates' career motivations. *The Urban Review, 27*(1), 51-75.

Paige, R. (2002). *Meeting the highly qualified teachers challenge: The Secretary's second annual report on teacher quality*. Retrieved from http://www.ed.gov/about/reports/annual/teachprep/2003title-ii-report.pdf

Paige, R., Rees, N. R., Petrilli, M. J., & Gore, P. (2004). *Alternative routes to teacher certification*. Retrieved from http://www.ed.gov/admins/tchrqual/recruit/altroutes/index.html

Pajares, F. (1992). Teachers' beliefs and educational research: Cleaning up a messy construct. *Review of Educational Research, 62*(3), 307-332.

Phuntsog, N. (1999). The magic of culturally responsive pedagogy: In search of the genie's lamp in multicultural education. *Teacher Education Quarterly, 26*(3).

Marx, S. (2004). Regarding whiteness: Exploring and intervening in the effects of White racism in teacher education. *Equity & Excellence in Education, 37*(1), 31 43.

Reynolds, A. (1992). What is competent beginning teaching? A review of the literature. *Review of Educational Research, 62*(1), 1-35.

Reynolds, A. (2000). Open the doors and see all the people. *Teaching and Change, 8*(1), 10-30.

Richardson, V., & Placier, P. (2001). Teacher change. In V. Richardson (Ed.), *Handbook of research on teaching* (4th ed., pp. 905-947). Washington, DC: American Educational Research Association.

Ridley, D. S., Hurwitz, S., Hackett, M. R. D., & Miller, K. K. (2005). Comparing PDS and campus-based preservice teacher preparation: Is PDS-based preparation really better? *Journal of Teacher Education, 56*(1), 46-56.

Rock, T. C., & Levin, B. B. (2002). Collaborative action research projects: Enhancing preservice teacher development. *Teacher Education Quarterly, 29*(1), 7-21.

Shultz, E., Neyhart, T., & Reck, U. (1996). Uphill all the way: an investigation of attitudinal predispositions of preservice teachers toward diversity in urban classrooms. *The Teacher Educator, 32*, 22-36.

Sirotnik, K. A., & Goodlad, J. (Eds.). (1988). *School-university partnerships in action: Concepts, cases, and concerns*. New York, NY: Teachers College Press.

Sleeter, C. (2001). Preparing teachers for culturally diverse schools: Research and the overwhelming presence of whiteness. *Journal of Teacher Education, 52*(2), 94-106.

Solomona, R. P., Portelli, J., Daniel, B-J., & Campbell, A. (2005). The discourse of denial: How White teacher candidates construct race, racism and 'White privilege.' *Race Ethnicity and Education*, 8 (2), 147-169.

Stairs, A. J. (2006). *Preservice teacher learning in an urban school-university partnership*. Unpublished doctoral dissertation, Boston College, Chestnut Hill, MA.

Teitel, L. (2001). An assessment framework for professional development schools: Going beyond the leap of faith. *Journal of Teacher Education, 52*(1), 57-69.

Thompson, S., & Ross, F. (2000). Becoming a teacher in a professional development school. *Teaching and Change, 8*(1), 31-50.

Weiner, L. (1990). Preparing the brightest for urban schools. *Urban Education, 25*(3), 258-273.

Weiner, L. (1993). *Preparing teachers for urban schools, lessons from 30 years of school reform*. New York: Teachers College Press.

Wideen, M., Mayer-Smith, J., & Moon, B. (1998). A critical analysis of the research on learning to teach: Making the case for an ecological perspective on inquiry. *Review of Educational Research, 68*(2), 130-178.

Wilson, S., Floden, R., & Ferrini-Mundy, J. (2001). *Teacher preparation research: Current knowledge, gaps, and recommendations.* Seattle, WA: Center for the Study of Teaching and Policy.

Wong, P. L., & Glass, R. D. (2005). Assessing a professional development school approach to preparing teachers for urban schools serving low-income, culturally and linguistically diverse communities. *Teacher Education Quarterly, 32*(3), 63-77.

Yeo, F. (1997). *Inner-city schools, multiculturalism, and teacher education: A professional journey.* New York, NY: Garland. Zeichner, K. (2003). Adequacies and inadequacies of current strategies to recruit teachers. *Teachers College Record, 105*(3), 490-519.

Zeichner, K. M., & Conklin, H. G. (2005). Teacher education programs. In M. Cochran-Smith & K. Zeichner (Eds.), *Studying teacher education: The report of the AERA panel on research and teacher education* (pp. 645-735). Washington, DC: AERA

PART II

RESEARCH ON URBAN TEACHER LEARNING

CHAPTER 3

"WE KNOW YOU'RE BLACK AT HEART"

A Self-Study of a White, Urban High School Teacher

Alyssa Hadley Dunn

Any teacher knows the awkward pause when you see a student outside of school, the moment when a student approaches you at a restaurant with a goofy smile and a halting hello as you introduce him to your companions. The day after one of these encounters, the student approached me in school and asked about a friend's daughter, a young Black child, who was sitting next to me in the restaurant. Except, he thought the child was mine. With a laugh, I told him that I have no children, and, importantly, that I am White, as if I needed to remind him. He laughed and replied, "That's okay, we all know you're Black at heart." What the student was attempting to say, I believe, was not solely about race; instead, by using race as a metaphor, he was indicating that I connected with my urban students and, somehow, understood them and identified with their experiences. This comical moment, intended as a compliment, was revealing; it challenged me to reflect on my journey to becoming an urban teacher.

Research on Urban Teacher Learning: Examining Contextual Factors Over Time
pp. 29–40

How had I, who knew nothing about urban or multicultural education a mere five years prior, become "Black at heart"?

The chapter that follows is a self-study of my progression into urban education. It begins with a discussion of my personal history and background, as understanding one's attitude and beliefs toward teaching is vital to becoming fully aware of one's place in the educational system (Pajares, 1992). I then highlight the onset of my journey into urban education at a teacher education program that was part of a school-university partnership. I track this progression by analyzing journals from my first prepracticum through my full-time work in an urban high school. My viewpoint is additionally informed by my master's and doctoral research in urban teacher education. I am able to reconstruct my process of transformation into an urban educator by categorizing my experience into three central themes. It is not my intention to generalize this study to a broad group, but rather to offer questions and suggestions for teachers and teacher educators.

CONCEPTUAL FRAMEWORK AND METHODOLOGY

This research is grounded in the literature of self-study. Briefly, a self-study is one's examination of one's own practice. Most commonly, teacher educators "engage in self-study both for purposes of their own personal-professional development and for broader purposes of enhanced understanding of teacher education practices, processes, programs, and contexts" (Cole & Knowles, 1996). The long-term goal of self-study is the improvement of teacher education. Self-study builds on the process of reflective inquiry developed by Dewey (1938/1991), but because of the difficulty of guaranteeing professional distance, validity, and generalizability, self-study is not often recognized as a prominent research methodology. However, as it gains momentum in the United States, as in England and Australia, I felt it was the appropriate methodology for my own observations because preservice teachers often need to hear the voice of more experienced practicing teachers mixed with research. Instead of distancing the theory of teaching, praxis, and contexts, this study attempts to weave all together through the experiences of one urban educator.

My self-study grew out of the reflective inquiry required during my teacher preparation. In accordance with Valli (1997), we participated in journal writing, mentoring and supervision, critical discussions, and action research in ways that allowed us to think critically about our work and how our own backgrounds and viewpoints informed our practice. Valli points out that, while reflection is inherent in teacher improvement, "it can also serve the broader goal of improving schools, human relations, and educational policy" (p. 86).

This self-study also operates from the perspective that teachers are informally inducted into and influenced by the profession through a process known as "teacher socialization" (Zeichner & Gore, 1990). Though there are many views of when and how teachers are socialized, this study agrees most closely with Feiman-Nemser (2001), in which socialization is an ongoing process throughout a career, including teacher preparation, professional training, and on-the-job education, and with Zeichner and Gore (1990), who posit that true teacher training begins as early as one's own childhood in schools, or pretraining influences. I also take a "critical view of socialization," that, according to Zeichner and Gore, means that I continuously reflect on and critique current education and seek to use my role as an educator as an agent for change.

I was able to critically examine my practice for this self-study because of the availability of journals, dating back to my first prepracticum in 2002. I kept weekly reflections for a class portfolio, and a researcher collected these journals for her own study and later provided them to me. I also kept reflections and observations during my two years teaching in an urban high school. Using this qualitative data, I looked for patterns in my writing and coded the data into three major themes. Before discussing these themes, I begin by examining the pretraining influences on my desire to teach.

"TWO FEET FIRST": LEARNING TO TEACH IN URBAN SCHOOLS

As discussed in the conceptual framework, there exist a multitude of contexts in which one learns to teach. As researchers note, beginning teachers often rely on the ways they were taught to inform their classroom practice (Yero, 2002). My own education about education began at an early age.

After my first day working in an urban school, I emailed my mother and touched on the common fears of many preservice teachers in a new educational setting:

> I felt like I was back in high school today. Except this time, it was a high school that I had always been afraid I would end up in if you hadn't had the money to send me to [a private school.] My first day at [BHS] was good, don't get me wrong, but it seemed like I was in an alternate universe or something. It was such a culture shock.... I just can't help thinking how much more comfortable and happy I would be had [my university] done the first prepracticum in a suburban or private school. Nothing like jumping in two feet first!

The feeling of "jumping in two feet first" stemmed from the disparity between the school in which I was teaching and the private, religiously-affiliated schools I had attended for 12 years. The public schools in my hometown were "bad," a sentiment that was unspoken among teachers, students, and their parents. I could not define what a "bad" school was at such a young age, but I knew that "bad" elementary schools did not prepare children for high school, and bad high schools did not prepare adolescents for college. The city where I grew up was diverse; however, because of racial and socio-economic divides that exist in education today, my own education was spent with upper-middle class, White peers.

Though, in hindsight, I can critically analyze my schooling, at the time, I was blissfully unaware of the divides outside the school walls, and I was content, as I imagine were the majority of my classmates. Teachers demonstrated their care for students by giving us a choice about project topics and holding fundraisers for classroom computers; parents served as volunteers and coaches; and administrators regularly checked on their teachers and observed classes. Every student was known by name and face.

Because of the caring and devotion of such teachers, I knew from a young age that I, too, wanted to be a teacher. I chose to attend a private university in a major metropolitan area, convinced that I could not find a better place to prepare me to teach in a private school like the one from which I had just graduated. Upon entering the program, however, I learned that my assumption could not have been further from the truth.

My classmates and I were embarking on a new program developed by the university and the local public school system. This school-university partnership meant that, for our first prepracticum experience, we would not have the "luxury" of choosing a placement and thus securing ourselves contentedly in a school similar to our alma maters. Rather, we were introduced to BHS, a school of 1,200 students, 100 faculty members, and a crumbling building with bars on the windows. Our program required us to attend class at BHS before and after school. During the day, we rotated between three cooperating teachers' classrooms. This partnership between the university and the school was part of a new focus on preparing professionals to work in urban schools. This was a surprising and unwelcome development for me because of my misconceptions about urban students. I believed they did not want to be in school and were taught by teachers who could not secure positions in "better" districts. I was angry at the program; but mostly, I was angry with myself because I was scared. I had always prided myself on being open-minded and anti-racist, but I began the semester fearing students who did not look like me.

On my first morning at this school, I passed through metal detectors and endured a bag search by a security officer before finding my way to where our class was meeting. Other college students milled around the tables, and I sensed uneasiness in the crowd. We were pleased to begin teaching, but *here*? Like the population of the teaching profession at large, the class of around 25 student teachers was predominantly White and female (U.S. Census Bureau, 2004). The hallways and classrooms of BHS were something entirely unfamiliar; the school was 95% students of color, and a majority spoke a first language other than English. As I wrote in a personal reflection at the end of the first semester,

> When I walked into [BHS] that first day, I was completely overwhelmed by the importance that diversity took in the classroom setting. There were accommodations made for ESL and special education students that were very foreign to me ... we didn't even have those departments at my high school, and here at [BHS], they seem to be two of the most important ones.

My first few weeks were immensely revealing. The teachers wanted to be there, the students wanted to learn, and I was actually enjoying myself. In my experience, my teacher preparation program effectively prepared me for almost every aspect of working in an urban school. This directly contradicts the work of Haberman (1994), an advocate of alternative teacher certification, who asserts that traditional programs do not prepare teachers for urban schools. The difference between my personal experience and his research could be that my university committed itself, in mission and action, to preparing teachers for multicultural, urban teaching.

Surely, my transformation into an urban educator did not happen immediately, or even within that first semester. However, beginning with that experience, there emerged several themes that have continued throughout my career: Developing Relationships with Students, "Managing" a Classroom, and Working Within the System.

Developing Relationships With Students

The most important part of a student-teacher relationship is building individual trust and respect, but how is this possible with so many students in one classroom? While research has shown that smaller class sizes lead to increased learning and teacher satisfaction, the reality is that many urban school systems lack the funding to decrease class size (National Education Association, 2002). Hence, I greet 32 students per class each day. It then becomes my responsibility to find a way to develop a relationship with each student and create a productive classroom culture.

Often, my students compare me to Michelle Pfeiffer's character from the film "Dangerous Minds," in which she plays a former Marine who becomes an English teacher in a gang and drug-riddled school. She "saves" her students and helps them academically through the power of poetry and bribery—literature alongside candy and amusement park trips. My students intend this as a compliment, but I tell them it is not. To imply that I am their "savior" suggests that they need saving, that there is something inherently erroneous within their culture or themselves that leads to failure. This deficit model of thinking is not a theory to which I subscribe. This realization was not immediate, because, for a while, I still believed that my students needed rescuing. For example, in a reflection written after my first prepracticum experience, I observed:

> There's a part of me that likes to read books like my new favorite, *The Freedom Writers Diary*, and longs to be like Erin Gruwell, the White girl from the suburbs who turns around the lives of L.A.'s most gang-ridden high school students and changes their world for the better. It may seem like a pipe dream, but the more people tell me I can't do it, the more I want to.

Implicitly, I was thinking more about myself than my students. Yes, I wanted to help them, but more than that, I wanted recognition for saving them from destruction as Michelle Pfeiffer did. Many young teachers enter urban schools motivated by this "savior model," and while there may be nothing wrong with this motivation if it brings qualified teachers into the classroom, it is important to look beyond the relationship of savior/saved to a more equitable relationship of mutual learning. I was, in a sense, overcompensating; I wanted to challenge the status quo and prove that "city kids" could succeed, but in the process, I was extending the deficit model. Ayers, Ladson-Billings, Michie, and Noguera (2008) reflect on this tendency:

> I have to know my students well enough to connect with them.... Like all teachers, I run the risk of not taking enough into account—every student is unique, none are exactly the same—but I also run the risk of taking too much into account, of leaping to shaky conclusions based on surface or superficial evidence. Even the phrase "city kids" can be reductive: narrow, stereotyped, filled with images of dread and danger and deficit. (p. 6)

Striking a balance between teaching my students to learn and learning from my students was not something I fully understood until I began teaching in a classroom of my own full-time. There, for example, I met students who knew more about life than I did. How was I going to teach them to "find" themselves in literature, which I espoused as one of my educational philosophies after my first semester in college, if they had lived through horrors and experiences of which I had never dreamed? Farisha,[1] a 22-year-old senior, had escaped Afghanistan only to see her father killed by the Taliban at a refugee camp. She was smuggled across borders, walked thousands of miles, and somehow ended up in my literature classroom with a zest for learning and a constant smile. The relationship that teachers develop with Farisha results from a healthy amount of admiration for her resiliency and determination. The language barrier has kept her in high school longer than she intended, but she has not given up. This has, in fact, made her more determined, and I, as her teacher, have become more determined to help her succeed. With Farisha, however, I refuse to pretend that I have all the answers. I teach her literary terms and reading comprehension strategies, and, in turn, she teaches me about self-motivation and empathy in an example of Freire's dialectial relationship (1970/2000). This is quite different from the attitude I held as a prepracticum student teacher, where I feared being "wrong" so much that I did not speak up as much as I should have. In fact, one student's end-of-semester reflection read, "I wish you would talk more! Don't be afraid."

The best way for me to develop relationships with students is by utilizing Ladson-Billings' (1994) culturally relevant pedagogy (CRP). This pedagogy, in which students are able to connect their outside lives to the classroom and are encouraged to see their cultures as educationally valuable, has enabled me to connect with many of my diverse students. In an early reflection from my preservice experience, I wrote that CRP is "the solution to urban students' apathy." Unfortunately, for many students, a culturally relevant curriculum is not enough to keep them inspired; however, for the majority of students, their ability to connect literature to their culture makes our relationships stronger and more meaningful.

Whether learning about the Harlem Renaissance, reading excerpts from Malcolm X and Toni Morrison, or discussing the cultural norms of Latino/a immigrants in Sandra Cisneros' *The House on Mango Street*, I encourage students to bring their lives into our discussions. Beyond simply the "heroes and holidays" approach to multicultural education (Lee, Menkhart, & Okazawa-Rey, 1998), my entire curriculum attempts to expose students of all cultures to the works of all cultures. In response, a student's mother wrote, "I am overjoyed that my son is learning about Black history in a month other than February." In an informal and anonymous online survey at the end of a semester, on a rating scale-type question, 95% of my students strongly agreed that, "My teacher wants me to connect my culture to what we learn in her class." To me, this speaks of a meaningful and academically productive relationship.

"Managing" a Classroom

The relationships that I developed with students directly affected and were affected by the classroom culture and my classroom management style. I wrote in a journal my sophomore year of college that "if I respect my students, they will respect me." I observed in my prepracticum experi-ence that, if teachers respected their students, students responded in turn. There did not seem to be any deviations from this norm. Observing a classroom for more than this hour per day, however, may have shown me differently. I also believed my coursework in classroom management had prepared me for students who did not behave properly. In a journal written only three weeks into my prepracticum, I observed:

> [Classroom management] is any way that a teacher sees fit to control the class: keep them on task, avoid confrontations between students, and effec-tively communicate the subject and goals without too many interruptions.

While I still agree with my previous assessment, I missed the broadest goal of classroom management: to develop an environment where learning can take place. As aptly stated by a fellow teacher, "Good teaching takes care of classroom management." Taylor Mali, a teacher-turned-poet, wrote about trying to get the undivided attention of his students who were distracted by the world outside the classroom windows as he was trying to teach math. His plea: "Let me teach like the first snow, falling" (Mali, 2002). If the classroom were as captivating as the first snowfall, would not classroom management "take care of itself"?

But what happens when good teaching is occurring, students are engaged, and one student prohibits the others from learning? In the words of a former teacher, "One bad apple can spoil the bunch." As a committed teacher, how do you get the student back on task while not los-ing the rest of the class? Each teacher has his or her own strategy, but I found my own by observing what *not* to do. This is the value of multiple preservice teaching experiences: Not every student teacher can be placed with a model professional at all times. In the case that she is not, there is still value in learning what strategies do not effect positive change. If one student is being disruptive, I learned that I am not the type of teacher to yell across the room. If it can be helped, I learned that I am not the type of teacher to publicly reprimand or to immediately kick the student out of class. Instead, I learned through observation and experimentation that I would rather move closer to the student, speak quietly to him/her, and, if the situation escalates, ask him/her to step into the hallway to calm down. One value of this discovery is that it came through a combination of observation and hands-on learning.

The most important lesson I have learned about classroom manage-ment is that sometimes I need to ask for help. As a new teacher—and a young teacher, at that—I did not want to appear unable to manage the classroom on my own. I did not want to give anyone—students, parents, other teachers, or the administration—the impression that I was unprepared and needed aid. After a confrontation with a student with an emotional-behavior disorder escalated to the point where I could not calm him and he was threatening another student, I finally learned that it was acceptable and necessary to ask for assistance. Just as I am not a "savior" for my underprivileged students, I am also not a magician who can make tension and anger disappear. The most effective classroom management happens, then, when not only a teacher is involved, but when the entire school and community are committed to making sure classrooms are safe and productive.

Working Within the System

The most difficult aspect of working in urban public schools is the bureaucracy that surrounds every decision, every day. The bureaucracy is stifling; whether it is excessive paperwork, backloads of meetings, or inane high-stakes standardized testing, the "system" seems unavoidable. Often, these top-down bureaucratic decisions have harmful effects on students. When I feel guilty for giving my students the dreaded "worksheets" more than one day in a row, I remind myself that, unfortunately, some things, such as the limitations of the No Child Left Behind Act of 2001, are out of my control. "Teachers are not the sole generators and advocates of uninspired pedagogy," writes Nieto (1999); "often, they are the victims of school policies and practices that restrict their freedom of choice by allowing few innovations, or of societal contexts that are difficult to change" (p. 77). Too often, teachers "teach to the test" because they know their job depends on student performance on standardized assessments. Too often, teachers are forced to forget the educational goal of encouraging critical thinking because constant testing forces teachers to ascribe to Freire's (1970/2000) "banking model" of education. Under this model, which many urban school systems seemingly encourage, "instead of communicating, the teacher issues communiques and makes deposits which the students patiently receive, memorize, and repeat ... the scope of action allowed to the students extends only as far as receiving, filing, and storing the deposits" (p. 72). According to Eisner (1994), this type of education neglects the whole child: "Schools are educational churches, and our gods, judging from the altars we build, are economy and efficiency. Hardly a nod is given to the spirit" (p. 96).

One example of a mandate that encourages "banking" education is a system-wide benchmark test that I have encountered during my professional teaching. The benchmark tests were intended to judge what the students were learning in each of the core subjects. Every three weeks, teachers distributed a pre- and posttest of 10 multiple-choice questions.

The pre- and posttests for each cycle were exactly the same, and the three week cycles matched the Curriculum Pacing Guide mandated by the county, in which teachers are told what to teach and when to teach it—a prime example of what Apple (1982/1995) calls "deskilling" of teachers. However, these tests do not actually measure achievement; instead, they measure how well students can memorize ten answers every three weeks. Many teachers ignore the pacing guides from the outset because they are not suited to every classroom. For example, in a classroom with 15 students who do not speak or barely speak English, what is the sense of beginning freshman year with *The Odyssey* or *Romeo and Juliet*? While these two seminal works undoubtedly need to be covered at some point in the year, beginning with such difficult texts is not the way to engage new high school students. Further, both native speakers and ESL students need scaffolding from the study of other pieces to comprehend and analyze those complex texts.

The great irony of testing is incisively discussed by Reich (2001). As a former U.S. Secretary of Labor, he realizes that the future for which we are preparing our children will not be based on standardization. Teaching all students the same thing—and then testing their ability to regurgitate this information—only made sense when "jobs were standardized [because] the largest pedagogical challenge was to train young people to sit still for long periods of time, be patient, follow directions, and be punctual" (p. 64). In today's economy, however, it is an injustice to prepare students for jobs like this because "many of the new jobs depend on creativity and out-of-the-box thinking" (p. 64). I have similar goals for my students: to think critically and analyze insightfully.

How, then, do teachers balance the constraints of the system with their goals for their students' education? From personal experience, I know this is a delicate and frequently frustrating balancing act. This was something for which my teacher preparation program did not prepare me. While I learned quickly that I should not "teach to the test," as this was seen as very un-culturally responsive, I did not learn how to teach what I *wanted* to teach if what I *wanted* to teach was something I was not *allowed* to teach. I refuse to teach only the contents of the textbook or the end-of-course and graduation exams. These tests merely examine reading comprehension and the ability to recall random facts. While these are valuable skills, they are not the only skills students should learn.

However, by not teaching urban students anything about standardized testing, we further disenfranchise them. While their wealthier counterparts have the means to pay for private test preparation tutorials, my students have neither the time nor the money. Because these assessments do not seem to be disappearing any time soon, if I do not teach them to navigate assessments, they will remain unprepared for their future. Thus, I teach test-taking strategies instead of rote memorization. I teach them how to analyze test questions in a way that gives them power, and instead of looking at a question and thinking they are not smart, they can look at a question as a puzzle to be solved.

Working within the system often seems like a hopeless endeavor. I have students who work diligently for four years, achieve high marks in all classes, but cannot pass the final graduation test. Hence, they receive a "certificate of attendance" versus an official diploma; their four years seem moot. I have to remember, however, that this is not the end of their story. If I have done anything for these students, it would be to show them that, in accordance with Hebert Spencer, "The great aim of education is not knowledge, but action." I want them to "recognize education as a possibility" (Freire & Macedo, 1995) and to use this possibility to make their own way in the world, no matter what the system tells them they can or cannot achieve.

FINAL REFLECTION

The journey to becoming a teacher who is "Black at heart" was a complicated one, and it still continues as I learn more about my students and myself in the ongoing process of teaching. My students' education informs my own, particularly as I learn to develop student relationships, manage a classroom, and work within the school system. In each of these areas, my primary goal has always been to imbue in my students a desire to learn and a way to connect their outside lives to those in the classroom. My teacher education program, by focusing on preparing urban teachers, began this process concretely by deliberately placing its student teachers in and educating us about urban schools. While intimidating at first, it undoubtedly instilled in me a desire to remain in urban education. It challenged my preconceptions about urban youth and teachers, and it showed me ways to navigate school bureaucracy to reach my students on a personal level. According to Henry David Thoreau (1910), "Things do not change; we change" (p. 433), and my practicum experiences are what began a lifelong change in my life as an educator. My full-time teaching has extended that change—and that challenge—and enabled me to make connections between my pedagogical instruction and the "real world" of urban schools.

NOTE

1. A pseudonym.

REFERENCES

Apple, M. (1982/1995). *Education and power.* New York, NY: Routledge.

Ayers, W., Ladson-Billings, G., Michie, G., & Noguera, P. (Ed.). (2008). *City kids, city teachers: More reports from the front row.* New York, NY: The New Press.

Cole, A. L. & Knowles, J.G. (1996). *The politics of epistemology and the self-study of teacher education practices.* Paper presented at the Self-Study in Teacher Education: Empowering Our Future International Conference. Retrieved from http://educ.queensu.ca/~ar/Ardra.htm

Dewey, J. (1991). *Logic: The theory of inquiry* (Vol. 12). Carbondale, IL: Southern Illinois University Press. (Original published 1938)

Eisner, E. (1994). *The educational imagination: On the design and evaluation of school programs* (3rd ed.). New York, NY: Macmillan.

Feiman-Nemser, S. (2001). From preparation to practice: Designing a continuum to strengthen and sustain teaching. *Teachers College Record, 103*(6), 1013-1055.

Freire, P. (1970/2000). *Pedagogy of the oppressed.* New York, NY: Continuum.

Freire, P. & Macedo, D. (1995). A dialogue: Culture, language, and race. *Harvard Educational Review, 65*, 377-402.

Haberman, M. (1994). Preparing teachers for the real world of urban schools. *The Educational Forum, 58*, 162-168.

Ladson-Billings, G. (1994). *The dreamkeepers: Successful teachers of African American children.* San Francisco, CA: Jossey-Bass.

Lee, E., Menkhart, D., & Okazawa-Rey, M. (1998). *Beyond heroes and holidays.* Washington, DC: Teaching for Change.

Mali, T. (2002). *Undivided Attention.* [Electronic Version]. Retrieved from www.taylormali.com

National Education Association. (2002). *Class size.* Retrieved from http://www.nea.org/classsize/index.html

Neito, S. (1999). *The light in their eyes: Creating multicultural learning communities.* New York, NY: Teachers College Press.

Pajares, M. F. (1992). Teachers' beliefs and educational research: Cleaning up a messy construct. *Review of Educational Research, 62*(3), 307-332.

Reich, R. B. (2001). Standards for what? *Education Week, 20*(41), 64.

Thoreau, H.D. (1910). *Walden.* Cambridge, MA: T.Y. Crowell & Co.

U.S. Census Bureau. (2004). *Facts for features: Special feature, teacher appreciation week.* Retrieved December 1, 2008 from http://www.census.gov/Press-Release/www/releases/archives facts_for_features_special_editions/001737.html

Valli, L. (1997). Listening to other voices: A description of teacher reflection in the United States. *Peabody Journal of Education, 72*(1), 67-88.

Yero, J. L. (2002). *Teaching in mind: How teacher thinking shapes education.* Hamilton, MT: MindFlight.

Zeichner, K., & Gore, J. (1990). Teacher socialization. In W. R. Houston (Ed.), *Handbook of research on teacher education* (pp. 329-348). New York, NY: Macmillan.

CHAPTER 4

BECOMING AN URBAN TEACHER IN A PROFESSIONAL DEVELOPMENT SCHOOL

A View From Preparation to Practice

Andrea J. Stairs

This chapter reports on a qualitative, collective case study conducted over five years with four White, middle-class urban teachers who prepared to teach in the same northeastern professional development school (PDS). These four teachers were tracked from their first teacher education experience in the urban PDS through their full-time student teaching in that same PDS to their teaching positions in urban high schools three years after graduating. Tracking teachers for five years provides a view of teacher learning over time that is not often found in the research literature. The purpose of this study was to examine urban teacher development and the role that PDSs might play in teacher learning by coming to understand the experiences of these four teachers.

Research on professional development schools suggest that they prepare preservice teachers well for the realities of teaching. Abdal-Haqq's

Research on Urban Teacher Learning: Examining Contextual Factors Over Time
pp. 41–60
Copyright © 2010 by Information Age Publishing
All rights of reproduction in any form reserved.

(1998) synthesis reported that preservice teachers prepared in PDS settings utilized more varied pedagogical methods and practices; were more reflective; knew more about school routines and activities beyond the classroom; felt more confident and experienced less "culture shock" when beginning teaching; and were more likely to seek employment in inner-city schools when their PDS setting was urban, among other findings (p. 15). Rock and Levin (2002) considered the role and outcomes of inquiry activities for preservice teachers in partnership and found they clarified personal teaching theories, gained a better awareness of themselves as teachers, acquired knowledge about teaching, curriculum, and inquiry, and gained a general appreciation for the inquiry process. Thompson and Ross (2000) and Reynolds (2000) noted the link between theory and practice in partnership teacher preparation as key to preparing successful teaching professionals.

Despite the positive findings about learning to teach in PDSs, very few studies explicitly state the school contexts in which they were conducted. That is, many PDS research studies assume that context is unimportant to report or neutral. If the assumption is that teacher learning is to some degree dependent upon the context in which the learning occurs, published studies should report whether the schools were urban, suburban, or rural and go on to describe the context and conditions in more detail. In light of this, it is unclear how effective partnership preparation is for developing professional educators for urban schools, for instance. A few PDS studies have considered urban teacher preparation. Groulx's (2001) study found that urban professional development school candidates in elementary schools "had changed their minds about the challenges of working with minority children, not denying the difficulties but clearly feeling more positive and efficacious" (p. 86-6). Similarly, Wong and Glass's (2005) research into a network of urban PDSs revealed that PDS-prepared graduates were initially more committed to teaching in low-income, culturally and linguistically diverse schools than were the non-PDS graduates. Finally, Beardsley and Teitel's (2004) evaluation of one university's reformed, urban-focused teacher education program conducted in two professional development schools resulted in not only more interns of color in the program, but also interns who learned to see color in teaching and learning, recognized their capacity to lead, and became change agents. The authors attributed these positive outcomes to strong, collaborative PDSs and attention to the diversity and equity standard for PDSs developed by the National Council for Accreditation of Teacher Education (NCATE) (2001). Nevertheless, Boyle-Baise and McIntyre (2008) suggest "attention to equity, diversity, family, and community needs to become an integral part of PDS principles, perspectives, and practices" (p. 326) more so than in the past.

Urban Immersion (UI) is a teacher preparation experience for secondary teacher candidates at the Lynch School of Education at Boston College (BC) offered in collaboration with Brighton High School (BHS) in Boston Public Schools. The university's long-standing relationship with the high school developed into a professional development school model where the school and university partners committed to the four primary goals of PDSs: preservice teacher education, inservice teacher education, collaborative inquiry, and improved student achievement (Holmes Group, 1990). Urban Immersion arose from a meeting called by the high school's administrators asking for further classroom-level support from their university partner. To address this need, the collaborators determined that all secondary teacher candidates would complete coursework and fieldwork one day per week at the high school. The dramatic increase in the number of preservice teachers in the building supported teachers and students operating in overcrowded classrooms. Boston College prepracticum (early field experience) students taught individuals, small groups, and whole classes of students depending on the classroom teacher's specific needs. This experience provided the mostly White, privileged preservice teachers an opportunity to become part of an urban school culture, with which few were familiar. This model has been successful in recruiting participants into full-time urban student teaching and urban teaching careers (Stairs, 2006).

The UI program was conceptualized around theories of urban education scholars who believe that there is specialized knowledge new teachers to the urban context must develop to successfully teach urban students, including identifying the resources and challenges urban teachers face (Donnell, 2007; Haberman, 1994, 1995; Ladson-Billings, 1995, 2000; Oakes, Franke, Quartz, & Roger, 2002; Weiner, 1993, 1999). The school and university partners determined that through their coursework and experiences in classrooms, UI participants should develop their knowledge of content and pedagogy, but more importantly, develop their knowledge of the urban context and how to balance the multiple demands so that all students might learn and improve their life chances. The four participants in the study described in this chapter were UI participants who chose to return to the PDS for their full-time student teaching and were teaching in urban high schools three years after completing their teacher education program. The overarching research question for this collective case study was, "What does learning to teach urban high school English look like over time?" Subquestions included, "How do these teachers enact their learning over time?" and "How does the PDS context influence these teachers' learning?" In the next section, the theoretical framework is described, followed by the research methodology, findings, and conclusions.

THEORETICAL FRAMEWORK

For the purpose of this study, I drew on Feiman-Nemser's (2001) theory of learning to teach as an ongoing process, what she calls "a professional learning continuum from initial preparation through the early years of teaching" (p. 1014). Feiman-Nemser suggests that there are central tasks of learning to teach attributed to each step in the process, from preservice preparation, to induction (the first three years), to continuing professional development.

Feiman-Nemser (2001) describes five central tasks of teacher learning during preservice preparation: analyzing beliefs and forming new visions; developing subject matter knowledge for teaching; developing understandings of learners and learning; developing a beginning repertoire; and developing the tools to study teaching. She acknowledges that the images and beliefs students bring with them to preservice preparation influence what they are able to learn, but she argues that well-designed teacher education programs can alter these images in meaningful ways. During this phase, preservice teachers analyze the assumptions they bring with them in order to develop images of what it means to be a successful teacher of all students. Preservice teachers must continue to learn about their content areas but begin to view their content through a pedagogical lens while at the same time developing their knowledge of learners and age- and culturally appropriate strategies for teaching students. Feiman-Nemser emphasizes that this phase provides a time to "*begin* developing a basic repertoire for reform-minded teaching" (p. 1018, emphasis in original) so that pedagogical variety is pursued for the sake of students' learning, not for its own sake. Finally, she argues that a central task of preservice learning is coming to view learning as an integral part of teaching—that the study of teaching leads to improved practice.

She goes on to outline six central tasks of the teacher induction phase: gaining local knowledge of students, curriculum, and school context; designing responsive curriculum and instruction; enacting a beginning repertoire in purposeful ways; creating a classroom learning community; developing a professional identity; and learning in and from practice. These central tasks have two end goals in common: "Becoming a teacher involves forming a professional identity and constructing a professional practice" (p. 1027). Getting to know the local context, preparing and conducting lessons that are responsive to students in that context while creating a sense of community in the classroom, and determining what kind of teacher one is and wants to be while developing an inquiry stance toward practice is no short order for the first three years of teaching. It is true that, as she argues, "New teachers have two jobs—they have to teach and they have to learn to teach" (p. 1026).

Finally, Feiman-Nemser makes clear that the process of learning to teach is not complete after the preservice and induction phases of one's career. She explains that after the third year, one can expect a stage of experimentation and consolidation followed by a stage of mastery and stabilization around the seventh year of teaching. In the phase of early professional development, she outlines four central learning tasks: deepening and extending subject matter knowledge for teaching; extending and refining one's repertoire; strengthening dispositions and skills to study and improve teaching; and expanding responsibilities for leadership development. With more experience, it is possible to expand pedagogical content knowledge and a repertoire of strategies for teaching content that works around prescribed curriculum and builds on students' interests. Deeper inquiry into teaching and pursuit of teacher leadership opportunities enhance experienced teachers' learning.

Feiman-Nemser's theory of teacher learning over time served as the theoretical framework for conceptualizing and conducting this longitudinal study. A primary purpose of employing this framework was to examine what these central tasks of teacher learning might look like in terms of the urban teaching context at the preservice and induction phases and the learning exhibited by the four case study participants.

METHOD

As stated earlier, the research question guiding this study was, "What does learning to teach urban high school English look like over time?" Subquestions included, "How do these teachers enact their learning over time?" and "How does the PDS context influence these teachers' learning?" A qualitative, collective case study approach was employed. Merriam (1988) defines a qualitative case study as "an intensive, holistic description and analysis of a single entity, phenomenon, or social unit" (p. 16). Stake (2000) defines a collective case study as one where several cases are examined "because it is believed that understanding them will lead to better understanding, perhaps theorizing, about a still larger collection of cases" (p. 437). Case studies are not generalizable to larger populations, but can be generalized to theoretical propositions. Here, the four participants serve as four cases of learning to teach urban high school English over time.

Contexts and Participants

Two research sites applied for each participant—first, the professional development school in which all four were prepared to teach, and second, their schools in which they taught full-time three years after graduating. The common site of the participants' teacher education experiences was Brighton High School in Boston Public Schools, discussed in this section. The contexts for their full-time classroom teaching in four different school sites are mentioned below with participant information.

Brighton High School's student demographics for the years in which the participants prepared to teach are as follows: 46% Black, 40% Latino/a, 8% White, 6% Asian. For more than half of the 1200 students, English was not their native language, and 20% received special education services. Most were on free or reduced lunch (75%). The partnership between the high school and the university met all four criteria for PDSs as described by the Holmes Group (1990), but struggled to enact collaboratively planned preservice and inservice teacher education as prescribed by NCATE's (2001) PDS standards. That is, the primary responsibility for planning preservice teacher education lay with the university, and the primary responsibility for planning inservice teacher education lay with the high school. Nevertheless, an inquiry atmosphere pervaded the school site where teachers and professors worked collaboratively on authentic issues of concern, particularly around student learning. These professionals met regularly during the school day and afterschool on school/university/community committees, often to look at student work samples and share promising instructional practices to better meet the needs of the students.

The participants in this study include four 2005 graduates of Boston College who became interested in urban teaching during their prepracticum and full-practicum field experiences in Brighton High School's professional development school program. The two women and two men were considered the most successful English student teachers at the school based on mentor recommendations and final ratings on the state's professional performance rubric, and all four have committed to urban education, meeting the two main criteria for selection from a larger pool of potential participants. The selection process for participants in this study was similar to that employed by Ladson-Billings (2000) who "worked backwards" by purposively selecting successful teachers of African American students for her study in order to come to understand the knowledge, traits, practices, and dispositions of these teachers. Here, I adopt a similar stance. By selecting four teachers who became interested in urban teaching during their PDS-based teacher preparation program and were teaching in urban high schools three years later, the education community can potentially learn more about teachers who develop this commitment and decide to teach in urban schools.

The four teachers were assigned pseudonyms to protect their anonymity. Sara, Paul, Kate, and Matt completed their Urban Immersion experience at the PDS between 2002 and 2003. All four also completed two other 70-hour field experiences in suburban and private schools, along with corresponding coursework, before student teaching at the PDS in fall 2004 or spring 2005, and all earned bachelor's degrees in English and education in spring 2005. In their first year after graduation (2006), all four earned master's degrees in education. Sara focused on educational studies, Paul focused on curriculum and instruction with an English as a second language concentration, Kate focused on moderate special education, and Matt focused on curriculum and instruction. After earning her master's degree, Sara was directly admitted into her university's doctoral program in education and attended full-time, also teaching an undergraduate, introductory education course. At the time of the third year follow-up, Sara was in her first year teaching at an urban high school in the southeastern United States, Paul was in his second year of teaching in a large, northeastern city school-within-a-school, Kate was in her third year of teaching in a mid-sized, northeastern city high school, and Matt was in his third year of teaching at a large, northeastern city high school (the site of Urban Immersion, Brighton High School).

Data Collection and Analysis

Multiple data sources were collected, including interviews, teaching observations, and artifacts, such as written reflections, syllabi, and lesson plans. Data were collected at three points on the participants' professional continuum, twice during preservice preparation and once during induction, allowing for richer evidence and greater triangulation. Data collected during the first two phases were part of a larger research project on Urban Immersion (Stairs, 2003, 2006). Data collected during the third phase were gathered during site visits and day-long shadowing of participants in their full-time teaching positions. Initially, an inductive approach to data analysis was employed to make sense of the multiple data sources (Hatch, 2002). This meant reading and rereading data several times for each participant and then conducting cross-case analysis to determine points of convergence and divergence in the four teachers' experiences. Then, to further clarify the cases, Feiman-Nemser's (2001) continuum theory was applied in the final steps of analysis. This allowed for deeper examination of teacher learning over time as the theory considers teacher learning as a developmental process. This chapter provides description and interpretation of the participants' journey to urban English teaching and their learning about urban teaching over time.

FINDINGS AND DISCUSSION

Each teacher has a very individual story about his or her journey to urban English teaching from preparation in an urban professional development school to practice in four different urban high school contexts. However, after conducting cross-case analysis, there were some commonalities evident. Using Feiman-Nemser's (2001) framework, the central task most evident in the data during their preservice learning phase was analyzing beliefs and forming new visions, and the central task most evident in the data during their induction learning phase was designing responsive curriculum and instruction. Both preservice and induction phases of learning are discussed with examples and vignettes from the data.

Preservice Learning: Analyzing Beliefs and Forming New Visions

The central task most evident in the data from participants' PDS teacher preparation was the first task of teacher learning during preservice preparation discussed by Feiman-Nemser (2001): analyzing beliefs and forming new visions (p. 1016). Evidence suggests that the participants examined their beliefs about urban students and related their altered beliefs to a vision of good teaching rooted in equity and social justice.

Prepracticum field experience. During their first field experience in the PDS, all four participants shared their developing beliefs about urban students. Two participants explicitly stated they brought negative assumptions with them to the experience and that these had changed, while two explained in a more nuanced way how their beliefs developed. For example, in reflecting back upon her semester, Sara stated, "I was making such horrible assumptions about inner-city high school students" (Reflection, 11/19/02, p. 2) and, similarly, Matt said, "During these last three months, my perception of urban students has changed dramatically. I have come to understand, appreciate, and respect these students and enjoy spending time with them ... urban students *are* intelligent" (Reflection, 4/24/03, p. 1). Paul's statement also expressed his changing beliefs:

> I feel like a different person now.... I have grown in many areas ... but most importantly, I think I have learned how to relate to these children. No matter how different I may be from some of these kids, I think that I have found ways of getting through to them and making the material interesting (Reflection, 12/4/03, pp. 1-2).

Kate said, "Coming from a high school where almost all of my classroom peers were White, I never realized how important culture could be in the classroom" (Course paper, 11/20/03, p. 2). Kate went on to share a conversation she had with a Brighton High School student about how he disliked one teacher who yelled at him when he spoke his native language in the classroom. The student explained that sometimes his native language just slipped out because it was the language spoken exclusively in his home. Kate explained how experiences like this made it apparent to her that "students' cultures cannot be taken away from them or outright rejected in school because it makes the students feel devalued" (Course paper, 11/20/03, p. 3).

As all four developed their beliefs about urban students, they focused on the relationship between teacher and students, which revealed their developing vision of good teaching as student-centered. Paul said that "it is important for a teacher to establish some type of personal connection with kids" (Reflection, 12/4/03, p. 4). Matt explained:

> Now, when I look at a student, I try to imagine what is going on in the back of their mind. I try to understand why the student might be acting a certain way. With this compassion, I believe I will reach more students. (Reflection, 4/24/03, p. 4)

Part of paying attention to students is noticing what learning activities excite and motivate them as learners and human beings. Kate admitted to carefully observing "the different learning activities to which the students responded most enthusiastically" (Journal, 12/4/05, p. 2) because "students can only do their best work when they do an assignment in a way in which they feel comfortable and confident" (Journal, 12/4/05, p. 3). Finally, Sara revealed that she planned to teach in an urban school upon graduating as "the students are AMAZING ... so accepting and so very intelligent" (Reflection, 11/19/02, p. 5). The students at Brighton High School provided learning opportunities that allowed participants to change their beliefs about urban students and their role in teaching them in the future.

Through cross-case analysis it became clear that these participants became committed to teaching in urban schools not only because of relationships they formed with students and their interest in keeping students' needs at the center of urban education, but also because of their developing vision of good teaching rooted in social justice and equity. Sara believed her early field experience made her a better person and helped her realize the type of teacher she wanted to become. She wondered, "Who knew that in three months I would grow to be so passionate about public education and the injustice that exists in the education system as a whole?" (Reflection, 11/19/02, p. 5). One pivotal moment she cited during her early field experience was when she explained to one of her mentor teachers she intended to teach in a private school like the one she attended. The teacher simply asked her, "Why?" She reflected upon this question during the semester and decided that the inequities were too great and she might make a real difference teaching in an urban school. She defined what being a socially just educator means to her:

> Making sure I'm not just teaching them what has been taught to me or what the textbook says I should be teaching them. Making sure that they're learning about themselves through the literature and making them better people, not just teaching them English. (Interview, 11/18/03)

The other three participants also revealed their desire to make a difference by teaching in urban schools. Kate admitted that she had been "an extremely naïve person when it comes to ideas of equality and fairness in America" (Course paper, 11/20/03, p. 4). She learned how strongly the collective White worldview influences expectations people from all cultures are held to and how this worldview is "completely capitalistic and power-driven" (Course paper, 11/20/03, p. 4). She realized that students from non-dominant cultures may not understand or relate to these values and may suffer as a result. Matt said, "More than anybody else, urban students need support ... the school systems are usually less supportive in urban areas. Therefore, the teachers take on even greater importance for the urban student" (Reflection, 4/24/03, pp. 3-4). Though Matt does not clarify what he means by "support," it is clear that he recognizes the need for strong teachers in urban schools. Paul simply stated, "Brighton High School has opened my eyes. The school has opened my eyes to the need for better education and better teachers in urban schools and new ways to motivate students in urban settings" (Course paper, 11/20/03, p. 1).

Full-practicum field experience. Though each teacher progressed on an individual journey of analyzing beliefs and forming new visions, what each had in common was meaningful clarification of beliefs early in their teacher education program. It may not be surprising, then, that after two more semesters of coursework and early field experiences in other school contexts, all four chose to return to the urban PDS for their full-time student teaching as seniors. All four participants also chose to student teach with one of their mentor teachers from the first experience. Feiman-Nemser (2001) argues, "Teacher candidates must also form visions of what is possible and desirable in teaching to inspire and guide their professional learning and practice. Such visions connect important values and goals to concrete classroom practices" (p. 1017). Evidence of participants' clarifying beliefs and conceptions of good teaching developed early in their urban PDS experience was confirmed by how they enacted these beliefs in their full-time student teaching at the PDS. The participants' visions of student-centered education rooted in social justice and equity were enacted through culturally responsive lessons (Villegas & Lucas, 2002). There were multiple examples of lessons embodying participants' beliefs and visions of good teaching, but only a few are shared here by way of illustration.

To explore the oppression of women with her tenth-grade students, Sara conducted a whole-class discussion of rapper Tupac Shakur's poem "The Rose that Grew from Concrete" followed by literature circle discussions using four vignettes from Cisneros' *The House on Mango Street*. Matt used the opening pages of Achebe's *Things Fall Apart* to model "social context questions" so that his tenth-grade students might learn to question and critique the beliefs and norms in society. Students practiced posing and answering social context questions in small groups using their whole-class text, Miller's *The Crucible*. Paul engaged his ninth-grade special education students with the concept of assimilation important to their whole-class text, Hansbury's *A Raisin in the Sun*, by reading aloud a passage on Native American assimilation three times and then asking students to independently represent what assimilation means through a drawing. Kate's twelfth-grade Writing for College elective covered traditional topics for a college preparatory writing course in engaging ways, such as her lesson on clichés where she provided a handout of common clichés and students composed short poems using only clichés as a way to discuss why originality in writing is important.

Changing beliefs is not enough—teachers must enact their new beliefs to solidify their new visions of themselves as teachers. Data analysis suggests this process began for the four participants during their first field experience in the urban PDS and extended through their full-time student teaching in the same PDS. Feiman-Nemser (2001) contends that there are major problems and obstacles to cohesive, reform-minded teacher education, but she suggests that the Holmes Partnership (a major proponent of PDSs), among other groups, laid important groundwork for preservice teacher education that can make a difference. Purposeful, integrated field experiences are one component she mentions "because of the critical and complex role that classroom experiences play in learning to teach during preservice preparation" (p. 1024). The PDS context where these participants learned to teach may provide the context and conditions for altering beliefs.

Preservice teachers may develop these same commitments and practices in any urban teacher education program, but I would argue the PDS program made the learning opportunities systematic. There was a common commitment among school-university partners that created conditions for preservice teacher learning. PDS teachers were constantly developing their professional knowledge and skills by, for example, enrolling in and/or co-teaching university courses regularly, meeting with school-university partners during the high school's common planning time, and mentoring two to six preservice teachers each semester. The culture of learning among mentor teachers promoted a culture of learning among the preservice teachers, and in turn, the high school students. The context of the PDS created positive learning about urban teaching for the study participants that they applied in their full-time teaching.

Induction Learning: Designing Responsive Curriculum and Instruction

It was clear from the data that the beliefs and visions formed during their preservice phase were maintained during their induction years. In this section, I share a vignette from each teacher's classroom as I shadowed them in the spring of 2008. These vignettes represent the way these teachers designed responsive curriculum and instruction during their induction phase of teacher development.

What's wrong with a bilingual class as long as they're learning? This subheading represents a comment Kate made during an interview on a day I shadowed her (Observation, 1.28.08). In her third year teaching, as in her preservice phase, Kate was primarily teaching senior classes. That day students were working on research papers about Shakespeare's *Hamlet*. She decided to teach a literary research paper because all the other senior teachers were doing the same assignment. The difference in her assignment was that the whole class was writing about the same text. She had tried having them do an independent book of their choice in the past, but the students had told her they hadn't read the book, just the Spark Notes before writing their papers. She wanted them to work from a common text that they had read aloud and studied together in class to make the paper writing process more meaningful.

Writing a literary research paper on *Hamlet* may not initially seem like curriculum and instruction designed with her students in mind. However, her students were planning on attending college the following year, and Kate wanted to be sure they were prepared for the kinds of assignments they would be expected to complete at the next level. The activities about the play to that point were drawn largely from the performance-based curriculum, *Shakespeare Set Free*, and *No Fear Shakespeare* texts with contemporary English language translations were also used to make the play more accessible for her students, many of whom were non-native English speakers. What was most noticeable and responsive about Kate's instruction, however, was the way she supported her students' work on their thesis statements that day in the library. Kate provided handouts and modeled her expectations for a strong thesis statement and then allowed guided practice time for students to review their sources and craft a thesis. Kate moved from table to table, kneeling down to students individually or pulling up a stool. Students worked diligently, sharing their developing thesis statements with each other in English, Spanish, or Portuguese. At moments she stepped into the periodicals room and found another resource for a student. One boy hadn't written anything several minutes into class. His hands were in his pockets, and he was staring straight ahead. Kate knelt down next to him, and he told her he didn't know what he was doing. "Yes you do," she replied. "What's your topic? The tragic hero? OK, let's talk about what you're proving." The next few minutes of their conference were inaudible, but as she got up from their conversation, he turned around smiling and began working.

As Kate concluded our interview about the seniors' lesson, she shared that she always tries to build off of students' native languages, helping them think of words in their native languages, even helping them print research articles off the computer in their native languages rather than asking them to read the English versions. She said, "At first, English-only made sense, starting college, then I went to [college] and student taught and taught here, and what's wrong with a bilingual class as long as they're learning?" (Interview, 1.28.08, p. 5). It seemed that her students agreed as several languages floated around the room in each of her classes in an English-only state. A boy who was sitting next to me during her first period class stated that her best quality was her patience: "She wouldn't be the same teacher is she weren't so patient."

Don't make it sound so simple. One day, more than a month after shadowing Kate, I shadowed Matt (Observation, 3.4.08), whose twelfth-graders had also just finished reading *Hamlet* and were working on thesis statements in class. Matt began each long block teaching twelfth or tenth grade with 20 minutes of independent reading time where students read books of their choice and take notes in reading journals. The class of seniors spent their 20 minutes completely silent, all students reading (with the exception of one struggling to stay awake). After reading, Matt provided examples of thesis statements and had students practice whether they met the three criteria he had laid out: clear, arguable, specific. After some time to practice analyzing thesis statements as a class, Matt placed students in pre-determined groups and gave each group a transparency with some student-written thesis statements without names attached. Matt explained that it should helpful for students to look critically at someone else's thesis, and all would receive advice on improving their statements. He instructed each group to make changes right on the overhead transparency and be prepared to make comments to the class about why these changes would improve the thesis. The seniors were eager to critique each other's thesis statements and worked diligently, loudly debating with each other about what needed to be improved about each statement. Used as the subheading for this section, one student stated, "We want the person to expand words and don't make it sound so simple."

This vignette captures Matt's ability to use the resources students brought with them to the classroom. He recognized he was working with seniors who had some years of experience with essay writing, and he wanted to draw students into improving their work by collaborating as a class. In a post-observation interview, Matt explained that he decided to teach *Hamlet* because it is "a staple in the twelfth-grade curriculum" at the high school, "the themes are rich and timeless," and "we want to teach students to make meaning of difficult language" (Interview, 3.4.08, p. 10). By teaching a challenging text, Matt was holding his students to high standards, a cornerstone of culturally responsive pedagogy (Ladson-Billings, 1995; Villegas & Lucas, 2002). Matt showed he understands how to make his curriculum and instruction appropriate for his students.

We're going to focus on the theme of alienation through racism. Shadowing Paul was a different experience from the other teachers in that he taught the same class—tenth-grade humanities—four times a day, and one shorter period of advisory and homeroom (Observation, 3.3.08). He was teaching Wright's *Black Boy* to all four classes. That day, the primary activity for students was to perform a scene isolation of pages 179-182. This activity had students read aloud a scene about the young, Black narrator accepting a ride with White boys in a car, being beaten badly, and learning from that moment how to observe and interact with White people. The scene included vivid description of the narrator's thoughts and actions and was stylistically complicated. Before reading, Paul explained that they were going to look at a time when the narrator experienced racism firsthand and relate this to the two major themes of the novel: hunger and isolation. As a student volunteer read the passage, one girl shouted, "This is messed up!" At the conclusion of the scene, Paul began a word web on the board centered with "alienation through racism." He invited the class to share moments in this scene, then others in the text, when the narrator experienced alienation through racism. As the word web grew with student comments—when he was stopped by police because of his race, when he doesn't call the White men "sir" and is beaten because of it, when store owners are openly mean to Black customers—one African American girl interrupted.

"Can I say something?" Paul nodded. "You know how some people say the definition of 'nigger' is 'ignorant'? I know it doesn't seem right, but it means ignorant, right?" Paul explained that he didn't know the exact answer to her question, but that the definition had changed over time. Another girl added, "People think that nigger means Black, dirty, but White is clean, pure." The first girl got up and walked to the back of the room for a dictionary. Paul asked for some more examples of alienation through racism and directed students to the handout they would be working on either individually or with a partner of their choice as the young woman looked up the words "black" and "white." In a few minutes she had located both and Paul allowed her to share with the class. "Black means black person, dirty, dark; white means a color of maximum lightness, the opposite of black, a member of a racial group, morally unblemished, pure." Paul thanked her for sharing, and the discussion ended there as students worked on their handouts. In the next minute, Paul stopped at a table where one girl was telling the two boys at her table that the police came to her house with guns drawn looking for her cousin because he had a warrant for his arrest. "I was scared! I've never been so scared in my whole life!" Very sincerely, Paul said, "That's terrible."

Paul showed he was not afraid to teach a book that deals with racism, allowing students space to process and connect with their daily struggles, which at times are race-related. When Paul told the class that they would "focus on the theme of alienation through racism," the heading for this vignette, he made explicit that they were not simply talking about the plot of a racially charged text. They were examining issues that many of his students could relate to, as evident in the concern over defining black and white.

It got things off my chest. Sara taught honors freshman English, a creative writing elective for 9th- through 12th-graders, and yearbook to 10th-through 12th-graders the spring when I shadowed her (Observation, 4.16.08). A quotation posted above the door to her classroom indicated Sara's commitments as a teacher: "The right of every American to first-class citizenship is the most important issue of our time." It may be that having just completed her master's in educational studies in a particularly progressive, social justice-oriented graduate program further influenced her identity as a teacher teaching more than just English, a comment noted above that she made during her preservice phase. When I shadowed Sara at her high school, the unit she was working on with her creative writing elective was "Creative Writing as Social Action: Using Writing to 'Bear Witness.'" The vignette described here reveals Sara's ability to design responsive curriculum and instruction.

The class began with a "Do Now" activity written on the board: If you could switch any of your identities for a day (& then switch back), which would you switch and why? Sara allowed her students to write for about eight minutes, then each candidly shared their responses with the class.

One boy said, "I'd be a woman for a day. Then I would understand what it would be like to be a mother and why my mother does so much for me." Another boy agreed that he would be a woman, too, "So that I could understand what women go through, like sexual things they have to deal with people saying." He went on to say that he wouldn't switch back to his own identity because he'd like to give birth to a child. A girl said, "I'd like to be a White American to see what the power is like." Another girl chose to be a man "to see what the power is like." One boy said, "I would be White for a day just to see if the media and racists—to see if the world opened up for me or to see if I had certain privileges. I'd call and see if I get the same offers, Black or White." This boy, however, said he would not want to stay White: "I'm happy with myself."

After this opening activity, Sara had students transition to their main writing for the day. Considering their Do Now responses and the homework they did about privileges in society, today students would write about prejudice. She reminded them that they had examined the difference between racism and prejudice the previous class. Race may be the topic of their writing, but it did not have to be. Sara told students to think about what other people don't know about them as individuals and what they should know. On the white board next to the day's agenda, Sara wrote "1. What they think. 2. What you actually are." When students finished writing two pieces on this topic, Sara invited them to sit on the stool at the front of the class and read one or both of their writings. As each read their stories of racial, sexual orientation, immigration, and religious prejudice, the class enthusiastically clapped. Sara focused them on listening not just as friends, but as writers, and they told each other frankly about the most powerful parts of their writing. As the activity wrapped up, Sara asked what they liked about this creative writing activity. One boy said, "They straight," and another said, "It got things off my chest," the subheading for this section as it represents the experience of the students that day.

Sara presented curriculum and instruction responsive to her students' interests and clearly rooted in the belief that education is a political act. She positioned herself as a facilitator of students' examining assumptions others make about them, which provided a cathartic moment for students who expressed their frustrations in a supportive learning environment. Students were literally applauded for being themselves and sharing their feelings aloud to the class by reading their writing. Oakes, Franke, Quartz, and Roger (2002) suggest that "capable and ambitious young people are eager to become social justice educators, even in the face of realistic portrayals of the political and economic realities that make urban schools so challenging" (p. 231). Sara's responsiveness was rooted in her identity as a social justice educator.

CONCLUSIONS AND IMPLICATIONS

Following Sara, Paul, Kate, and Matt over time has allowed us a glimpse into what urban teacher learning looks like over time. In terms of Feiman-Nemser's (2001) framework, participants exhibited the most evidence of analyzing beliefs and forming new visions during the preservice phase and designing responsive curriculum and instruction during the induction phase. This is not to suggest that the teachers did not learn about aspects of teaching described in other areas of Feiman-Nemser's framework, but the data did not reveal whether (or the degree to which) these participants developed in those areas. The strongest evidence of learning was revealed in participants' evolving beliefs and responsive pedagogy.

Though the main research question for this study asked what learning to teach urban high school English looks like over time, it seemed that participants' teaching identities were less related to their content area and more related to their commitment to urban education. All four were meeting state and national standards for English teaching with academically challenging yet culturally appropriate tasks, but as Sara stated, she saw herself as "not just teaching them English" (Interview, 11/18/03). Oftentimes high school teachers are known for love of their content area above all other factors, but these four participants revealed an interest in their students' learning and development as human beings and a commitment to teaching for social justice.

The subquestions for this study considered how participants enacted their learning over time and the influence of the PDS on their learning and practice. I argue that these PDS-prepared urban teachers learned about effective urban teaching during their preservice phase when they developed appropriate beliefs, and they successfully translated their learning and beliefs into practice during their induction phase. This finding suggests an important outcome of learning to teach in the urban PDS context. If teacher preparation is designed for urban PDSs with inquiry-oriented, learning-focused conditions, graduates may be more likely to enact their beliefs and learning in practice even several years after graduation. More longitudinal research on urban PDSs is necessary to further examine this possibility.

Context matters in urban teacher learning. It may be assumed that the four participants in this study seamlessly applied what they learned from their PDS teacher preparation in their full-time teaching positions because the contexts were congruent. However, McKinney, Haberman, Stafford-Johnson, and Robinson's (2008) study comparing traditional and PDS internships in urban schools found no significant difference in pre and posttest scores on the Urban Teacher Selection Interview. They concluded that the internship was a short-term experience that did not adequately prepare preservice teachers for urban teaching, asserting that "critical resurrection and reframing of teacher preparation programs are necessary to better prepare teacher candidates for the urban school context" (p. 78).

The PDS at the center of this study did provide urban coursework and fieldwork from the first semester candidates entered teacher preparation, with the option of returning to the PDS for full-time student teaching. The Urban Immersion program during the first semester allowed preservice teachers the opportunity to explore urban teaching. Candidates completed two other field experiences in suburban and private/parochial schools (and other teacher education coursework) before selecting student teaching contexts senior year. The four participants in this study, then, made informed decisions about where they saw themselves as teachers for their student teaching—in the urban context—and remained committed to urban teaching after graduation. McKinney et al.'s (2008) assertion that teacher preparation programs need to be "reframed" for urban teacher learning is a reality at this university, and this small study shows the promising nature of urban teacher learning over time from preservice to inservice teaching for urban PDS graduates.

This study confirms previous PDS research that preservice teachers prepared in an urban PDS are more likely to seek employment in city schools (Abdal-Haqq, 1998; Wong & Glass, 2005). It also confirms Groulx's (2001) finding that more positive and efficacious beliefs are developed by urban PDS preservice teachers, but this study goes further to suggest that PDS-prepared teachers can enact these beliefs in practice over time.

A main implication of the current study is that teacher preparation in urban professional development schools may effectively recruit and prepare strong urban teachers when candidates are introduced to the urban context early in their teacher preparation program and are allowed multiple opportunities to explore various school contexts before choosing to student teach in urban schools. More research that examines urban PDS graduates' learning over time would contribute to our understanding of the outcomes of PDS preparation.

REFERENCES

Abdal-Haqq, I. (1998). *Professional development schools: Weighing the evidence*. Thousands Oaks, CA: Corwin Press.

Beardsley, L. V., & Teitel, L. (2004). Learning to see color in teacher education: An example framed by the professional development school standard for diversity and equity. *The Teacher Educator, 40*(2), 91-115.

Boyle-Baise, M., & McIntyre, D. J. (2008). What kind of experience? Preparing teachers in PDS or community settings. In M. Cochran-Smith, S. Feiman-Nemser, D. J. McIntyre & K. E. Demers (Eds.), *Handbook of research on teacher education: Enduring questions in changing contexts* (3rd ed., pp. 307-329). New York, NY: Routledge and the Association of Teacher Educators.

Donnell, K. (2007). Getting to we: Developing a transformative urban teaching practice. *Urban Education, 42*(3), 223-249.

Feiman-Nemser, S. (2001). From preparation to practice: Designing a continuum to strengthen and sustain teaching. *Teachers College Record, 103*(6), 1013-1055.

Groulx. J. G. (2001). Changing preservice teacher perceptions of minority schools. *Urban Education, 36*(1), 60-92.

Haberman, M. (1994). Preparing teachers for the real world of urban schools. *The Educational Forum, 58*(2), 162-168.

Haberman, M. (1995). Selecting 'star' teachers for children and youth in urban poverty. *Phi Delta Kappan, 76*(10), 777-781.

Hatch, J. A. (2002). *Doing qualitative research in education settings*. Albany, NY: State University of New York.

Holmes Group (1990). *Tomorrow's schools: Principles for the design of professional development schools*. East Lansing, MI: Author.

Ladson-Billings, G. (1995). Toward a theory of culturally relevant pedagogy. *American Educational Research Journal, 32*(3), 465-491.

Ladson-Billings, G. (2000). Fighting for our lives: Preparing teachers to teach African American students. *Journal of Teacher Education, 51*(3), 206-214.

McKinney, S. E., Haberman, M., Stafford-Johnson, D., & Robinson, J. (2008). Developing teachers for high-poverty schools: The role of the internship experience. *Urban Education, 43*(1), 68-82.

National Council for Accreditation of Teacher Education (2001). *Standards for professional development schools*. Washington, DC: Author.

Oakes, J., Franke, M. L., Quartz, K. H., & Roger, J. (2002). Research for high-quality urban teaching: Defining it, developing it, assessing it. *Journal of Teacher Education, 53*(3), 228-234.

Reynolds, A. (2000). Open the doors and see all the people. *Teaching and Change, 8*(1), 10-30.

Rock, T. C., & Levin, B. B. (2002). Collaborative action research projects: Enhancing preservice teacher development. *Teacher Education Quarterly, 29*(1), 7-21.

Stairs, A. J. (2003). The controversy around defining "highly qualified" teachers and one university's definition in practice. *Teacher Education and Practice, 16*(4), 384-398.

Stairs, A. J. (2006). Urban Immersion: A prototypical early clinical immersion experience. In K. R. Howey, L. Post & N. L. Zimpher (Eds.), *Recruiting, preparing, and retaining teachers for urban schools*. Washington, DC: American Association of Colleges for Teacher Education.

Stake, R. E. (2000). Case studies. In N. K. Denzin & Y. S. Lincoln (Eds.), *The handbook of qualitative research* (2nd ed., pp. 443-466). Thousand Oaks, CA: Sage.

Thompson, S., & Ross, F. (2000). Becoming a teacher in a professional development school. *Teaching and Change, 8*(1), 31-50.

Villegas, A. M., & Lucas, T. (2002). Preparing culturally responsive teachers: Rethinking the curriculum. *Journal of Teacher Education, 53*(1), 20-32.

Weiner, L. (1993). *Preparing teachers for urban schools: Lessons from thirty years of school reform*. New York, NY: Teachers College Press.

Weiner, L. (1999). *Urban teaching: The essentials*. New York: Teachers College Press.

Wong, P. L., & Glass, R. D. (2005). Assessing a professional development school approach to preparing teachers for urban schools serving low-income, culturally and linguistically diverse communities. *Teacher Education Quarterly, 32*(3), 63-77.

CHAPTER 5

NAVIGATING THE FIRST YEAR

The Experiences of Alternatively Certified Urban Teachers

Katie Tricarico and Diane Yendol-Hoppey

Because alternative certification is a rapidly growing pathway to teaching, school administrators and teacher educators need to understand the difficulties these novice teachers experience during their first year on the job, especially when those teachers are working in the most challenging urban schools. The National Commission on Teaching and America's Future (2002) states that nearly one fourth of new teachers leave the profession within their first three years. In urban areas, the attrition rate is even greater since about half of these new teachers leave the profession within five years (National Commission on Teaching and America's Future, 2002). Furthermore, teachers working in schools in which the minority enrollment is greater than 50% tend to leave at rates more than twice those of teachers in schools with fewer minorities (Haycock, 2000). In order to learn how to support and retain novice teachers working in challenging urban schools, this paper explores two urban teachers' experiences as they navigated the first year.

Research on Urban Teacher Learning: Examining Contextual Factors Over Time
pp. 61–78
Copyright © 2010 by Information Age Publishing
All rights of reproduction in any form reserved.

As we entered the research context, we initially intended to study how first-year teachers perceive and experience the support systems that are available to them. However, early data analysis quickly indicated that even in a district that dedicated substantial resources to teacher induction and mentoring, support was extremely limited. These teachers felt overwhelmed and virtually unsupported. As a result, rather than investigating the nature of support, we constructed a research question that would allow our participants to share the dilemmas they found pressing. Our investigation shifted to the question, "How do new, alternatively certified teachers experience and navigate their first year as teachers of record in an urban school?"

METHOD

Grounded within an interpretivist framework (Crotty, 1998), this qualitative study helped explore how these two teachers experienced their first year of teaching in an urban school. The participants in this study were newly certified teachers named Sandy[1] and Bruce who completed the University of Florida/Duval County Public School Collaborative 2006-2007 *Transition to Teaching* Apprenticeship Program. This federally funded program targeted recruiting, training, and retaining second-career candidates to teach in high-needs areas. Therefore, the schools in which these teachers were employed were Title I schools where more than 90% of the student population qualified for free or reduced cost lunch. This Apprenticeship program provided a year of "on the job experience" paired with 15 credits of coursework. During this year, these novices taught side-by-side a mentor teacher in an elementary classroom and received coaching from the university instructor who spent approximately 30 hours per week at their school. It was during the following year, their first year as teachers of record, that we conducted this study.

Participants

The two participants were purposefully selected (Patton, 2002) from a pool of 15 candidates, all former apprentices, in order to represent variation in age, gender, and socioeconomic status.

Sandy is a White woman and single mother of two in her fifties who came to the profession after earning her MBA and working in the corporate world. Sandy describes herself as growing up poor and putting herself through school as a "way out of poverty." When asked what brought her to education, she responded:

Because my children are grown. So now I get to, call it selfish, but I get to have my dreams now. And do what I want to do, versus, you know, my life is no longer driven by how much money I make because I don't have to provide for my children. Now I can do whatever I want and focus in on the things that interest me and that I love. (Interview 1)

Sandy lives out her dream of being a teacher by beginning her career in the same urban school where she completed her apprenticeship. This school is classified as a turn-around school, meaning the school has not made adequate yearly progress (AYP) and is being given additional support by the district. The school is in transition, made visible by the change in principal at the start of the school year and the number of district personnel bringing new mandates to the leadership team on a regular basis. Sandy teaches kindergarten at her school.

Bruce is a White man in his twenties and earned his bachelor's degree in business management information systems. He has moved through many careers since then, working at an animal hospital, as a dairy manager in a grocery store, off shore in the Gulf of Mexico, and then in staffing for a hospital and a bio-pharmaceutical company. His school is also a Title I school, but the principal has been there for several years and the faculty is generally stable. Bruce teaches third grade.

An important part of both teachers' backgrounds is a long-standing desire to be teachers. Sandy's desire to teach existed for many years, but barriers such as family commitments and lack of educational availability prevented her from moving into the classroom sooner. Bruce cited his parents as one reason he did not become a teacher sooner: "I've always thought about teaching, but I was discouraged from going into teaching by parents for economical reasons, and then eventually came to my senses and just did it" (Interview 1). As is visible in their statements, the aspiration was there, but both teachers needed to reach a point in their lives where they were able to take the step and join the apprenticeship program.

Data Collection and Analysis

Data collection consisted of four interviews held in September, October, November, and April (see Table 5.1) which asked Sandy and Bruce to make sense of their first year as teachers. Because we knew and had studied these teachers during their apprenticeship year, we already possessed a trusting relationship with both teachers, allowing them to provide candid answers to our questions. Each of the four interviews asked them to

Table 5.1.   Summary of Data Collection by Interview

Interview	Date	Interview topic
1	September 25, 2007	Background
2	October 23, 2007	Support mechanisms
3	November 27, 2007	Identity and efficacy
4	April 9 and 10, 2008	Teaching and mentoring

Table 5.2.   Emerging Themes Framed as Questions

Emerging Themes	Questions
Image of teaching	What is "good" and "bad" teaching?
Challenges	What perceived challenges do they face?
Stance	How do they perceive their students and the school environment?
Response to complexity	How do they respond to the complexity of teaching?
Satisfaction and perseverance	What makes them satisfied and persevere?
Role of relationships	How do relationships influence their success and survival?
Barriers	What are the barriers to success and survival?
Self-efficacy	What is their sense of self-efficacy?
Future	What are their future plans?

identify specific dilemmas each teacher experienced during his or her first year, but the first interview also included identifying what they believed was a "good" or "bad" teacher. The remaining interviews consisted of questions on topics such as support systems, mentors, school-related stress, and other similar issues.

Each interview was transcribed and coded by identifying a preliminary list of domains (see Table 5.2). The transcribed interviews were used to create probing questions for subsequent interviews. These questions were identified due to a need to capture missing information from the first two interviews. The researchers identified a set of elements that captured the experiences of Sandy and Bruce during their first year as teachers.

Given that these participants began teaching careers in high-poverty, urban contexts, the onus of responsibility will be the reader's to determine if the issues faced by these teachers are the same issues faced by the new teachers in other elementary schools.

FINDINGS: SANDY AND BRUCE'S SENSE-MAKING

Sandy and Bruce differed in gender, age, and life experiences. However, they found themselves in very similar situations as first-year teachers who went through the same alternative certification program, teaching in high-needs schools. No matter how their backgrounds differed, at the start of their first year of teaching, Sandy and Bruce claimed that their main task was to figure out how to navigate this first year of teaching in their urban elementary school by coping with stressors created by the organizational environment, while at the same time making sure that their students were learning. This navigation task described by Sandy and Bruce is similar to the discussion of success and survival, discussed by Yendol-Hoppey et al. (2008):

> Survival and success are two different things. Survival means that you are pleasing the system and abiding by the many expectations that are important to the administration and bureaucracy of the system. Succeeding is the important part, but it is very different. Succeeding is about the kids' learning. (p.11)

Sandy and Bruce both discussed the tension that they felt between meeting the demands of the system, surviving, and making sure that children learned.

Although the first-year experiences of these two teachers were very similar, the way they formed their own professional identity through those experiences is significantly different. The following sections will discuss seven themes that emerged during the analysis that relate to the experiences that shaped Sandy and Bruce's professional identity: (1) What is "good" and "bad" teaching?, (2) What makes them satisfied and persevere?, (3) What is the role of relationships?, (4) What support do they need and receive?, (5) What are the barriers to success and survival?, (6) What is their sense of self-efficacy?, and (7) What are their future plans? These seven themes provide insight into how each teacher makes sense of their success and survival as they navigate their first year. From these themes, three assertions were drawn that suggest how these novice teachers learned to navigate their new positions as classroom teachers.

What is "Good" and "Bad" Teaching?

Important to these two teachers' conceptions of success during their first year of teaching were their visions of "good" or "bad" teaching. After their 16-year "apprenticeship of observation" (Lortie, 1975) as public school students themselves, and then serving as a teacher's apprentice for an additional year in a high-poverty school, both teachers had clear ideas of what they considered successful and unsuccessful teaching. On the whole, they both cited some of the same "good" teacher characteristics, including "that they're honest, that they believe in their children regardless of where their children live or what their background is. And that they're always driven to ensure that their children learn" (Sandy, Interview 1). Bruce added, "They seem to be very aware of the subject matter and the students" (Interview 1). Other shared descriptors for what makes a good teacher included: "patience, open-minded, creative, intelligent, quick-witted, energetic, determined" (Bruce, Interview 1). In sum, both of these new teachers felt that a teacher should care about his or her students, as well as understand and be able to appropriately teach subject matter so students can learn.

As for what constitutes a "bad" teacher, both teachers marked attitude as the strongest indicator. According to Sandy, "I consider someone a bad teacher, or has a bad attitude which lends itself to bad teaching, when they go around the school and go, 'I hate this school; I don't have bad kids, I have stupid kids'" (Interview 1). She continued to say, "That's all you hear, and that carries over to the kids because you're not willing to put as much into teaching them, or even doing engaging activities" (Interview 1). Bruce added, "I guess a bad teacher is someone who doesn't care about the kids, one way or the other" (Interview 1). Other adjectives used to describe poor teachers included being unprepared, having poor classroom management skills, and complacency.

As indicated, both Sandy and Bruce discussed a strong link between "good teaching" and caring for students whereas "bad teaching" emerges from an attitude of disrespect for the children and the profession. This information is crucial to understanding their personal philosophies which guide their teaching and their emerging conception of success in teaching. Both of these teachers identified both relational and pedagogical characteristics of teaching that they believe would facilitate their success.

What Makes Them Satisfied and Persevere?

Both Sandy and Bruce took pride in their new positions as teachers. One of the greatest differences between Sandy and Bruce as teachers was the type of goals they had for themselves as teachers. Sandy stated very measurable goals for student learning, while Bruce was striving for goals that could be considered life skills, such as values and making wise choices. An example of Sandy's stated goals for her students was evident when she said the following:

By the time they leave me, I'd like them to have the basics, the core, so that when they move on to first grade, they're ready to write a story, they're ready to begin addition. They at least have a working knowledge of comprehension strategies and those type things that they can continue to build on. (Interview 3)

In an earlier interview, Sandy also stated that she would know she had succeeded in her first year teaching when,

My students meet the performance standards set by the state. When my kindergarteners at the end of the year know how to read at least at a level C, and I certainly hope higher than a level C because that's not the goal I set for them, that they know all their letter sounds, that they can write a narrative story with a beginning, middle, end ... that they can do logical thinking on their manipulatives. (Interview 1)

Most of Sandy's goals are measurable, either by state or in-class assessments, so she was able to gauge her progress and adjust her teaching to help all of her students learn.

Bruce, on the other hand, described several goals that were far less measurable. The majority of his goals concern life skills, such as this example: "I hope to instill values in them, worthwhile values to help them become successful in life and society" (Interview 3). Bruce also stated,

I really hope what they take away from class is that you get more flies with honey than with vinegar, or however that saying goes. Because, I try to teach them that kindness gets you a lot of places. We'll talk about jobs, and is it a matter of what you know or who you know, and you have to be able to interact with people. It's not just about book smarts; it's about working with others in life. So, I think that's one of the most valuable things they take away from here. (Interview 3)

Unlike Sandy's learning goals, which were more academic in nature, Bruce's stated affective goals were very difficult to assess. Since it was not easy for him to determine whether students were reaching these affective goals, it was difficult for him to gauge his own success as well as adjust what he was doing to meet his students' needs.

What is the Role of Relationships?

Bruce and Sandy both recognized that in order for them to be successful with their students they must develop trusting relationships by building community. Bruce frequently asked for student input and put things to a vote. He generally felt that he and his students had a good relationship where it was "not so much a superior and subordinate" (Interview 3). Sandy felt that her biggest strength was her obvious caring for her kinder-garteners, who knew they were safe in her classroom and could confide in their teacher (Interview 3). She built this relationship through "a lot of one-on-one conversations, you know just talking to them and finding out what they wanted and what concerns they might have and what they expected" (Interview 3). When asked specifically about student relation-ships, Sandy focused on the community that her students have built. The nature of Sandy and Bruce's relationships with their students was differ-ent; while Sandy worked from an ethic of care, Bruce worked to democra-tize the relationship with his students.

As they discovered, relationships were often easier to foster with the students than with the students' parents. Both teachers discussed the diffi-culty they had with contacting some parents, often those with whom they were in most need of speaking. Sandy stated, "Some of my parents, [I have] a real good relationship. They'll call me, I'll call them; we don't have any problem calling late in the evening. And then I have others that could seem to care less" (Interview 3). Bruce noted similar difficulty with parents who are out of reach due to drug rehabilitation programs, jail, or other circumstances that make it impossible to communicate (Interview 3). Sandy stated that she was trying, constantly, to make contact with her students' parents; Bruce, on the other hand, acknowledged that although he knew it was important, he was probably not in as much contact with parents as he should have been. What seems to set these two teachers apart from each other is Sandy's persistence.

What Support Do They Need and Receive?

A substantive difference between Bruce and Sandy is in the degree of support they perceive they need and receive. Although both teachers sought support from their grade-level team and school coaches, Bruce found much greater access to support from these colleagues than Sandy. Bruce stated, "So, I go to coaches, and then people at my grade level or other grade levels, depending on circumstances and what my question is" (Interview 2). He was better able to navigate who to ask for help because he had been successful on past requests, even if the answer took time. On the topic of timeliness, Bruce said that he got "better results going to peo-ple on my grade level because they're there living day in and day out with my similar situation, so they respond much more quickly to my needs" (Interview 2). He established a mutually beneficial relationship with his colleagues, as he was able to assist them with technology issues while they gave him "ways to do things to prevent [him] from reinventing the wheel"

(Interview 2). His colleagues provided Bruce with assistance with his class-room management, curriculum, and paperwork needs, as well as offered a calming word during times of frustration: "So, it's good to have their support. I'm glad there's somebody there, because they can calm me down in situations, for example with the learning schedules. Trying to stay 3 weeks behind is more comfortable than trying to be on target, because I know things aren't going according to schedule" (Interview 2). In many ways, his colleagues were instrumental to his survival.

Sandy's school environment was much less conducive to providing her with support. Although she received requested help from other former apprentices and her former university coaches, she received little support from colleagues in her school. She said, "I do the talking and don't get much response. So, basically I'm told to figure it out by myself" (Interview 2). Because her calls for help were not usually answered, Sandy expressed that the lack of support "contributed to [her] feeling of floundering" (Interview 2), but she believed this lack of support from school-based coaches was understandable:

> Everybody's doing multiple jobs. Like my senior mentor, 5 days a week, she's covering classes for cluster meetings. Our reading coach and our standards coach, they're running PLCs in the morning and other programs in the afternoon. So, everybody's just wearing multiple hats and so they don't have the time. (Interview 2)

However, lack of time does not account for the minimal respect she received from some of her fellow teachers. Although she requested help with specific needs, Sandy gave up stating, "I'm really tired of having demeaning comments made to me. And I mean, they've made some pretty demeaning comments" (Interview 2). Sandy's lack of support from colleagues made her completely responsible for both her survival and success within a highly challenging context.

By April, both Sandy and Bruce were given new school-based mentors. Bruce explained that his first mentor did not work in his grade level and could not provide him with specific advice that would apply to his situation. His new mentor, who taught in a room across the hall from his own, could help with "the subtleties I am missing" (Interview 4). Sandy also was provided more useful support with her new mentor. Sandy described her new mentor as, "Phenomenal. She at least stops in everyday for at least 15 minutes to see how things are going.... She comes in when I am in the middle of a lesson—she doesn't interrupt, but I'll go down and see her ... she'll give me little hints or tweaks on something I may have done" (Interview 4). For both teachers, support from their new mentor was crucial to knowing that they could find help, thereby removing a great deal of isolation and helping them figure out how to be successful while surviving their first year of teaching.

What are the Barriers to Success and Survival?

Sandy and Bruce identified several different barriers to their survival and success that they faced as first-year teachers. Sandy primarily named barriers that were within her control once she gained experience as a classroom teacher. Bruce, in contrast, named barriers that were out of his control. The two barriers that Sandy most frequently mentioned were materials and student behavior issues. During our first interview, Sandy said, "To be honest with you, I didn't expect all the behavior related issues that I have" (Interview 1), but she remained confident that once she figured out what works for her students, she would be able to move to other issues. Sandy also faced resource challenges and found ways to provide for her students even if there was a shortage of materials available at school. She mentioned that her school was short on basic supplies such as paper and pencils, but she took trips to the store to purchase these items rather than have her students go without. Sandy overcame barriers because she took responsibility for seeking out ways to overcome success and survival barriers.

Time was Bruce's greatest barrier at the end of his first year. Starting with his first interview in September, Bruce noted that "what's expected of you is more than what's possible when you look at your learning curriculum and the blocks of time they've set aside is 10 hours and the school day is 7 ½ hours" (Interview 1). The time barrier continued to be Bruce's main difficulty throughout each interview as he tried to balance learning and community building: "We could spend a whole day doing bonding exercises, but there's not enough time because I have to do 10 hours worth of work in seven hours, and it never gets done, so ..." (Interview 3).

Another major barrier for Bruce was the freedom to teach what he felt "is necessary to teach at the time rather than following the prescribed lessons in a certain time and a certain order" (Interview 3). His ideal environment would be one in which the students' needs more often guided what the teacher taught:

So maybe the students are ready to learn about...the water cycle, but ... It's not on the list, so rather than when the kids have a question about why it's raining so hard and why is the ground flooding, I can't really take a science lesson for that day and just really run with that. Instead I'm teaching about coniferous and deciduous trees because that's what we're supposed to teach. (Interview 2).

For Bruce, he believed that the majority of barriers to both his survival and success are external and out of his control. Although Sandy and Bruce both describe similar barriers they faced during their first year, their responses to how they faced and resolved those barriers were quite different.

What is Their Sense of Self-Efficacy?

When talking about themselves as teachers and how they felt about the job they were doing compared with the job they would like to be doing, Sandy was resoundingly more positive than Bruce. Even though she struggled with the staff at her school, she felt that she was in the right place: "Anybody can go to an A school. I belong here" (Interview 3). Although she felt that she was "floundering" (Interview 2) and "isolated most of the time" (Interview 2), she was persistent in finding ways to improve her situation, stating, "That's the type of person I am. I don't give up. I try something else to see if that works or if it doesn't" (Interview 2). Sandy took pride in her ability to "find out anything and get the information so it benefits the kids" (Interview 1). She also had faith that her relationships with her colleagues would improve once they got used to the many adjustments being made in her turn-around school. Most of all, however, Sandy kept in mind that she was "here for [the children], not for all the other things" (Interview 2).

When asked if it was difficult for them to tell how they were doing as teachers, both Sandy and Bruce answered yes (Sandy, Interview 3; Bruce, Interview 3). However, Sandy then described when she was able to tell how she was doing, referencing the same measurement tools she brought up when talking about her goals:

> And until you do a formal assessment or an informal assessment, or you just have a child blurt out something and you thought maybe you weren't reaching that child, and all of a sudden the window's open, and you go, Yes, I did! (Interview 3)

Bruce, however, described a reliance on the feedback of others to know whether he was doing a good job, stating, "I have virtually no feedback. It's hard for me to know if I'm doing a good job or a bad job, or where there's room for improvement" (Interview 3). He furthered his thinking by saying, "Granted, a video camera may be beneficial, but again, without having enough experience … I need somebody with experience to critique what's going on. I could say I did a great job, but you [the researcher] would say, do you realize…?" (Interview 3).

Bruce demonstrated low self-efficacy in regard to his abilities as a teacher. Aside from his need for others' feedback to determine his success, he also stated, "The further I get along, the less well-prepared I feel I am as a teacher. I mean, things come together slowly but surely, but I still feel that I'm nowhere near where I want to be" (Interview 3). He also pointed out that his classroom management was weaker than he at first thought and that he should have been in better contact with parents than he was. Although he plans to be successful as a teacher, his comments about his performance do not indicate that he felt successful throughout the school year.

Reflection on practice is another key piece of self-efficacy. For example, Sandy showed a great deal of reflection and learning about herself and her students. Sandy took the opportunity to observe other teachers who worked with her students to try to pick up some management strategies. She spent time each night reflecting on how the day went in order to improve the next, and throughout the school year used this reflection to guide her practice. She shared, "I am always reflecting on...what can I change? What else can I do? That phoneme segmentation exercise didn't work. What else can I do?" (Interview 4). Although Sandy was able to describe her reflective practices from the start of the school year onward, Bruce did not consider reflecting on practice to be an important part of his life as a beginning teacher. In April he explained, "Occasionally, I'll look back and look at, like if something goes really badly, I'll sit back and think, whereas if something goes really well, I don't need to reflect on it so much as say I have to do that again" (Interview 4). Although he actively "improvised" as he went (Interview 4), Bruce's lack of conscious reflection differs quite distinctly from Sandy's reflective stance. The sense of efficacy that each of these new teachers feels may influence the degree of success as well as their survival as a first-year teacher.

What are Their Future Plans?

Although both of these teachers shared the immediate goal of being a classroom teacher, Sandy and Bruce had very different ideas of where they saw themselves in five years. Although she was at first hesitant to teach kindergarteners, Sandy said she loves it now, "because kindergarteners aren't jaded when they come into school. And even those that have been retained, you still have the opportunity to turn around their thinking and how they feel about school" (Interview 3). In five years she sees herself "in the classroom, with the kids, only better than what I am right now" (Interview 3). Sandy continued to say, "My goal is to be in the classroom with them, and hopefully if—is still here, you know, you never know with schools…But hopefully, still here, with the urban kids" (Interview 3). It took Sandy many years to reach her goal of being a classroom teacher, and it is clear from her statements that she has no intention of leaving.

Bruce, on the other hand, expressed his desire to leave the elementary school environment to teach older students or move into a more technology-based position. He cited the students' ability to think on a higher level as his reason for the potential grade switch, and his interest in technology along with other previously discussed frustrations will likely cause him to transfer out of the elementary setting within the next five years. The degree of satisfaction with their current positions is evident in Sandy and Bruce's future plans. Together, these themes suggest that when a teacher has a clear understanding of what he or she believes is good teaching, can identify progress their students are making, is able to form supportive relationships with colleagues, works around barriers, and believes that change is within their control, they are likely to both survive and feel successful in teaching which in turn encourages them to remain committed to teaching.

INSIGHTS: LOOKING ACROSS THE TWO CASES

Three assertions became apparent when looking across these two teachers' experiences, most of which tied their experiences to the self-efficacy statements made by both Sandy and Bruce over the course of the four interviews. Specifically, major differences found between the two participants in this study stem from the types of goals they set for themselves and their students, along with the successes they felt they were having in meeting those student goals. The other main difference between them was the control they felt they had in breaking through the survival barriers they faced in becoming teachers. Again, the concept of self-efficacy comes into play here, as they tried to overcome barriers they identified. These three interrelated assertions provide insight into the dispositions that influence these two teachers' perceptions of and satisfaction with their success and survival during their first-year teaching.

Assertion 1: Sandy and Bruce's degree of satisfaction with the profession stems from the types of goals they set for themselves and their students, along with the successes they perceived in meeting those goals.

Although both teachers espouse teaching values as an important part of their job, only Bruce states that improving students' values and ability to make wise choices is what will make him successful. This begs the question of whether the fact that his goals are so difficult to measure is contributing to his feelings of dissatisfaction. Sandy shows that she places importance on values, but she does this more by her actions than by her goals; her goals remain academic in focus. Because Sandy's goals are easy to measure through formal or informal assessment, she is able to gauge the progress, however small, that her students are making. Being able to capture progress allows her to celebrate successes. Bruce cannot do this as easily because his goals are very subjective. For example, what constitutes a wise choice, and how can it be documented? Additionally, students may make a "wise" choice one day but not the next, so it may seem that no progress towards this goal is being made. Perhaps Bruce finds it difficult to remain optimistic in terms of progress when the goals set are subjective and growth is difficult to measure.

Assertion 2: The degree of control Sandy and Bruce felt over improving their own teaching influenced their ability to break through the barriers they faced in the first year of teaching.

Sandy takes great pride in her ability to solve problems for herself. She states that she may not be doing something right, but she's giving it a shot and people can correct her later if necessary. Although she would like more feedback and visits from experienced practitioners so she can improve as a teacher, she does not let this desire get in the way of her work to create engaging and meaningful learning experiences for her students and instead uses reflection to understand what she needs to do next. Bruce, on the other hand, uses the lack of feedback as a crutch: "If I had some feedback, it would help me be more successful and therefore more satisfied" (Interview 3). Additionally, he seems to view feedback from others as the primary tool for improving his instruction. His requirement for feedback from others with more experience takes away his own control over his improvement, thus lessening potential efficacy he may feel when he is able to grow on his own accord. Since self-reflection does not play a significant role as a means to improve his instruction, he further loses control over his own growth as he continues to turn that responsibility over to others.

In discussions about their students, Bruce and Sandy approach the subject from two different directions. Although both clearly enjoy working with the high-need, urban student population, Sandy uses a strength model to describe her students, while Bruce takes a deficit approach. This is evident when he says,

> You can just look at some of them and you can see that, unless their life changes, you can see that certain kids are on their way to jail, more or less. I know it's only third grade, but you can look at some of them and see that

they have no social skills. They think that the way they handle things is by getting in someone's face, or taking what they want or doing what they want. (Interview 3)

Bruce also talks about how his students are not capable of thinking at higher levels: "If I had my druthers, I would prefer to be teaching more along the lines of the high school level. Something a little more intellectual where you could engage in meaningful conversations" (Interview 3). Bruce does not discuss any attempts he may have made to engage his third graders in upper level conversations, but it seems that from his comment, he is assuming that this would not be possible.

Conversely, Sandy acknowledges that some of her students and their families may not be as experienced academically as others. Instead of planning to leave the grade level, she is entertaining the idea of providing after school help for the student and parent together, saying,

If a parent can't help their child with homework because maybe they have difficulty reading or writing, then I'd welcome them coming in after school and working with them so they could build their skills up too, you know, kind of involving everyone in it and trying to see who needs what. (Interview 3)

In this manner, Sandy is showing a desire to help students' families gain needed skills, rather than simply thinking they can't. By working towards strengths, and assuming that there are strengths and abilities waiting to be found, Sandy knows that when there is a success, it is because she has tried everything to make it happen. Bruce, on the other hand, doesn't try to engage in the higher level conversations that he wants, and so both he and his students fail before even beginning.

Assertion 3: Sandy and Bruce's sense of self-efficacy was influenced by the differing degrees of success they experienced in overcoming barriers and deficits they identified.

Finally, the emphasis Bruce places on external barriers makes it difficult for him to take control of his situation. It is not until April that he is able to move beyond the fact that there is 10 hours worth of work to do in a 7-hour day and that prioritizing is the only way to get things done. Instead of taking control and doing as much as he can do in the time he has, for much of the year he used the lack of time available as an excuse for not getting everything done. His other main barrier is the freedom to teach what he wants, when he wants to, another barrier that is out of his control. Again, placing the power for these barriers in an external position takes away his control of his own situation. If he fails, he is able to blame something besides himself: I could have taught this, but there simply wasn't enough time.

Sandy, on the other hand, took matters into her own hands when she felt she wasn't getting the assistance she requested. She purchased her own supplies, made her own copies, and forged ahead with lesson plans, keeping her students' needs at the forefront of her actions even when she wasn't sure the administration would approve of her choices. By taking ownership of situations she could control, Sandy was able to see the effects of her actions on her students' achievements. This, in turn, increased Sandy's feelings of self-efficacy.

CONCLUSIONS

What have we learned about urban teacher learning from this study? First, we learned that the degree of satisfaction with the profession stems from the types of goals the novice teachers set for themselves and their students, along with the successes they perceived in meeting those goals. This has important implications for teacher learning as teachers who are successful, self-directed learners must have the ability to set measurable, substantive goals. Sandy was more successful in setting these kinds of goals and thus had more success learning along the way.

Second, we learned that the degree of control Bruce and Sandy felt over improving their own teaching influenced their ability to break through the barriers they faced in the first year of teaching. This also raises an important implication about learning within challenging urban schools. If novice teachers believe they have little control, then little professional learning within that context is likely to occur.

Third, we learn that the degree of self-efficacy that teachers possess is key to teacher learning. As indicated, this study identifies a coupling between a teacher's perception of their success and the degree of self-efficacy they possess. Since self-efficacy in teaching is the measure of how well an educator believes he or she is able to engage all students and help them learn (Hoy, 2003-2004), Sandy and Bruce's stories indicate that self-efficacy is an important factor related to new urban teachers' feelings of success. That feeling of success requires teachers to be able to learn within their context, and, as a result, is important to consider when studying teacher retention as well as teacher learning in urban schools. The main difference between Bruce and Sandy was the control they felt that they had in breaking through the barriers they faced in order to survive their first year of teaching. Again, the concept of self-efficacy comes into play here, as they experienced differing abilities in overcoming the barriers that interfered with their learning.

These findings suggest that teacher educators and school leadership need to seriously identify ways to make success and survival an and/both proposition rather than an either/or proposition if they want teachers to grow professionally. A culture of support created within an urban school can facilitate both success and survival for new teachers. Survival and success need to not become two different things. If survival means that you are pleasing the system and abiding by the many expectations, then that survival must not be at odds with the success of children learning. By creating a context where survival is supported rather than inhibited, Bruce, and others in his same position, might be freed to recognize the factors within their control and take responsibility for learning how to meet their students' needs.

Although more time and freedom might solve some problems, without attending to control and responsibility issues there will be barriers to learning that novice teachers like Bruce may not overcome. Additionally, this study also raises the possibility that Bruce's goals and inability to assume responsibility are part of his personality. In other words, these are dispositions or the way he approaches life, and not just his teacher persona. If that is the case, coaching and efforts to develop these capacities may not change his outlook, and ,thus, learning within his context may be problematic. In any case, this study could be used to open a line of conversation with new teachers about self-efficacy and how their outlook, both in terms of the goals they set and how they think about what they can and cannot control, can really influence the way they view themselves as teachers and their ability to learn how to better support their students.

This study raises further research questions. How do we prepare each new teacher for both success and survival for teaching in urban contexts when they enter the profession with such different abilities, orientations, expectations, and dispositions? Does the new teacher's understanding of success create some of the vacancies schools see each year? If so, how do we work with new teachers to help them set and reach more manageable goals? How can we assure that new urban teachers recognize how these concepts of success and survival interfere with them reaching the goal of learning how to better meet the needs of their students? Are survival skills something that can be taught, or is this also a disposition?

Alternative certification is a rapidly growing pathway to teaching. Bruce and Sandy are products of this movement. This study helps school administrators and teacher educators understand the difficulties these novice teachers experience as they try to continue their learning during their first year on the job. Almost every teacher education program in the country claims that life-long learning is essential to the profession, and being an alternatively certified teacher is no exception. In fact, due to the abbreviated nature of the preparation period for many alternatively certified teachers, teachers like Bruce and Sandy enter the profession with an incomplete knowledge base which requires on-going learning if they intend to meet the needs of their students. By better understanding how urban teachers experience their first year of teaching, we can help those working in the most challenging urban schools continue to learn by both surviving and succeeding.

NOTE

1.   Pseudonyms.

REFERENCES

Crotty, M. (1998). *The foundations of social research: Meaning and perspective in the research process.* Thousand Oaks, CA: Sage.

Haycock, K. (2000). No more settling for less. *Thinking K-16, 4*(1), 3-12.

Hoy, A. W. (2003-2004). Self-efficacy in college teaching. *Essays on teaching excellence: Toward the best in the academy, 15*(7).

Lortie, Dan C. (1975). *Schoolteacher: A sociological study.* Chicago, IL: University of Chicago Press.

The National Commission on Teaching and America's Future (2002). *Unraveling the "teacher shortage" problem: Teacher retention is the key.* Retrieved from http://www.nctaf.org/resources/research_and_reports/nctaf_research_reports/index.htm

Patton, M. Q. (2002). *Qualitative research and evaluation methods* (3rd ed.). Thousand Oaks, CA: Sage.

Yendol-Hoppey, D., Dana, N., & Jacobs, J. (2009). Critical concepts of mentoring in an urban context. *The New Educator, 5*, 22-44.

CHAPTER 6

THE IMPACT OF TEACHER PREPARATION FOR HIGH-NEED SCHOOLS

Dorene D. Ross, Stephanie L. Dodman, and Vicki Vescio

Despite the critical importance of preparing teachers to teach in high-poverty schools serving predominately children of color (high-need schools), there is relatively little research on the impact of teacher education as preparation for these contexts. Of these studies, the majority have focused on changes in student teachers' attitudes about teaching in urban, high-need schools. Few have focused on the impact on teaching practice, acceptance of jobs in urban contexts, or the teachers' perceptions of success when teaching in high need contexts.

Studies focusing on changes in attitudes and commitment to urban teaching show mixed impact of teacher education. Studies have shown that students believe an urban experience enhances the development of knowledge and enthusiasm for teaching (McKinney & Finke, 2004/2005; Thompson & Smith, 2004/2005), leads to declines in stereotypical attitudes toward diversity (Conaway, Browning, & Purdum-Cassidy, 2007; Olmedo, 1997), and develops skills to successfully teach in diverse settings (Wiggins & Follo, 1997; Wiggins, Follo, & Eberly, 2007). However, others reported that students' understanding of the challenges K-12 stu-

Research on Urban Teacher Learning: Examining Contextual Factors Over Time
pp. 79–101

dents face often are superficial (Cross, 2003; Dorrington & Ramirez-Smith, 1999) and that urban experiences do not increase graduates' commitment to teach in urban contexts (Olmedo, 1997; McKinney & Finke, 2004/2005; Wiggins & Follo, 1999).

Five reviewed studies investigated the impact of teacher education on teaching practice and/or acceptance of jobs in urban contexts. Not surprisingly, the studies show differential impact. Still the findings are promising. Two found attitude change and more openness to teaching children from other cultures (Nelson, 1997; Zygnunt-Fillwalk & Leitze, 2006). Nelson (1997) found participants better able to develop culturally responsive lessons and Ross, Halsall, Howie, and Vescio (in press) reported the majority of the participants developed a "no excuses" commitment to student achievement and stated an intent to teach in high-need contexts. Leland & Harste (2005) reported that 50% of their most resistant cohort accepted jobs in urban schools and Zygmunt-Fillwalk and Leitze (2006) reported that 47% of their graduates were still teaching in high-need classrooms after five years. These studies suggest the promise of an urban focus in teacher education, but several also note that the impact varied, and only two had a sample size larger than 10 participants.

This chapter describes the content and process of a one-semester experience designed to prepare elementary teacher education students for high-need contexts (i.e., high levels of poverty/high minority enrollment) and presents the results of a survey and interview-based study examining impact. This internship program takes place within the context of the Unified Elementary Proteach Program at the University of Florida. This five-year program, which culminates with a master's degree and certification, is designed to prepare elementary teachers for inclusive schools by equipping them with expertise in elementary education, special education, and English as a second language. All students in the program complete their full-time internship at the graduate level. The graduate elementary internship typically completed during the first semester of the master's year is accompanied by a companion course that supports the development of the interns. Following a description of the High-Need Internship Program, the methodology for the mixed-methods study is presented. Presentation of the findings is organized around the research questions for the study.

DESCRIPTION OF THE HIGH-NEED INTERNSHIP PROGRAM (HNIP)

Although the University of Florida has always placed some interns in high-poverty elementary schools, prior to the development of the High-Need Internship Program (HNIP) the support for interns in such experiences was no different than the support for other interns. The HNIP was designed as a one-semester experience to support preservice teachers during internships in high-poverty schools. The semester experience (internship, seminar, and the companion 3-credit course) was redesigned to establish a collaborative learning community to help interns demonstrate the "no excuses" philosophy set forth by Corbett, Wilson, and Williams (2002). In a study of effective urban teachers, Corbett et al. (2002) found that teachers' assumptions about the capability of low-income students impacted teaching practice and subsequent student learning. They reported that effective urban teachers believed all children can succeed and "it's the educator's responsibility to see that they do" (p. 13). Teachers scaffold student learning by providing time and support and by continually seeking ways to "unlock the door" to learning for each student. Their underlying philosophy was, "There is a way to reach [every student] and it's my job to find it" (p. 18). In contrast, less effective teachers made excuses for why some students didn't learn. Rather than believing they could reach ALL children, these teachers believed they could reach children who tried and/or children whose families were supportive.

In the HNIP a team of faculty and graduate students build on the interns' prior knowledge and experiences with culturally responsive pedagogy to increase their knowledge of conceptual and practical tools connected with culturally responsive pedagogy. Each semester the 18-24 interns who are placed in full-time internships in poverty schools simultaneously take a graduate course focused around the development of culturally responsive pedagogy and a weekly seminar focused around issues of context and teaching. The graduate course instructor coordinates the experience. Graduate students and/or adjunct faculty supervise the field component, teach the seminar, and participate in the graduate course.

Course Content

The course and seminar were organized to help interns develop perspectives and skills demonstrated by effective teachers of diverse populations of children living in poverty (Corbett et al., 2003; Ladson-Billings, 1994; Weinstein, 2002). Specifically the program helps interns:

1. Develop greater knowledge about how their own entering assumptions about race, class, parental involvement, achievement, motivation, and appropriate behavior are influenced by the culture and background of the interns and in turn impact instructional practice.

2. Collaboratively push one another toward "no excuses" beliefs and actions.

3. View teaching as a continual process of inquiry around questions of engagement, equity, and learning.

4. Increase conceptual knowledge of culturally responsive pedagogy (CRP).

5. Develop and experiment with CRP (practical tools) such as:
    *   Establishing a strong ethos of care and respect that undergirds both instruction and management (Irvine, 2003; Ladson-Billings, 1994; Weinstein, 2002);
    *   Developing the skills of a "warm demander" in order to provide a collaborative classroom structure where children work together so everyone succeeds (Bondy, Ross, Gallingane, & Hambacher, 2007; Ladson-Billings, 1994; Weinstein, 2002);
    *   Providing instruction that is culturally familiar, sensitive to student difference, explicit, and focused on mastery for all students (Corbett et al., 2002; Irvine, 2003; Ladson-Billings, 1994).

Course Pedagogy

Here, the five core elements of pedagogy used within the course and seminar are briefly described. It should be noted that, during weekly meetings, the course instructor and the intern supervisors talk about the focus of current class sessions and the pedagogical strengths and weaknesses of each intern. These sessions shape the planning of subsequent course sessions and the nature of feedback and support for the interns during supervision and seminar sessions and ensure that the internship experience is coordinated and coherently focused.

The experience is designed as a professional learning community. Overarching structures of the internship experience support the interns within the context of a professional learning community (Newmann & Associates, 1996). First, the teaching team operates as a learning community. Collaborative planning and weekly reflective assessment of the learning of each of the interns make our practice public and keep us focused on intern learning. Second, the class and seminars are organized to create opportunities for interns to function as critical friends working to solve instructional and management problems. Critical friends conversations are structured using protocols for the analysis of student work, for surfacing implicit assumptions, and for addressing instructional dilemmas (McDonald, Mohr, Dichter, & McDonald, 2007; National School Reform Faculty, 2007).

Reflective focus on intern assumptions about race, social class, and expectations. Numerous readings and class activities help interns examine the impact of their entering assumptions on their perceptions of students and on their teaching practices. For example, class members read *It's the Little Things* (Williams, 2000), an interview-based account of the "little things" that divide Blacks and Whites. In groups that represent diverse perspectives, interns examine how their assumptions impact their perspectives about the book and create personal commitments to action. Interns are required to "take action" (i.e. implement strategies connected to their personal commitments) and to reflect about what they learn.

Varied exemplars of culturally responsive pedagogy. To provide concrete pictures of CRP, we supplement readings with videos such as *Good Morning Miss Toliver,* a video of classroom instruction by a middle school teacher from East Harlem who exemplifies the characteristics of a culturally responsive educator. Additionally, each intern observes two accomplished teachers in the internship schools to help interns "see" the pedagogy recommended in the literature and believe that it is possible and effective with students like theirs.

Scaffolded development of practical tools (CRP). The interns' use of CRP is carefully structured to require them to implement practices that have been identified in the literature as successful for low-income, minority children. For example, in a prior study we found that a number of interns were afraid of parent contact (Ross et al., in press), so several related assignments scaffold their connections to children and families and help them address fears of parent contact. Each intern is required to create a child study notebook in which they document their learning about each child. They are challenged to find strengths, especially "out of school" strengths, and collecting information from families is strongly encouraged. Additionally, each intern is required to attempt a positive face-to-face or telephone contact with every child's family and to write at least one note relating a positive story about the child to every family. These notes and contacts ensure that their first contacts with families are positive.

Inquiry stance. Interns are required to take an inquiry stance toward their pedagogy with a focus on who is and is not learning and what can be done to enhance learning. Interns are regularly required to try strategies and report the outcome for every child and to conduct formal inquiries in a lesson study project and an inquiry project. The lesson study requires the use of CRP and collaborative analysis of evidence of the learning of every student. Despite repeated focus on assessment throughout their teacher education program, during the lesson study interns often learn that their assessment provides too little information about student learning. By the second round of the lesson study, interns think much more carefully about assessment, focusing on how the lesson and assessment are linked to teacher learning about student learning. This enables interns to move from thinking about lessons as "performances" toward thinking about lessons as scaffolds for student learning. For the inquiry project each intern selects a dilemma she/he has faced, explores strategies for addressing the dilemma, and tries and assesses the impact of one or more strategies. Intern inquiries are presented to other interns, preinterns (earlier practicum students), mentor teachers, and university faculty in a formal poster session.

METHOD

Data for participants in the HNIP were compared with data from program graduates completing the same Internship Program (IP) but in more heterogeneous schools to determine differential impact. High-need schools were defined as schools with both a high percentage of students on free/reduced lunch and a high percentage of minority children. The free/reduced lunch population in the HNIP schools ranged from 74% to 94% (average 84%); the non-White population ranged from 59% to 94% (average 78%). In contrast, in the heterogeneous schools (IP) the free/reduced lunch population ranged from 16% to 88% (average 50%); the non-White populations ranged from 27% to 67% (average 46%).[1] Specifically, when comparing interns who completed the HNIP with students who completed the IP, we addressed the following four research questions:

1. Are there differences in reported self-efficacy for teaching in high-need schools?
2. Are there differences in reported openness to teach in high-need schools?
3. Are there differences in rates of acceptance of jobs in high-need schools?
4. What are beginning teachers' perceptions of the challenges of and their preparedness for teaching in high-need schools?

Participants

Participants were students who completed their full-time internships as part of the master's year of a five-year teacher education program and graduated between 2005 and 2008. Students were assigned to complete their internships in local elementary schools that serve a high-need population or more heterogeneous populations.[2]

Students in the HNIP and the IP completed a graduate internship, a student teaching seminar, and a section of the 3 credit-hour graduate course. In both programs interns completed the same key assignments and both instructors focused on the development of practical tools. A university faculty member taught the HNIP course; an experienced principal of a high-need elementary school taught the IP course. Both instructors had high commitment to preparing interns to work with minority children in urban environments and high instructor ratings. The main differences between the groups were the sites of the internships, the number of readings focused on high-need students, and the level of coordination between the course instructor and the intern supervisors. As noted earlier, in the HNIP the instructional team met weekly or bi-weekly to coordinate their work. In the IP the intern supervisors were given information about the course content but the team of instructors did not meet. Class size for the HNIP ranged from 16 to 29 (average 22); class size for the IP ranged from 17 to 24 (average 21).

The interns were predominately female (range across sections 95%-100%) and predominately White (range across sections was 82% to 95%). For 2007 graduates the percentage of interns identifying as African American, Hispanic, or other was higher for HNIP (12%) than IP program (5%); for 2008 graduates more IP interns than HNIP self-identified as African American, Hispanic, or other (HNIP 14%; IP 18%).

Data Collection and Analysis

This longitudinal, mixed-methods study was designed to investigate the impact of a high-need internship experience on participants' reported self-efficacy and intent to teach in high-need schools (2007 and 2008 graduates), participants' acceptance of jobs in high-need schools (2005-2007 graduates), and participants' perceptions of success and key challenges in the first two years of teaching. The study involved the collection of both quantitative and qualitative data. The quantitative portion of the study involved the analysis of descriptive statistics from two instruments, Intern Survey and Follow-up Survey.

Intern survey. This survey, completed by 94 interns who graduated in 2007 and 2008, contained nine efficacy statements on a 5-point Likert scale that ranged from *strongly agree* to *strongly disagree*. Statements were drawn from a survey developed by Louis and Marks (1998). For the purposes of scoring, all numerical responses were adjusted such that lower efficacy measures correlated with number one and higher efficacy measures correlated with number five. This yielded one score representing the intern's efficacy. In addition, the survey contained questions about teaching intentions.

The intern survey was administered in fall 2006 and fall 2007 as both a pretest and a posttest given on the same days by both HNIP and IP instructors. Administration of the pretest was delayed until three weeks into the semester so that interns would have time to get to know their students and their contexts before responding. The posttest was given on the last day of class. All interns present on the data collection days completed the survey.

Follow-up survey. This survey was divided into two parts. Part 1 included 8 items about the demographics of the graduate's current teaching situation. Part 2 included questions on their satisfaction with teaching and the nature of support they experienced. Due to space limitations, only results from Part I are included in this chapter. The survey was completed by 34 HNIP students who graduated in 2005, 2006, and 2007 and 19 IP students who graduated in 2006 and 2007.

The follow-up survey was mailed to the 101 interns who graduated in 2005, 2006, or 2007. A repeat mailing was completed to increase the response rate. Return rate for the 61 HNIP graduates was 55.7%; for the 40 IP graduates the rate was 47.9% (average across groups—53%). Data from the two surveys were complemented with data from interviews for the qualitative portion of the study.

Interviews. The qualitative portion of the study investigated the similarities and differences in the challenges, supports, and perceptions of success faced during the first year of teaching in high-need schools by three graduates of each program who were teaching in high-poverty schools. In our analysis we used 60% free/reduced lunch population as the threshold for a high-poverty context. This is lower than the average percentage in the HNIP internship schools, but this threshold was used because it is a context where a clear majority of the students were living in poverty. Moderate levels were 40-59%. Schools with below 40% free/reduced population, the threshold for Title I, were considered low-poverty schools. The same percentage breakdowns were used to examine minority population.

Each graduate completing the follow-up survey was invited to volunteer to participate in an interview about her/his experiences during the first year of teaching. From the volunteers, we selected graduates who were teaching in high-poverty schools for the interviews. Only three graduates from the IP program teaching in high-poverty schools volunteered to participate. In contrast, seven graduates from the HNIP program who were teaching in high-poverty schools volunteered. From these seven we selected three whose teaching contexts matched those of the IP graduates, giving us six participants for the qualitative interviews. At the time of the interviews, all participants were completing either their first or second year of teaching. One participant from each group was teaching in each of the following contexts: rural—high White student population, urban—high African American student population, urban—high student population of English language learners.

Three researchers interviewed participants and collaboratively analyzed data. Using an inductive approach (Hatch, 2002), each researcher independently reviewed two interview transcripts to develop codes that described the teachers' perceptions of students, challenges, successes, supports, and preparedness for teaching. Researchers compared codes and developed a comprehensive set of domains to guide analysis with each transcript analyzed by at least two researchers. The research team collaboratively identified broad themes and conclusions. Findings about challenges and preparedness from this study (Dodman, Ross & Vescio, 2009) are summarized in this chapter. In the next section, results and the discussion of results are organized around the four research questions.

RESULTS AND DISCUSSION[3]

Are There Differences Between HNIP Interns And IP Interns In Reported Self-Efficacy?

Table 6.1 provides the average efficacy scores pre and post for each group, showing that entering efficacy scores vary by group. T tests indicated that pre and posttest scores were significantly higher for IP interns than for HNIP interns in both years ($p < .05$). Both groups showed statistically significant increases in efficacy scores from pre- to posttest during both years ($p < .05$).

Data indicated that HNIP interns began their internships with lower reported self-efficacy than IP interns in both years studied. The groups showed comparable growth in efficacy over the internship semester, but

Table 6.1. Average Efficacy Scores by Group and Year

Graduation Year	Group	Pretest	Posttest	Difference Pre/Post
2007	HNIP	3.78	3.87	+.09
	IP	3.89	4.05	+.16
2008	HNIP	3.88	4.08	+.20
	IP	4.07	4.26	+.19

the average posttest efficacy scores of HNIP interns were lower than the average posttest efficacy scores of IP interns in both years. It makes sense that HNIP interns reported lower levels of initial and final efficacy. These are novice teachers, learning and testing their skills in challenging contexts. The higher levels of classroom management challenges and the intense pressure to help struggling students perform on high-stakes testing in these schools are factors that might explain these findings. The data also suggest that for all interns, successful experience increases efficacy, validating the importance of internships in high-need schools.

Are There Differences Between HNIP Interns and IP Interns in Reported Openness to Teach in High-Need Schools?

Interns were asked how likely it was that they would accept a teaching position in a high minority/low SES school. Table 6.2 presents answers to this question on pre and posttests. Combining the top two answers conveyed a probability that they would accept jobs in a high need environment (probable); combining the bottom two conveyed it was highly unlikely they would accept a job in a high need context (unlikely). Results were inconsistent across the two years.

For the 2007 graduates the number of HNIP interns indicating they would probably accept a high poverty job decreased slightly from pre (68%) to posttest (63%); for IP interns the number increased dramatically from 38% to 68%. The number of interns indicating it was unlikely they

Table 6.2.   How Likely are You to Accept a Job in a High-Poverty/High-Minority School?

	2007 Graduates				2008 Graduates			
	HNIP		IP		HNIP		IP	
	Pre (n = 22)	Post (n = 19)	Pre (n = 21)	Post (n = 22)	Pre (N = 28)	Post (N = 26)	Pre (N = 22)	Post (N = 21)
Highly likely	23%	26%	5%	14%	39%	35%	23%	14%
Probably	45%	37%	33%	54%	39%	46%	23%	29%
Only if no other offer	27%	21%	33%	18%	22%	19%	50%	38%
Very hesitant to accept	5%	11%	24%	14%	0%	0%	4%	14%
Would not accept	0%	5%	5%	0%	0%	0%	0%	5%

would accept a high-poverty context demonstrated similar trends. Thus data from 2007 graduates suggested HNIP interns became less inclined to report that they would accept positions in high-poverty contexts, whereas the IP interns became more inclined to report they would accept such positions.

For 2008 graduates the percentage of HNIP interns who would probably accept a high-poverty internship increased slightly from 78% (pre) to 81% (post). In the IP, participants indicating interest in poverty contexts decreased slightly from 46% (pre) to 43% (post). The numbers indicating that accepting a job in a high-poverty school was unlikely demonstrated similar trends. These data suggested HNIP became slightly more inclined to report that they would teach in poverty contexts, whereas IP interns became less inclined.

In 2007 reported increases in the willingness to teach in poverty contexts for the IP interns were large enough that the percentage of graduates willing to teach in poverty contexts was comparable across the two groups on the posttest. Data from the 2008 graduates suggest changes were slight but showed a different trend. Although changes were slight, at the end of the internship the percentage of HNIP interns indicating willingness to teach in high needs schools was almost twice that of IP interns.

We cannot explain these differences. Most puzzling is why IP interns working with the same instructor in similar internship contexts increased dramatically in their willingness to teach in poverty contexts in 2007 but not 2008. Across the two years, the IP interns began the semester with comparable levels of interest in teaching in poverty contexts. The only pedagogical difference across these two years was to make the course readings more similar across the two sections meaning that the 2008 IP graduates read more about culturally responsive pedagogy and management. We wonder whether it is possible that reading about meeting the challenges of teaching diverse populations without a context for practical experimentation increased anxiety about high-need contexts.

Are There Differences Between HNIP Interns and Other Interns in Rates of Acceptance of Jobs in High-Need Schools?

It should be noted that the response rate for the survey varied by group. The response rate for the HNIP interns was 56% while the response rate for IP interns was only 48%. Therefore, confidence about the representativeness of the sample is lower for IP interns than for HNIP interns. The survey provided information about whether interns who graduated in 2005/6/7 accepted jobs in high-poverty and/or high-minor-

Table 6.3.   Poverty Rate by Group

	HNIP (N = 34)	IP (N = 19)
High poverty Free/reduced lunch rate > 60%	47.1%	42.1%
Moderate poverty Free/reduced lunch rate 40-59%	23.5%	10.5%
Low poverty Free/reduced lunch rate < 39%	29.4%	47.4%
High plus Moderate poverty	71%	53%

Table 6.4.   Minority Rate by Group

	HNIP (N = 34)	IP (N = 19)
High minority enrollment Percentage of minority students > 60%	44.1%	36.8%
Moderate minority enrollment Percentage of minority students 40-59%	20.6%	5.3%
Low minority enrollment Percentage of minority students < 39%	35.3%	57.9%
High plus moderate minority enrollment	65%	42%

ity schools. Data for 2005 graduates were only available from HNIP graduates. As noted previously, high-poverty schools were considered schools with higher than a 60% free/reduced lunch population. Moderate levels were 40-59%. Schools with below 40% free/reduced population were considered low poverty schools. The same percentage breakdowns were used to examine minority population. Tables 6.3 and 6.4 provide percentage data by group for poverty and minority levels in schools where the graduates are teaching.

The data indicate that HNIP graduates were more likely than IP graduates to teach in settings with high poverty (47% HNIP; 42% IP) and moderate poverty (23% HNIP; 10% IP). Conversely, IP graduates were more likely to teach in low-poverty settings (47%) than HNIP graduates (29%). Findings related to minority populations showed similar differences. HNIP graduates were most likely to teach in high-minority schools (44%) and IP graduates were most likely to teach in low-minority schools (58%).

The stated intent to teach in poverty schools means little unless graduates actually accept these jobs. The data indicated that graduates from the

HNIP were more likely than IP graduates to teach in settings with high and moderate poverty and in settings with high minority populations. IP graduates were much more likely to teach in low-poverty settings and in low-minority schools. The lower response rates from IP graduates mean these findings should be interpreted with caution; however, the data suggest that scaffolding and support while interning in high-poverty/high-minority settings may increase the likelihood that graduates will accept or seek teaching positions in high-need schools. These findings are encouraging, as is the fact that regardless of preparation program or school context, fewer than 10% of the graduates from either program expressed doubt about their career choice.

What Are Beginners' Perceptions of Challenges and Preparedness?

Data about the beginners' perceptions come from the qualitative interviews, and a summary of the stance of each teacher in relation to the factors described in this section is presented in Table 6.5. The novices' challenges were discussed in terms of students' family issues, school issues, academic achievement, and behavior. Participants described these challenges in intertwining ways. The results included here report on the challenges related to families and student behavior, challenges with academic achievement, and feelings of preparedness.

Challenges with families and student behavior. While there were some differences apparent in the challenges experienced by participants in differing contexts (schools with either high student populations of English language learners in urban settings, African Americans in urban settings, or Whites in rural settings), overall the differing poverty contexts of the participants did not seem to affect the kinds challenges that they experienced. What did seem to affect their challenges across the two participant groups, however, was prior experience working with children from poverty. Only one participant lacked any prior experience with this population, and she expressed the most struggles in her teaching. This participant, whose comments suggested negative assumptions about families, was especially struck by what she described as family issues and by student disruptive behavior in her classroom.

My one thing is that I never really understood what a [poverty] school meant until the first day and within five minutes I had an issue. I think if it had been mandatory to go to a [poverty] school it would be really important. I had all these wonderful ideas and things from [my teacher education program] and it all went out the window the first day.... A lot of times with some of my worst problems I just buzz the office. I have kids that are vio-

Table 6.5.   Summary of Qualitative Factors by Participant

	HNIP 1	HNIP 2	HNIP 3	IP 1	IP 2	IP 3
	High ESOL	Rural/ High White	High African American	High ESOL	Rural/ High White	High African American
HNIP	✓	✓	✓			
Other HN experience				✓	✓	
Frustration with family support	✓			✓	✓	✓
Links family support to misbehavior						✓
Links family support to poor academic achievement	✓			✓	✓	✓
Describes student behavior as a challenge	✓	✓		✓	✓	✓
Describes student behavior as a success story	✓	✓		✓		
Describes strategies for addressing students' challenges in achievement or behavior	✓	✓	✓	✓	✓	✓
Wants to return to same or similar context next year	✓	✓	✓	✓		✓

lent—things I've never seen before. They will hit someone and then go to the corner and cry. (IP Participant 3)

When this participant described her challenges with student behavior, she communicated her expectations for help from parents/guardians. These expectations often were not fulfilled.

One of them [the students], the grandma left when I tried to tell her what her kid has been doing. He is very gifted in reading but he flies, twirls, and can't sit still. I'm successful in one area—I know he likes me and tries sometimes but he is angry, but I can't be his therapist—I can't be his personal therapist/teacher throughout the day and I need that support from the parent. It's like a light bulb will turn on and he loses it and lashes out. He is in a guidance program. I'm trying as many things as I can with him but academically he misses so much. I try my best to keep him in the classroom and not buzz the office. He only had grades for two out of seven math tests because he is out so much. I feel like I need support outside the home but I felt like she doesn't care. I have the rest of my class to deal with. (IP Participant 3)

The other five participants all had prior experience working with students from poverty either in their full-time internship, in smaller practicum settings, or in prior full-time teaching. Of these five participants, two HNIP graduates did not mention families as challenges. The two remaining IP graduates and the one other HNIP graduate did mention families or home lives as a challenge, but they did not express a view that families are responsible for student disruptive or anti-social behavior as did the one IP graduate who lacked prior experience with children from poverty. When these three graduates talked about families, they focused on the connections between families and academic achievement. Their comments, however, suggested concerns about familial commitments to academic learning. The two IP participants expressed concern that they could not expect students to do homework. IP Participant 1 stated "[I] didn't do a lot with homework because I didn't know who was doing their homework, brothers/sisters doing it, sometimes home was not conducive to doing the work." IP Participant 2, who had previously taught in a more heterogeneous university partnership lab school before transferring to a high-poverty rural school, echoed this response. She described her students' family challenges as different from those she had previously experienced.

> The difference I believe is parental support. The difference is at [her previous school] there is no bus system. Kids have to be dropped off and picked up. Somebody had to be involved. There is a bus system here. There are kids here who don't have someone to pick them up. They have nothing to go home to, they eat by themselves; they do their homework by themselves. It's different. I can't have those same at-home expectations.

The HNIP graduate who mentioned home issues as significant was in a school with a high population of ELL students, and she talked about language barriers and a lack of familial and student priority for school. This participant made statements such as, "I feel for him because I try so hard to help him and he is not going to learn how to read by next year. There is just no way and his parents only speak Spanish at home" (HNIP Participant 1). She also explained students' lack of motivation for learning by connecting some students' attitudes to parents' modeling.

> Generally, I think that is one of the things that really holds them back, is that they are not … what I have noticed is that in their home lives they are not made to be motivated, you know their parents are not on top of them to

do their homework. They don't think homework is important because their parents don't show them that it is important for example.

For the four students who talked about family challenges, the three with prior experience with children from poverty did not demonstrate an assumption that families were to blame for student misbehavior; the one without experience clearly blamed student behavior at least in part on the families. However, statements about the roles they expected families to assume in supporting academic achievement suggested that prior experience did not diminish the graduates' tendency to see family patterns as a factor in low student achievement.

Although only one IP graduate directly linked family patterns to student behavior, five of the six graduates talked about student behavior challenges. The types of student behavior challenges that were discussed across the participant groups were those related to Attention Deficit Hyperactivity Disorder, emotional volatility, and bullying. Only one participant did not mention student behavior as a challenge in any way (HNIP Participant 3). For three participants (IP Participant 1, HNIP Participant 1, and HNIP Participant 2) these challenges were described either as part of stories of success that concluded with participants indicating how they overcame the behavior barrier or as part of larger stories that did not suggest the behavior was a continuing challenge. HNIP Participant 2's discussion exemplifies this finding.

> I have this one student and she was very angry for some reason when she started off. She wouldn't do her work, talked bad about us. I couldn't deal with her anymore. She totally shut me out; she wouldn't listen to anything that I said. We had a conference with her mom, she was bullying with other kids. I decided not to give up on her, there was something cool about her but I couldn't figure out what it was. I started to treat her like an adult, being really positive about her behavior. It was hard to find positive things, talked to her like a person, like a friend sort of. She did a complete 180, straight A's, not bullying anyone anymore. I looked at previous years and she was failing everything. I was so close to saying there is nothing I can do with this kid.

She went on to describe her behavior challenges in terms of one student's struggles with the effects of ADHD and several other behavior challenges with this same student. She linked these behavioral challenges to poor student achievement and indicated that she had tried, and was still trying, multiple methods to modify his behavior for success.

> He's just way different than anyone I've ever worked with. I don't feel like I understand him. And that makes it challenging for me to teach him, even understand him. Mom says he's had ADHD, but I just think there's more

going on there than ADHD... As a teacher I want to be able to figure out where he is and to differentiate. But it seems like every day it's something different. And mom doesn't want him tested for anything. Academically, he is one of the most intelligent children I have ever seen. His grades are not good though, because he doesn't do a lot of the work and it takes him 30 extra minutes to do something.

Only IP Participant 3, who lacked any similar contextual experience, described her behavior challenges as more difficult and challenging than the other participants. (The findings and representative quotes from her responses were included above.)

Challenges with academic achievement. All six participants described challenges in fostering student learning and increasing achievement. The particulars of the challenges did not seem unique to either participant group. These challenges included student factors such as lack of motivation for learning and work, first language to second language transfer issues, learning disabilities, below grade level achievement, learned helplessness, and inconsistent learning performance. Statements related to these challenges are represented by quotes such as the following.

- They [students] come to us with a lot of ... I'm not saying it's any other grade's fault...but not knowing a lot of basics, like multiplication. There are a select few, like 4 kids, that no matter how I explain, they don't grasp it.... I struggle with kids that I know have the ability to do it, but don't know how to get them there (HNIP Participant 2).

- There are children who I'm struggling to find ways to reach them, to get them motivated and more successful. [One student in particular] He is just so inconsistent—A for two days, F for four days, every time (HNIP Participant 3).

- Some of my other special ed kids, when they hit a block about something, they're done. That's one thing I've learned. Another one... his math skills were on par or above but every day at the beginning of a lesson he would say "I don't get it very much." Every day! He was inconsistent, sometimes he would soar.... But he was exceedingly up and down, like many of the special education kids that I have worked with. Once they feel that they can't do it, they're done (IP Participant 1).

Working with students in poverty schools where many students are below grade level, it is hardly surprising that graduates face challenges supporting children's achievement and behavior. In fact, these challenges are often expressed by teachers working in poverty schools (Corbett et al.,

2002). What is more important is whether teachers view these challenges as reasons that their children cannot achieve or as factors that must be addressed in order for their children to achieve. Corbett et al. (2002) describe this later perspective as the defining characteristic of a "no excuses" teacher.

Despite their descriptions of challenges, all of the graduates expressed an emerging "no excuses" approach to teaching more often than not in their interviews. An emerging no excuses perspective is described by Ross et al. (in press) as characterized by an approach to teaching in which novice teachers do not give up on their students by blaming home contexts or lack of student motivation even though they occasionally make statements that suggest they are placing blame. Although they saw student behavior and family involvement as factors in the academic challenges faced by students, they did not suggest these factors justified low student performance. Instead they expressed persistence in seeking alternatives for success. Even IP Participant 3 who stated she "had the rest of her class to deal with" and she couldn't be a student's "personal therapist," talked about how she has learned how to continually adapt to her students.

> Figuring out how to make them feel successful. A lot of them come from horrible home lives. I had one whose younger brother was really sick and he felt left out ... and just giving him reinforcement throughout the day just turned him around—he stopped talking and started listening and he is one of my best kids. Just figuring out how to work with each child [is the key]. Realizing how to stroke them throughout the day is making them have more success.

In addition, while recognizing the hard work of students, all six participants attributed a large portion of student success to teacher controlled factors such as using a variety of strategies, believing in students, being patient and following through, pushing students to develop responsibility, building relationships, and differentiating instruction. In addition, as they described students who were not succeeding every participant's comments demonstrated that she was working to find keys to student success despite the obstacles encountered. Five of the six reported they were well prepared with strategies to enhance student success, discussed in the next section.

Preparedness. As stated previously, all three HNIP graduates and two out of the three IP graduates believed they were well prepared for the challenges they faced. These feelings of preparation were represented in such statements as those that follow:

- I don't know how I would do it if I did not have the preparation I had; I would not have made it (HNIP Participant 1).

- No matter what internship you have my main focus was school. [During an internship] you don't have the pressures of grading, of parents. It's like going from babysitting to being a parent... [One high poverty school in particular] helped in that I felt comfortable and accepted and it helped to change some of my [ways of thinking]" (IP Participant 1).

IP Participant 3, who lacked prior experience working with children from poverty, was the only participant who did not feel prepared for her initial teaching context. She expressed, however, that she had learned so much during her first year that she planned to remain her school. The same was true of four of the remaining five participants. They planned to either remain at the same school or transfer to a school with a similar student population. The sixth participant (IP Participant 2) desired to move to a school with more monetary support for teachers and greater parental involvement. Interestingly, this was a teacher who had taught for one year in a school where she had experienced this support.

SUMMARY AND IMPLICATIONS

This mixed-methods study addressed questions related to the preparation of teachers in the High-Needs Internship Program (HNIP) as compared to those who interned in more heterogeneous contexts (IP). Importantly, the qualitative portion of the study suggests that some form of prior experience with children living in poverty, even a part-time experience, helps novice teachers adjust to teaching in a high-poverty context more easily, particularly in the area of classroom management. However, a key issue is whether novice teachers will seek and accept teaching positions in these challenging schools. The quantitative portion of the study shows that students who experience a coordinated internship in poverty schools are more likely to accept initial teaching positions in schools with high and moderate poverty levels than those who do not. The findings suggest that designing coordinated internship experiences that ensure interns have successful experiences in high-poverty schools can be an important and successful strategy in recruiting and retaining high quality teachers for urban schools.

Quality teachers are the single most important factor and make the biggest difference in determining student success and achievement (National Commission on Teaching and America's Future, 1996). Yet, the literature suggests that it takes approximately five years for teachers to become able to maximize the achievement of children (Johnson and the Project on the Next Generation of Teachers, 2004). And although many novice teachers are placed in poverty schools, these schools have difficulty recruiting and retaining them. Consequently, the problem of attrition in high-poverty, urban schools becomes one of critical significance. The high rate of teacher turnover results in situations where students in urban schools are less likely to encounter experienced and highly qualified teachers. Combined with the additional risk factors associated with poverty (Rothstein, 2008), teacher attrition contributes to a cycle of low achievement. Change requires that we help teachers succeed, reduce the stress they feel as beginners, and help them want to stay in high-need settings.

The literature regarding attrition indicates that a lack of adequate initial preparation and a lack of mentoring for new teachers in the profession contribute to the high rates of turnover (Darling-Hammond, 2003; Johnson et al., 2004). All six participants interviewed, regardless of their internship, described a successful year, demonstrated an emerging "no excuses" approach to teaching, and expressed high levels of commitment to student success (Corbett, et al. 2002). All six were judged successful by their principals and were eligible to return for the subsequent year.[4] In addition, five of the six intended to continue to teach in a high-poverty context.

In considering the experiences of these beginning teachers, however, it is important to remember that 47% of IP graduates were teaching in low-poverty schools and 58% were teaching in low-minority schools. Thus, as a group they were much less likely to teach minority children living in poverty. From the qualitative interviews it is not possible to know whether all graduates of IP would experience similar success in poverty schools. The same point could of course be made about the interviews of the graduates of the HNIP; however, it is clear that the majority of graduates of the HNIP accepted jobs in schools with student populations from high to moderate poverty. These data suggest that the HNIP with strong support for the interns' success enables them to graduate with the confidence to accept positions in high-need, urban schools. In addition, findings from the qualitative portion of the study suggest that prior experience teaching children from poverty lessened the frustration during the first year of teaching in a poverty school. In combination, these data suggest that the context of teacher preparation does indeed matter. If we hope to prepare novice teachers for high-need contexts, it is important to provide teacher education experiences within such contexts.

Finally, it seems important to note that the qualitative findings repeat findings from an earlier study of this program (Ross et al., in press) that the biggest challenge for the interns is confronting their assumptions about families. Despite at least two courses that deal extensively with family involvement in education and alternative perspectives about family involvement, the teachers still found it difficult to step outside the boundaries of their own values (Ladson-Billings, 1994; Thompson, 2003). They clearly needed more support in their interactions with families. Ross et al. (in press) generated several strategies for helping teachers develop conceptual tools (e.g. readings and discussions designed to increase knowledge about their own entering assumptions about race, class, and parental involvement) and practical tools (e.g. child study notebooks, home visits, early and positive family contact) for learning about and building upon family assets. Although these suggestions, mentioned earlier in the chapter, are now incorporated into the companion course taken by interns, this study suggests more support is needed. A strategy we are currently studying is the impact of involving preservice teachers in running Family Math Nights at local high-poverty schools. We hope that these events, which are drawing record numbers of families to the schools, will challenge the preservice teachers' entering perspectives about the willingness of families to be engaged in their children's education and thus encourage them to adopt the same kinds of problem solving approaches to parent engagement that they use related to instruction.

NOTES

1. Some of the schools serve rural populations where the proportion of students on free/reduced lunch is high but the majority of the population is Caucasian.
2. Some, but not all, were placed on the basis of stated preference for one kind of school context, a specific teacher, or a specific school.
3. Because the number of interns who were students of color was so small within each cohort year, we did not separate their results for analysis.
4. Because enrollments shift, especially in poverty schools, "eligible to return" is the designation for beginning teachers that principals would like to keep in their schools.

REFERENCES

Bondy, E., Ross, D., Gallingane, C., & Hambacher, E. (2007). Creating environments of success and resilience: Culturally responsive classroom management and more. *Urban Education, 42*(4), 326-348.

Conaway, B. J., Browning, L. J., & Purdum-Cassidy, B. (2007). Teacher candidates' changing perceptions of urban schools: Results of a 4-year study. *Action in Teacher Education, 29*(1), 20-31.

Corbett, D., Wilson, B., & Williams, B. (2002). *Effort and excellence in urban classrooms: Expecting—and getting—success with all students.* New York, NY: Teachers College Press.

Cross, B. E. (2003). Learning or unlearning racism: Transferring teacher education curriculum to classroom practices. *Theory Into Practice, 42*(3), 203-209.

Darling-Hammond, L. (2003). Keeping good teachers. [electronic version]. *Educational Leadership,* 60(8).

Dodman, S., Ross, D.D., & Vescio, V. (2009, April). *Student teacher to urban teacher: The impact of internship context on beginning teaching experiences in high-need schools.* Paper presented at the annual meeting of the American Educational Research Association, San Diego, CA.

Dorrington, A. E. L., & Ramirez-Smith, C. (1999). *Teacher educators: A minority perspective on preparing majority preservice teachers for diverse classrooms.* Newport News, VA: Christopher Newport University.

Hatch, J.A. (2002). *Doing qualitative research in educational settings.* Albany, NY: SUNY Press.

Irvine, J. J. (2003). *Educating teachers for diversity: Seeing with a cultural eye.* New York, NY: Teachers College Press.

Johnson, S. M. and the Project on the Next Generation of Teachers. (2004). *Finders and keepers: Helping new teachers survive and thrive in our schools.* San Francisco, CA: Jossey-Bass.

Ladson-Billings, G. (1994). *The dreamkeepers.* San Francisco, CA: Jossey-Bass.

Leland, C. H., & Harste, J. C. (2005). Doing what we want to become: Preparing new urban teachers. *Urban Education, 40*(1), 60-77.

Louis, K.S., & Marks, H.M. (1998). Does professional learning community affect the classroom? Teachers' work and student experiences in restructuring schools. *American Journal of Education, 106*(4), 532-575.

McDonald, J.P., Mohr, N., Dichter, A., & McDonald, E. C. (2007). *The power of protocols: An educator's guide to better practice.* New York, NY: Teachers College Press.

McKinney, S. E., & Finke, J. A. (2004/2005). A comparison of the internship experience for student interns placed in different urban school environments. *Professional Educator, 27*(1/2), 51-57.

National Commission on Teaching and America's Future. (1996). *What matters most: Teaching for America's future.* New York: National Commission on Teaching and America's Future. Retrieved from http://www.tc.columbia.edu/nctaf/publications/whatmattersmost.html

National School Reform Faculty. (2007). *NSRF materials.* Retrieved from http://www.nsrfharmony.org/protocols.html

Nelson, R. F. (1997). *Teaching student teachers how to promote cultural awareness in urban and suburban schools.* Paper presented at the Annual Meeting of the American Association of Colleges for Teacher Education.

Newmann, F.M. & Associates. (1996). *Authentic achievement: Restructuring schools for intellectual quality.* San Francisco, CA: Jossey-Bass.

Olmedo, I. M. (1997). Challenging old assumptions: Preparing teachers for inner city schools. *Teaching & Teacher Education, 13*(3), 245-258.

Ross, D.D., Halsall, S., Howie, S., & Vescio, V. (in press). No excuses: Preparing novice teachers for poverty schools. *Teacher Education and Practice.*

Rothstein, R. (2008). Whose problem is poverty? *Educational Leadership, 65*(7), 8-13.

Thompson, S., & Smith, D.L. (2004/2005). Creating highly qualified teachers for urban schools. *Professional Educator, 27*(1/2), 73-88.

Weinstein, R. S. (2002). *Reaching higher: The power of expectations in schooling.* Cambridge, MA: Harvard University Press.

Wiggins, R. A., & Follo, E. J. (1999). Development of knowledge, attitudes, and commitment to teach diverse student populations. *Journal of Teacher Education, 50*(2), 94-105.

Wiggins, R. A., Follo, F. J., & Eberly, M. B. (2007). The impact of a field immersion program on pre-service teachers' attitudes toward teaching in culturally diverse classrooms. *Teaching and Teacher Education, 23*, 653-663.

Williams, L. (2000). *It's the little things.* New York, NY: Harcourt.

Zygmunt-Fillwalk, E. M., & Leitze, A. (2006). Promising practices in preservice teacher preparation. *Childhood Education, 82*(5), 283-288.

CHAPTER 7

CONNECTING TEACHING AND LEARNING

A Comparison of First- and Second-Year Urban Teachers

Jennifer Mueller, Debora Wisneski, and Nancy File

At the University of Wisconsin–Milwaukee (UWM),[1] teacher candidates can complete an undergraduate professional preparation program that will certify them as early childhood (birth–age 8) teachers in Wisconsin. At UWM, teacher education programming is undergirded by the School of Education (SoE) mission, which is to prepare highly qualified teachers who are well-positioned toward professional competence in the urban context.

In the early childhood education (ECE) program, we also extend our responsibility to include support for our program graduates so that they can remain in the urban context as effective educators who enact equity-informed teaching practices and improve the educational outcomes of the children with whom they work. We see ourselves as on a continual journey of program improvement and development—both inservice and preservice. Here we share part of our journey in coming to understand what this

Research on Urban Teacher Learning: Examining Contextual Factors Over Time
pp. 103–118

might mean, in more concrete terms, for our urban-focused teacher education programming and pedagogy.

In this journey, we realized the need to become more deliberate, intentional, and evidence-based in our decision making. The voices of our students always ring in our heads. We decided to examine some of our graduates' experiences as new urban teachers to provide insight about steps to take toward program improvement. For a year, we worked with eight of our graduates who were first- and second-year teachers in Milwaukee, WI. We talked with them, interviewed them, and observed them. We shared their struggles and their triumphs. We sought to gain a sense of their development as educators, and to better understand the factors that appeared important in their trajectories as professionals.

These overarching questions guided our inquiry:

1. What were our participants experiencing as new teachers in a large, urban school district?
2. What factors were salient in their trajectories as developing teachers?
3. What might we learn from these teachers to support teacher education program improvement?

In the following section we overview our theoretical perspectives for this work. We then describe in more detail the professional contexts of our participants, and the methods for data collection and analysis for the study. We share our emergent findings, including the ways we saw the urban context spurring our teachers' growth.

THEORETICAL PERSPECTIVES

We especially concerned ourselves with what we could learn from our graduates to support us in developing our teacher education programming in specific and evidentiary ways. The theoretical frameworks from which we draw highlight two issues that guided our inquiry—the variability of the urban context, and a desire to help our teachers begin to connect teacher education with pupil outcomes.

First, for the study and in our work, we draw from socio-cultural theories of teaching and learning where "learning and development take place in socially and culturally shaped contexts, which are themselves constantly changing" (Palincsar, 1998, p. 354). More specifically, theories of situated and distributed cognition guided our inquiry (Brown, Collins, & Duguid, 1989; Brown et al., 1993; Lave & Wenger, 1991; Putnam & Borko, 2000; Salomon, 1993). This perspective suggests that cognition, learning, and expertise are situated within socio-cultural contexts and distributed across individuals, activities, and resources within a context (Salomon, 1993).

Applying this lens, Wang, Odell, and Schwille (2008) suggest that "teaching practice and teacher learning are culturally scripted activities ... and that what and how beginning teachers learn ... grow out of the context" (p. 148) in which teachers function. Liston, Whitcomb, and Borko (2006) note how the "central tasks" of learning to teach take place in a variety of contexts and with varying supports. The sociocultural lens we employed supports the idea that the "urban" context would shape teachers' learning in a variety of ways. Those contexts and what teachers draw from them are varied and variable, as we shall see, and it is important to understand the nuances and inherent complexity.

Second, Darling-Hammond (2006) explains how "powerful" teacher education has the capacity to impact teaching practice and, thus, ultimately the outcomes for children. Guarino, Santibanez, and Daley (2006), however, point out that while "recent research suggests that teachers exert an influence on student learning ... the evidence is not always clear regarding the observable characteristics of effective teachers" (p. 176). Despite this, the job of a teacher education program is, presumably, to develop those effective teacher characteristics. Thus, we undertook this study with an eye toward developing initial insight into the characteristics that seemed effective for our participants, and how those might ultimately connect with positive pupil outcomes.

METHOD

Participants and Context

Participants for the study were recruited via the SoE's Administrative Office where records of graduates are kept. Criteria for recruitment included that participants be graduates of UWM's ECE certification program, in their first or second year of teaching, teachers of children pre-school–third grade, and employed in an urban school preferably in Milwaukee. The eight volunteer participants (Allison, Seneca, Angelica, Andi, Rebecca, Karaline, Nora, and Kelly) are all White females, hailing from lower-middle to middle-class families.[2] Six taught in schools in Milwaukee Public Schools (MPS) and two in private "schools of choice" within the city (see Table 7.1). Four of the teachers were in their first year of teaching, and four were in their second.

Milwaukee schools present a wide variety of school contexts, though the majority of schools in the district serve predominantly students of

Table 7.1. Participant Information

Name	Grade Level	School Type	School Demographics	Year Teaching	Curriculum
Allison	4-year-old kindergarten	Private/MSD Choice	97% Latino/a 100% free and reduced lunch	2nd	Scripted direct instruction
Seneca	1st/2nd grade resource teacher (special ed.)	MSD Public	94% African American 95% free and reduced lunch	1st	Scripted direct instruction
Angelica	Substitute in 4th grade/2nd grade	MSD Public	80% Latino/a, 10% African American 95% free and reduced lunch	1st	Self-chosen
Andi	4-year-old kindergarten	MSD Public	94% African American 93% free and reduced lunch	2nd	Self-chosen
Rebecca	Multiage 4/5-year-old kindergarten	Private/MSD Choice	99% African American 100% free and reduced lunch	2nd	Self-chosen
Karaline	4-year-old kindergarten	MSD Public	97% African American 97% free and reduced lunch	2nd	Scripted direct instruction
Nora	3rd grade	MSD Public	20% White, 80% Students of Color 73% free and reduced lunch	1st	Self-chosen (reading first school)
Kelly	4-year-old kindergarten	MSD Public	17% White, 76% African American. 69% free and reduced lunch	1st	Self-chosen

color from low-income families. Milwaukee is home to a comprehensive school voucher program where low-income families can access tuition vouchers that allow their children to attend designated private and parochial "schools of choice" throughout the city. There is an income ceiling for participation; thus, all of the families who utilize the voucher program also qualify for free and/or reduced lunch. Table 7.1 is included to illustrate the range of teaching contexts of the participants.

In order to further contextualize our teachers' work, we provide an overview of some of the main features reported by the participants. We include these because these elements were shaping how our teachers considered and enacted teaching and learning in their classrooms. Cataloguing them helped us to understand our teachers' experiences. We believe that many of these elements are common to, if not over-represented in, urban school settings.

Our teachers' reports indicated *challenging and ambiguous hiring practices in MPS* where after a complex application and interview process, hiring might come with little notice before a start date. There was *uncertainty of position once hired and placed.* As enrollment numbers stabilize, an official "count" occurs in the third week of school. Teacher positions may be shifted at this point; teachers often experience stress prior to this finalization of the job placement. Like many urban districts, MPS tolerates *teaching out of certification area.* This occurred in our sample where Seneca was hired to a special education position, and Angelica began teaching in a fourth-grade classroom. Our teachers were required to *learn to manage "staff."* In MPS many of the ECE graduates are hired for preschool positions.[3] Many of them are provided a paraprofessional, but there was often tension reported in the relationship between the teacher and the paraprofessional. MPS experiences *large class sizes,* larger than the surrounding suburban schools, particularly at the preschool level.[4] Our teachers reported a *perceived lack of administrative support,* where the administration had little experience or understanding of issues relative to the youngest students. The participants felt the need to advocate for appropriate early childhood pedagogy at the building and district levels. There was a *lack of curricular resources or, alternatively, strictly scripted curriculum.* The preschool classrooms in MPS provide fewer curricular mandates (and resources) on average. However, in some schools teachers are required to deliver scripted direct instruction curricula, even in the preschool classrooms, for up to several hours per day. The children had access to *no or few "specials."* With budget cuts, fewer schools offer music, art, or physical education classes. As a result teachers have fewer opportunities during the day for planning and preparation. Finally, the participants' accounts included their need to attend to the *stressors of families living in poverty and in high crime areas.*

Data Collection and Analysis

The data corpus includes individual interviews, group interviews, classroom observations (both videotaped and recorded in fieldnotes), and artifacts. All participants were individually interviewed in-depth three times—September, January and June—using a structured protocol (Patton, 1990). The initial interview was designed to gather a range of individual background information, to elicit participant dispositions about connections between teaching and learning, to discern participants' views on their teacher preparation and how it was shaping their practice, to elicit their views about the support and professional development needs of new teachers, to generate discussion about issues of culture within their teaching, and to allow them to talk about the experiences that they found salient. Subsequent interviews built upon ongoing data collection.

Group interviews were conducted once per semester with the content partially determined by the individual interviews and insights gathered during classroom observations (detailed below). The participants also determined portions of these interviews, as they took the lead in designating the topics and flow of the conversation. This allowed them to generate discussion about what was salient to them in their classrooms.

The classroom observations took place twice per semester at a time the participant chose. Each participant was observed for 2-4 hours with fieldnotes collected. The observations provided alternate sources of data such that participants' renderings of their own experiences could be cross-checked, and collaborative understandings of experiences and phenomena could be developed.

The teachers were also videotaped during a "lesson" of their choosing. Two of these tapings were completed per participant—one in each semester of the study. These lesson tapings lasted from one-two hours. Following the taping, the teacher viewed the videotape of the lesson with a researcher and commented on the lesson while viewing the tape. Participants were asked to simply comment on the content of the tapes, expressing their ideas of what went well and what they wanted to work on in terms of teaching and learning. These interviews were open-ended, allowing us to capture what the participants found salient in viewing a specific segment of teaching and learning in their classrooms. The interviews were audio-recorded.

All data were transcribed verbatim and coded beginning with a provisional start list of codes (Miles & Huberman, 1994) rooted in the conceptual framework of the study. Analytic memos (Strauss, 1987) were generated to foster the inductive development of additional codes. Once coding categories were finalized, both within-case and across-case analyses were conducted to identify themes. Within-case analysis allowed us to capture change over time in the approaches toward teaching and learning. Responses were examined at particular points in time across several types of data and also then over the course of the year. Cross-case analysis revealed the overarching themes among the cases.

FINDINGS

The process of listening to and spending time with our graduates was perhaps the most important part of this project for us. For instance, it was one thing to hear them talk about their struggles with the scripted curriculum, but it was another to see and experience with them how that shaped their teaching. The power of their stress, anxiety, and triumphs was only heightened and helped us to better understand what framed their work. Spending time with them in their classrooms helped us to come to fuller perspectives of their challenges and the issues that consumed their time.

As we analyzed the data, some differences began to emerge between the first- and second-year teachers in what they centered on when discussing and considering teaching and learning in their classrooms. As we will show, the first-year teachers, for a good portion of the year, tended to focus on the technical aspects of their teaching—for example, classroom management and organization, lesson delivery, and day to day tasks and procedures that were new to them. (This finding supports other research on new teacher development. See Liston et al., 2006.) Smooth delivery of these technical aspects was their main teaching goal. This focus tended not to include consideration of how these actions of teaching might connect to student learning. By the end of the year, however, these new teachers were beginning to more explicitly consider how students and student learning might shape their instructional and management decision making.

The second-year teachers began their year overtly reflective about their self-proclaimed previous year's focus on classroom management and organization, and they quickly began to consider student learning the basis of their management and instructional decision making. In other words, rather than the "well managed" classroom as their main goal, they viewed student learning as their main instructional objective and classroom management organization as means to that goal.

The First-Year Teachers

For first-year teachers, lessons "went well" when they perceived the children to be well behaved or if they "got through" a lesson plan. When we asked "how things were going," their conversations drifted toward, in Kelly's words, how they were "keeping on top of things"—or not.

For example, in Seneca's initial interview we asked how her students were doing in her class. She immediately began talking about the things *she* was struggling with in her first few weeks of teaching. She noted:

> Classroom management, like discipline, yes ... but where to put folders ... or do you put the pencil sharpener over here so they don't electrocute themselves or do you leave it over there so they don't bother you every two seconds.... It's just little things that you kind of pick up on more ... do you put crayon boxes at each desk or do you have like a crayon caddy? You know, it's just like the really minor things that I never would have thought about. (Interview, 9/22/06)

Here, Seneca equated "how the students were doing" with her organizational struggles.

In another example, Nora specifically requested that the observer come during her reading block because that was when she felt like she "had it together, and the kids would be really good." In the discussion following the observation, Nora expressed that she "really liked" her reading series because all the materials were "right there" and it helped her to be "more organized." We asked Nora how she thought the lesson went. Nora noted that "the kids seemed to really get it. They were super today." The researcher asked what it was the kids "really got." Nora focused on the fact that the children were able to stay on task while she was working with another group, and that they were really "getting how to organize their materials" and "get their work done in their groups." We noticed here that when we provided Nora with an opening to talk about student learning, her concern remained with the organizational aspects of her teaching (Fieldnotes, 10/5/06).

When the first-year teachers watched the videos of their teaching they tended to focus on the classroom management aspects of the lesson rather than on lesson content or student learning. For example, in one viewing Angelica watched the video anxiously wondering when one of the children "[was] going to act up." Her viewing became focused on detecting students' behavior that she had not noticed while actually teaching the lesson. Angelica expressed her dismay with this lesson because she had not been able to "keep a lid on those four [children] in the back" (Interview, 1/11/07).

The Second-Year Teachers

We found with the second-year teachers a self-awareness, in the first interviews, of their previous years' focus on management and technicality. This indicated their belief that they had begun their professional work with a technical focus similar to the first-year teachers in the study. An informal conversation with Allison was illustrative of this. She noted how in her first year she had been "so obsessed" and "so worried about" managing her classroom, that that was "all [she] could focus on." She worried that, because of this, she had just "taught right out of the book" and had not tried to "change things up" in terms of her curriculum. She noted, "I don't even think I cared if the kids learned anything or not. I just wanted it to look pretty" (Fieldnotes, 9/8/06).

The discussions of the second-year teachers, however, more explicitly included attention to students and student learning in relationship to teaching actions. For example, in her first interview, Rebecca reflected on how her focus on classroom management in her first year had kept her from fully appreciating the freedom she had at her school to craft her own curriculum. She noted that in her second year she was able to appreciate the decisions *she* could make in order to "get [the kids] where they needed to be" suggesting that she was explicitly considering the needs of the students as she made curricular decisions (Interview, 10/31/06).

Later, Rebecca asked to have her afternoon "carpet time" taped so that she could watch to see how students understood a concept she was trying to teach. In this viewing she noticed a point where she felt that she explained something in a way that impeded student learning of a math concept, indicating her focus on something other than the management aspects of the lesson. She watched as a student answered a question not quite correctly and she did not address it. She reflected: "Ooo, I need to listen to [the students] more. [He] really didn't get that, and umm … I didn't, I didn't pay attention" (Interview, 1/2/07). She realized that her lack of attention meant that she missed prompting a learning opportunity for this student. This excerpt shows that she was aware that the steps she took as a teacher connected to how a student engaged with her lesson. Further, she suggested a way to rectify what she saw as an error on her part, based on a student response.

During this year Rebecca placed a priority on developing her curriculum particularly related to math and science. Toward the end of the year she noted that she felt that she could "look at each of the areas, now" and see "where the kids were, and really do a better job with making sure that learning is going on" (Fieldnotes, 4/30/07).

Karaline similarly noted her own focus on behavior management in her classroom in her first year of teaching. When she reflected back on her first year she noted, "I think I just realized that I was way too focused on the behavior stuff" (Interview, 9/21/06).

Karaline was in a school where she was required to enact scripted curriculum. She was expected to use this type of instruction throughout most of her day, and she often lamented about how she didn't have time to let the children "explore and play." Early on, Karaline talked about wanting to alter her curriculum to include content and instructional strategies that she felt were more appropriate "to meet the learning needs" of her 4-year-olds because she felt that the scripted instruction "made it seem like they all learned in the same way" (Fieldnotes, 9/15/06). She began to experiment with the use of learning centers during her block of scripted reading instruction in an effort, by her report, to better meet children's individual learning needs and styles. "Then they can learn some of the skills and concepts in different ways," Karaline explained. She specifically asked us to observe during the center time and then *she* asked the observer questions about how the activities she had planned for the centers were supporting students in understanding particular concepts (Fieldnotes, 3/19/07). Throughout the year our observations and Karaline's discussions showed how she was developing methods to come to understand what and how her children were learning and how she could shape her instruction to better meet their learning needs.

Understanding the Difference in Focus

What were the factors that supported teachers to begin to explicitly consider the connections between teacher action and student learning? There was one exception amongst our second-year teachers—Andi—that helped us to consider what might be supporting our teachers' development. Andi's story shows how perceived lack of support in her context impeded her in shifting toward the focus on student learning that the other second-year teachers evidenced. She reported that in her first year of teaching she struggled with a classroom of 32 four-year-olds, little paraprofessional support, and limited curricular resources. Additionally, she reported experiencing what she felt was a grave breach of trust on the part of her principal. Andi felt as though her expectations for her second year from her principal were to "get things under control" in her classroom. She became almost paranoid in her focus on this, as she felt more highly scrutinized in her efforts to improve her classroom, so much so that, after one observation, she would not allow the researchers to observe in her classroom. The stress became so overwhelming that in the middle of her second year, she was granted an interdistrict transfer to an open first-grade position in a different school within MPS. In this new setting, she reported feeling as though she "really needed to prove" herself, and that proving herself meant that she continued to "really show" her ability to manage the class.

We suggest that this situation for Andi perhaps kept her from engaging in the difference in focus we witnessed in the other second-year teachers.

Certainly the other participants reported less than supportive administrators and stressful situations in their schools. However, Andi seemed to move into a mode of perceiving her contexts as a set of obstacles and failures, while the other participants did not.

We also saw evidence by the end of the year that the first-year teachers were beginning to shift their thinking to include student learning, especially when they talked about what they might like to improve in their classrooms in their final interviews. For example, Angelica talked about how she was coming to better understand how assessment could support student learning. She noted that she had learned about assessment in her undergraduate preparation, but she "never got what it would be like in a classroom to do that and to really even like [understand] the daily informal tests." She noted:

> 'Cause you can...talk or present something to them and they can all go, "Uh-huh." You know.... Because it would happen where I, I would test them later on or say something to them and they would just, just sit there and like stare and I'm like, "You totally missed what I was going for." But, never did I stop to check [if they understood]. (Interview, 6/26/07)

We turned to elements that were similar between our first- and second-year teachers to deepen our understanding of what may have engendered the shifts in their thinking—elements of their urban context.

Supports of the Urban Context

Two issues emerged from the data and were specific to the urban context that seemed to support our teachers to more explicitly consider student learning. First, all the participants (including Andi), reported that given their backgrounds in early childhood education, they felt they entered teaching with a strong knowledge base of appropriate early childhood pedagogy and practice. In addition to this, all of the participants reported on multiple occasions they were required to explicitly *advocate* for appropriate early childhood education. This put the teachers in positions in which they were oftentimes uncomfortable to have to speak up as a new(er) teachers. However, they felt strongly enough that their students needed certain things that they did take those stands. Across the group they shared stories of feeling surprised at how much they had to, as Nora put it, "speak up for what we knew was the right thing to do." Andi shared her thoughts on how she felt she had to advocate in her teaching, and what it required of her as a new teacher:

Just to be confident in what you're doing 'cause you've gotta start there, I think, before people are gonna do what you're asking them to do. That you gotta feel strongly enough that you're doing a good job and that you can do it better if these things happen. That's kind of my thing. (Interview, 10/17/06)

We suggest that in being put into these kinds of positions early, and what the teachers felt was often, necessitated an ability to articulate and justify their practice to administrators and colleagues. For example, they spoke of advocacy to keep rest time in the full-day preschool, or to have instructional play be a part of the children's daily experiences, or for third-graders to be read aloud to, or for second graders to have a dramatic play area. And because they did feel that they had some background, if not expertise, they were willing to take the stands about their teaching they felt were necessary. The need to be convincing pushed them to think about their students more explicitly as learners and to carefully consider how they would best craft an effective learning environment. In some ways, the unsupportive administrator—as long as the teacher did not feel overly scrutinized—pushed the teachers to be very conscious of and articulate about the kinds of learning environments that would most benefit their students.

Another element common in the urban setting that supported our teachers in coming to think more carefully about the individual learning needs of children was the need for our teachers to engage with cultural difference and diversity. Our teachers reported that they felt they were prepared in their teacher education to think about urban school issues as they began their teaching. They generally felt as though, while not experts, they had some strategies that supported them. We suggest that a confidence in this area, in combination with the need to advocate for their students, supported them in coming to more explicitly consider students' needs.

For example, Karaline talked at length about her conflicted feelings about the appropriateness of the required scripted curriculum for her 4-year-olds. She reported that in her school, the parents were not always in support of the curriculum, but they did not have a voice in the school space to express their concerns. She admitted that she began her teaching career very judgmental of the families of her students, given the differences in cultural and social background between herself and her families. She came to realize that in the effort to focus on her students' learning, she would have to address her presumptions about the families and rethink her approach to partnering with them, something "we talked about all the time at UWM." This task did not daunt her, and Karaline reported feeling as though she had the tools to advocate for students and their families:

> Now more than ever, I'm starting to realize that ... it's... the schools are not really even showing parents how to advocate. Like they just send their kids to us trusting that we're doing the best things for them.... And just, you know, like educating parents. I mean, I think that's huge...teaching them to be advocates for the kids and like just informing them that they have the right to speak up and should speak up about things...(Group Interview, 4/21/07)

Karaline's discussion suggested that she felt a responsibility, given the learning needs of her students, to support families in navigating school and accessing learning opportunities for their children. This, in turn, helped her to focus even more on the learning needs of her students.

DISCUSSION AND CONCLUSIONS

In this study we found that our newest teachers demonstrated a focus on the technical aspects of teaching, particularly classroom management. For these teachers, organizational and management aspects of their teaching were the goal, seemingly with little focus on how their teaching actions connected to student learning. We saw a shift in our first-year teachers, and a focus from our second-year teachers, with more explicit consideration of how their teaching actions shaped student learning, and how student learning could be considered in the instructional and management decisions they made. One of our second-year teachers was not able to make this shift, which prompted us to further explore the teaching context that may have supported the teachers to make these shifts. The participants' reports suggested that they felt they had a knowledge base from their undergraduate preparation of appropriate early childhood practice and issues of culture and diversity in their settings. They had to overtly advocate for early childhood, and address issues of culture and diversity, which we argue supported them to make more effective connections between teaching actions and student learning.

The ability to more explicitly consider student learning as part of the process of instructional and curricular decision making emerged here as a characteristic of effective teaching, with the potential to affect student outcomes. To see this shift in focus evolve in our teachers was exciting. It has helped us to more carefully consider how, programmatically, we might better prepare our teacher candidates in terms of thinking more explicitly of these connections, and how they might put them into practice. Additionally, the study has helped us to see the importance of including explicit attention to these connections as we mentor our new teachers. In other words, through the highlighting of this connection in our teachers' development, we have come to understand the importance of the same connections for ourselves as teacher educators.

This inquiry has also helped us to reframe our ideas of what our teachers will face as early career professionals in urban schools. Here, the challenges of the urban context actually supported our teachers to develop more effective practice. The struggles that our teachers encountered in their first years of teaching provided the context for them to understand what is needed to be an effective teacher. Inadequate support for curriculum development and overcrowded classrooms pushed these teachers to recognize the importance of learning principles in early childhood education that focus on the learner and to become advocates for their students. The struggles of the families of the students helped the teachers review their role in relation to families and partner more with family members in advocating for the individual children's needs.

The literature on new teacher attrition in urban schools is rather dismal, often with a focus on the challenges that prompt them to leave. Through this inquiry, we came to see, in more nuanced ways, that the struggles teachers may face in urban education can be opportunities to learn and define themselves as professionals. Understanding that struggle is part of the process of learning to teach, and not an indication that teachers are incapable or ineffective, is powerful. However, we are not sure that this would happen when teachers work in isolation. We suspect that the processes of our inquiry that asked the teachers to explain how they understood their experiences actually allowed the teachers to become more conscious of the connections between their teaching actions and their effects on students. This suggests that creating meaningful opportunities for teachers to talk about and examine their practice over time has the potential to develop those characteristics of effective teachers that will shape positive student outcomes.

What was, perhaps, most exciting for us was finding eight of our teachers committed to urban schooling. Though some of the participants have by choice or by force switched schools,[5] they all, with one exception, remain in Milwaukee schools.[6] These teachers' accounts suggest that they remain dedicated to being effective urban teachers.

NOTES

1. A mid-sized, research-extensive university.
2. As are the overwhelming majority of candidates who go through the ECE teacher preparation program.

3. Unlike surrounding districts, MPS engages in universal, full-day prekindergarten. Full-day programming was implemented in 2004.
4. Despite being a full-day program, prekindergarten is not fully funded by the state, and MPS only receives .6 full-time-equivalent per preschool pupil. Given this, class sizes are often very large (28-32), and there are often not resources available to support curriculum development.
5. Karaline and Andi both changed schools within MPS. Andi's switch was explained above. Karaline changed schools after her third year to a school that did not use the scripted curriculum that was required in her first placement. Angelica has now been twice moved to a different position within MPS based upon enrollments.
6. The exception is Seneca who had her first baby shortly after the data collection was complete. She switched to a daycare job within the city and was still working with children in the urban environment.

REFERENCES

Brown, A., Ash, D., Rutherford, M., Nakagawa, K., Gordon, A., & Campione J. (1993). Distributed expertise in the classroom. In G. Salomon (Ed.), *Distributed cognitions: Psychological and educational considerations* (pp. 188-228). New York, NY: Cambridge University Press.

Brown, J., Collins, A., & Duguid, P. (1989). Situated cognition and the culture of learning. *Educational Researcher, 18*(1), 32-42.

Darling-Hammond, L. D. (2006). *Powerful teacher education: Lessons from exemplary programs*. San Francisco, CA: Jossey-Bass.

Guarino, C., Santibanez, L., & Daley, G. (2006). Teacher recruitment and retention: A review of the recent empirical literature. *Review of Educational Research, 76*(2), 173-208.

Lave, J., & Wenger, E. (1991). *Situated learning: Legitimate peripheral participation (Learning in doing: Social, cognitive and computational perspectives)*. New York, NY: Cambridge University Press.

Liston, D., Whitcomb, J., & Borko, H. (2006). Too little or too much: Teacher preparation and the first years of teaching. *Journal of Teacher Education, 57*(4), 351-358.

Miles, M., & Huberman, A. M. (1994). *Qualitative data analysis: An expanded sourcebook*. Thousand Oaks, CA: Sage.

Palincsar, A. S. (1998). Social constructivist perspectives on teaching and learning. *Annual Review of Psychology, 49*, 345-75.

Patton, M. Q. (1990). *Qualitative evaluation and research methods*. Newbury Park, CA: Sage.

Putnam, R., & Borko, H. (2000). What do new views of knowledge and thinking have to say about research on teacher learning? *Educational Researcher, 29*(1), 4-15.

Salomon, G. (1993). Editor's introduction. In G. Salomon (Ed.), *Distributed cognitions: Psychological and educational considerations* (pp. xi-xxi). New York, NY: Cambridge University Press.

Strauss, A. (1987). *Qualitative analysis for social scientists*. New York, NY: Cambridge University Press.

Wang, J., Odell, S., & Schwille, S. (2008). Effects of teacher induction on beginning teachers' teaching: A critical review of the literature. *Journal of Teacher Education, 59*(2), 132-152.

CHAPTER 8

MAKING THE TRANSITION FROM PRESERVICE TO INSERVICE TEACHING

Critical Literacy in an Urban Elementary Classroom

Wendy B. Meller

There are more than 24 million children under age 6 in the United States. Douglas-Hall, Chau, and Koball's (2006) report for the National Center for Children in Poverty (NCCP) states that the proportion of young children living in low-income families is rising and the largest percentages come from urban and rural areas. The National Center for Educational Statistics (NCES) reported that 42% of public school students were considered to be part of a racial or ethnic minority group in 2005. Of U.S. public schools, 63% also had students designated as limited English proficient (LEP), while 11% of all public school students were LEP. Teachers, however, do not possess the same characteristics. Strizek, Pittsonberger, Riordan, Lyter, and Orlofsky (2006/2007) report that among public school teachers, 83% were non-Hispanic White. Only 8% were non-

Research on Urban Teacher Learning: Examining Contextual Factors Over Time
pp. 119–131
Copyright © 2010 by Information Age Publishing
All rights of reproduction in any form reserved.

Hispanic Black, 6% were Hispanic, and there were small percentages of other groups.

The mismatch between racially homogeneous teachers and students from increasingly diverse backgrounds, as stated earlier, is a critical issue in teacher education (ukpokodu, 2004, p. 19), which is evident based on the preceding statistics. This supports the finding that "many student teachers report feelings of helplessness in confronting issues of cultural difference because of their limited exposure to anything other than White, middle-class cultures" (Dozier, Johnston, & Rogers, 2006, p. 9). Children's literature however, can serve as a bridge between teachers' and students' backgrounds. Literature that emphasizes critical issues such as race, poverty, and difference can offer preservice teachers opportunities to confront those issues before being on their own in the classroom. It also provides them with a starting point for having dialogue with others about critical social issues. Having these critical conversations can become one of the many layers of critical literacy. In this study, I chose to examine how a first-year teacher from a White, middle-class background implemented critical literacy strategies in her classroom after exploring that concept through the use of children's literature during her teacher preparation. The first-year teacher and I coconstructed answers to the following questions: (1) What happens to a first-year teacher's perceptions of critical literacy from preservice preparation to inservice teaching? (2) What influences impact this teacher's development of critical literacy perspectives? (3) How did this teacher implement critical literacy?

CRITICAL LITERACY READING THEORY

Serafini (2003) considers critical literacy to be "an approach that addresses the social, historical, and political systems that affect literacy and what it means to be a literate person in contemporary society" (¶30). Paolo Freire is often referenced in order to understand critical literacy as a literacy approach (Dyson, 2004; Knobel, 2007; Luke & Freebody, 1997a; McDaniel, 2006; Stevens & Bean, 2007). Freire's central approach to education is based on his model of emancipatory literacy. Based on this perspective, Giroux (1987) describes literacy as more than the process of acquiring a technical skill enabling one to read. Rather, he believes it serves as a necessary foundation for cultural action toward freedom. Luke and Freebody (1997b) view reading as a social practice because it uses "written text as a means for the construction and reconstruction of statements, messages, and meanings" (p. 185). From a critical literacy standpoint, these practices become an everyday function tied up in politics and power.

Serafini (2003) believes that the reading processes associated with critical literacy practices are intended to help teachers and students "understand the variety of meanings that are available during the transaction between reader, text, and context, and the systems of power that affect the meanings constructed" (¶30). During this process, he believes the reader is invited to question issues of power and engage in a "social practice of constructing meaning that cannot be separated from the cultural, historical, and political context in which it occurs" (¶12). Texts, therefore, are interrogated by focusing on issues of gender, social class, race, and ethnicity.

The teacher in my study confronted cultural/racial differences in her classroom every day. She chose to read books to her students that addressed various social issues. It was her perception of this process that I wanted to explore. Because her students came to school with various experiences and background knowledge, they naturally had different "answers" during their read-aloud discussions. How she responded to them became our main topic of discussion. Jennifer,[1] the participant in my study, was not seeking "one answer" or "one main idea" during her read-alouds. Her theoretical perspective embraced student differences and enabled them to have a voice in literature discussions.

RESEARCH METHOD

This was a qualitative case study supported by a critical/feminist research stance. Throughout the study, I sought to raise my participant's "consciousness of those being oppressed because of historically situated structures tied to race, gender, and class" (Hatch, 2002, p. 17). This case study included multiple sources of data, which helped me build a rich picture of our coconstructive process (Creswell, 1998). Data consisted of reflections (R), text connections (TC), a pre-(SF) and post-(SS) survey, recorded planning meetings (PM), observations (O), interviews (I), lesson plans (LP), and class products (CP). During 15 months of data collection I followed Jennifer from her preservice preparation into her own classroom.

Participant Description

Using criterion sampling, I chose a participant based on predetermined characteristics for in-depth qualitative analysis (Patton, 2002). There were four main criteria that I used in participant selection: prior experience with critical literacy; interest in using critical literacy during the first year of teaching; displaying an emergent philosophy of critical literacy; and a willingness to work closely with researcher. Based on my observations during Jennifer's preservice year, I felt that her teaching style, attitude, and willingness to participate made her an appropriate participant for the study.

Jennifer Rossini is a White, middle-class female who grew up in a suburban area in the southern United States without much diversity. She earned her bachelor's degree in healthcare marketing. I met Jennifer at the start of her coursework in an urban multicultural teacher education program. She was pursuing her master's degree in education for a career change. Jennifer entered this program looking for a challenge. She was 23 years old at the start of her internship.

School Context

Jennifer was hired to teach first grade at Lafayette Elementary School. This is an urban elementary school that also served as Jennifer's primary placement for her year-long internship the previous year. Lafayette Elementary serves students in prekindergarten through fifth grade. The student population includes more than 650 students, most of whom are African American. These demographics serve as a contrast to the county's 80% White population (U.S. Census Bureau, 2006). The school is open to students from all areas of the county, although many students live in close proximity to the school. The socioeconomic status ranges from poverty to middle class, with 83% of the students receiving free/reduced lunch based on their family income. These factors qualify Lafayette as a Title I school. At the beginning of the school year, Jennifer's class consisted of 2 White girls, 3 Black girls, 12 Black boys, and 1 Hispanic boy. The age of Jennifer's students' was typical for first grade.

Data Collection

Qualitative data were originally collected from Jennifer's cohort of 12 preservice teachers in the urban multicultural teacher education program at a large southeastern university during the 2006-2007 school year. Jennifer's data were later disaggregated as I followed her into her first year of teaching. Data from her preservice year included three main sources: reflections, text connections, and a pre- and postsurvey. Utilizing various read-aloud strategies with her peers, Jennifer was exposed to eight critical literacy stories. Following each read aloud, she wrote her connections to the stories on Post-it notes and shared them amongst her cohort (Wooten, 2000). Reflecting in an online journal followed each read aloud session.

At the beginning and end of this preservice year, Jennifer completed a survey, which included questions regarding her attitude and beliefs related to critical issues in an urban community and a teacher's role in that environment.

Data collection continued during Jennifer's first year of teaching from August to December of 2007. As noted earlier, data were collected from five main sources: recorded planning meetings, observations, interviews, lesson plans, and class products. Jennifer and I met weekly to discuss upcoming lessons and reflect on previous lessons. We discussed the literature, classroom dynamics, behavior management, school policies, inside and outside influences, and her personal thoughts. During these conversations, I sought to raise Jennifer's awareness and understandings of social change. I also observed her for a total of 15 times before, during, and after what she considered to be critical literacy lessons. I tape-recorded three scheduled formal interviews with Jennifer, which included open-ended questions to capture her thoughts on the process of teaching critical literacy as a first-year teacher. I received a copy of her lesson plans and I took photographs of some class products such as writing samples and artwork.

Data Analysis

I primarily based my data analysis on two models: typological and inductive data analysis. I began with typological analysis, as LeCompte and Preissle (1993) describe, assembling the pieces like a jigsaw puzzle, continually shifting my attention from whole to part. I reread the data, checking it for completeness and to reacquaint myself with it, this time with the wisdom of hindsight. I chose my research questions as my main typologies (Hatch, 2002; LeCompte & Preissle, 1993), which would guide me through this process. I highlighted entries throughout the data related to these typologies and then created summary sheets, which allowed me to physically move and sort the data to identify my codes. I then shifted to an inductive analysis model.

At this point, I began utilizing my summary sheets. I proceeded with an approach aligned with Strauss and Corbin's axial coding (1990), which enabled me to develop categories and look for relationships among them. This occurred by continually examining my summary sheets, referring to the original data, and collapsing the categories, always looking to develop central themes. I marked highlighted excerpts with a code, leading me to develop a code book. Next, I created a conceptual outline. I filled in the outline with salient excerpts and began to make generalizations. Making generalizations led me to make sense of this process as I began to make connections among my research questions. During the last phase of analysis, I interpreted my generalizations to explain the story (Hatch, 2002). Throughout this process, I stayed focused on the critical/feminist paradigm, representing my voice along with Jennifer's.

FINDINGS AND DISCUSSION

The findings of this study are based on two overarching themes: *Influences impacting critical literacy development* and *implementing critical literacy*. It will become evident that the development of Jennifer's critical perspective was emerging as she made the transition from preservice to inservice teaching. The findings show that while Jennifer took some initial steps toward critical literacy practices, several areas remain that need strengthening.

Influences Impacting Critical Literacy Development

Data revealed two contrasting influences impacting Jennifer's development: obstacles Jennifer faced causing her to be reluctant as she implemented critical literacy and support Jennifer received encouraging her to continue implementing critical literacy. These influences played a large role, pushing and pulling Jennifer's development and implementation of critical literacy.

Obstacles. There were a few obstacles that Jennifer faced during her first year of teaching related to critical literacy: lack of peer support and parental influence. The first obstacle was related to other teachers' lack of support. They rarely encouraged her use of critical literacy literature and talked her out of using such books for an administrative evaluation. When she told them she planned on using a Patricia Polacco book, her peers made comments such as, "You know, we know you have a really low class," and "That's going to be too hard" (I). When she took their advice and used a more traditional book, she found that her students were not on task and she regretted taking her peers' advice: "I should have gone with my own gut instinct knowing that these kids were going to be bored ... I knew that it wouldn't be [too hard] for my kids, because they are used to this stuff" (I). She had high expectations for her students and they were used to engaging in more real-life conversations. Not having the support and encouragement of her peers was one obstacle that caused a delay in Jennifer's development.

Another obstacle Jennifer faced was related to parental influence. She constantly grappled with two main issues related to parents: How did they discuss race at home? How would they perceive her having such discussions in the classroom? This caused Jennifer some reluctance as a new teacher. The cultural/racial mismatch between Jennifer and her students' parents illuminated the complexity of the situation. This reluctance limited her development as a critical educator. As a new teacher trying to establish relationships with parents, she feared being questioned by them about the content of her read alouds and also felt guilty when she blamed parents for their children's comments. Because of such obstacles, Jennifer did not want to take ownership for having conversations related to race. If parents were to question her use of such books, Jennifer felt she would respond as follows: " 'This is an author that we read, the children brought it up, I did not in any way'—because I really didn't" (I).

She was prepared to blame the direction of such conversations on her students rather than honoring her own lesson plans. This concern prevented her from being comfortable enough to engage her students in deeper conversations.

Jennifer found through her students' comments that parents played a role in predisposing children to seeing race as a dividing line. After reading *The Other Side* (Woodson, 2001), she was surprised when she discovered that parents told their children not to play with others based on the color of their skin:

> I've had comments like, "Well, my mom says I don't need to hang out with the Black people cause I'm peach." And I was like, "Oh gosh, what do I do now?" Because you don't know what to say.... And some of the other kids were like, "Well my mom says I don't need to play with White people." It was kind of an eye opener for me cause I'm like "look at how these parents— look what they're telling their kids." (I)

Jennifer realized that some of her students' parents were teaching their children to discriminate against others based on the color of their skin. This was an unforeseen topic of discussion for her. Even though she was surprised and unsure about how to react, she allowed her students to express themselves without driving the conversation to a more critical level. Jennifer also felt that resources were limited, she had concerns about the young age of her students, and she never had enough time. However, these reasons were not enough to discourage her from trying to move forward.

Support. In order to engage in critical literacy as a first-year teacher, Jennifer relied on sources that supported and motivated her. Her three main sources of support were the researcher, student engagement, and books. At times, these three sources were challenged as some also served as obstacles. Because of these dynamics, there was a constant push and pull movement in Jennifer's development. Being that I was there as a consciousness-raiser, I had to be aware of these conflicting elements.

I, as the researcher, served as a support system to Jennifer. However, she felt that I was one of the only people consistently supporting her during her first year:

> You were pretty much the only support that was there. I mean, people here knew I was doing it, but…. It was pretty much like, "Wendy's coming," and I knew that if you found anything, or if you saw anything, or if I had a question about a book. (I)

I not only provided her with feedback and books for critical literacy, but I offered suggestions about teaching, school politics, behavior management, and other issues related to the profession.

At one point, Jennifer and I began coconstructing questions for some of her read-alouds. I suggested this as a way to raise her consciousness about ways to ask critical questions. I introduced the idea as follows: "I thought maybe if we took one of the books and wrote questions to them … you know see where they go with it. Not just the whole 'who, what, where, why'" (PM). I made a list of questions and discussed them with her. For the book *Always My Dad* (Wyeth, 1995), I suggested questions such as *"What do you think the author wants you to think about this story?" "What do you think she would say [to dad] if we heard her voice?"* and *"How would you write the ending of the story?"* Jennifer then went on to create her own based on my list and the book.

> It helped me actually in thinking about questions and helping me get to more critical questions…. I could have asked general questions like, "Oh, how does this connect to you?" Or, "What do you see?" but I wanted to think about some more things so I looked at these…. First I thought, "Okay, can't keep a steady job." But then in the story it even shows like five different jobs he had … and so I initially thought of a question. (PM)

She felt that this process supported her critical development: "You gave me that outlined list of questions, and then my questions got better" (I). As a first-year teacher, Jennifer was eager to have my support to help increase her confidence and knowledge. However, while there was progress, her questions never seemed to mirror those I suggested and remained within the context of the stories.

Another motivating factor was that her students were well-behaved and engaged during their read-aloud discussions. Data revealed some instances when Jennifer used more traditional books and her students were off task. She believed that using critical literacy books helped her students cope with issues they faced in real life: "Last week I had three kids bring in letters their dads wrote them from jail … they all wanted to read them…. Because of that book [*Visiting Day* (Woodson, 2002)], they're not embarrassed that their dad's in jail anymore" (I). She also found that her students wrote in response to the books and became better communicators through this process. "I see how they talk to one another now... maybe they've grown too.... They're learning from one another" (I). One of Jennifer's obstacles was that she felt her students were too young to deeply engage in critical conversations. However, the outcome of her lessons and the interest level of her students when reading critical literacy literature encouraged her to continue this pursuit.

Having prior knowledge about critical literacy literature and continually learning how to use such books enabled Jennifer to initiate conversations that initially seemed taboo. While locating such books was an obstacle for Jennifer, she still felt that these books supported her and her students.

> Those books will be in my class no matter what, as long as I'm a teacher, because that's important stuff for my kids, no matter if they're Black, or if they're White, because that's stuff that happens in our world every day. (I)

As a new teacher given a classroom with limited books, Jennifer had a large task to find new books. She relied on my suggestions, books fairs, and the public library to help her seek out additional literature. However, she felt that she was building a foundation that would support her career. Support from the researcher, engaged students, and knowledge about critical literacy books all served as sources of support for Jennifer as she continued with this push and pull process.

Implementing Critical Literacy

During Jennifer's first year, I observed her on a weekly basis looking to see how the elements of her lessons developed into patterns forming her critical literacy curriculum. Jennifer's critical literacy curriculum was based on three main units: "Friends," "Family," and "Being Thankful." Her read-alouds were the primary element in her critical literacy curriculum. A secondary element was a written response during writer's workshop. Other than writer's workshop, limited activities were implemented before or after her read-alouds.

Throughout this process, I observed and discussed various elements of Jennifer's curriculum. We coconstructed questions to books, reviewed transcripts, reflected, planned for the future, and introduced each other to new literature. However, even with my support and suggestions, there were opportunities Jennifer missed in her implementation. Jennifer limited her students' writing to aesthetic (feelings) or efferent (knowledge) responses (Rosenblatt, 1978) rather than encouraging them to take on a critical perspective. Together, we discussed engaging her students in activities to extend and enrich her lessons. However, she rarely implemented activities beyond her read-alouds. We talked about getting her students involved in taking action for social change; yet, that never occurred even though she exhibited excitement and enthusiasm while brainstorming ideas for such an activity. She would use her students' ability level as reasons to not try some activities: "I would love to do that, but right now some of my kids can't even—they don't know their letters" (PM). Rather than think of how she could modify activities, or even use my suggestions for invented spelling or illustrating, she would not go further.

Jennifer missed these opportunities for various reasons, some of which are related to the trials and tribulations of being a first-year teacher. Others are related to the challenging and political nature of critical pedagogy. Jennifer also lacked peer support and had concerns about parental perceptions; she had limited literature and rarely found the time to take a trip to the public library; and her planning time was often interrupted and the school had numerous testing days and unexpected assemblies. At the same time, Jennifer was trying to assimilate into the school culture and wanted to establish relationships within and beyond the school community. Taking on a "critical" curriculum can make these typical challenges even greater for a new teacher.

DISCUSSION

As Jennifer engaged in critical literacy practices, talked with me, and self-reflected, she was able to explore her comfort level. This led her to gain confidence in talking about sensitive social issues, and in doing so, she no longer perceived such issues to be inappropriate for discussion. However, she still felt she would only have conversations about such issues through the use of books. Davis, Brown, Liedel-Rice, and Soeder (2005) stated that preservice teachers need to become familiar with social issues in order to help their students confront them. During her preservice year, Jennifer was exposed to children's literature that encompassed many social issues. She used many of those same books during her first year of teaching. This provides evidence that some of the information she acquired during her preservice year related to using books focused on social issues proved helpful during her first year of teaching.

The support and confirmation Jennifer received helped offset the obstacles. Had she not had someone there pointing out all of the good things taking place, the obstacles may have forced her to give up on critical literacy. Jennifer started off with great intentions and had important discussions around her read-alouds, yet she became passive when the activities moved away from the books. This passive behavior speaks to the vital nature of taking critical literacy from text talk to hands-on activities. Praxis, which according to Freire (1970/2005) involves the transformation of consciousness through the process of self-reflection, can lead to taking action to positively change the world. However, taking action for social change would come as a result of a high degree of reflection, which occurs over time. Jennifer was in the early stages of becoming a reflective practitioner and developing her critical perspective. It is understandable that as a new teacher she was not at a level to take on such a challenge. As Jennifer continues to reflect on this process, becomes better acquainted with her urban school community, and further explores critical literacy practices, she may gradually build on what she missed during her first year.

CONCLUSIONS AND IMPLICATIONS

Implementing critical literacy is difficult for new urban teachers. They are confronted with many challenges as they try to deliver thoughtful and purposeful instruction to their students. Critical literacy practices do not come with instructions, teacher's guides, or a checklist. Teacher education programs typically provide traditional reading instruction to their teacher education candidates (Broemmel, Meller, & Allington, 2008). Those that incorporate a critical perspective cease their support once coursework is complete, leaving new teachers on their own to develop a framework. Implementing critical literacy as a first-year urban teacher is a difficult and complex process. However, with time, support, and reflection, new teachers are capable of moving toward critical literacy practices. Engaging in conversations, reflecting, and reading professional literature about this process helps move teachers forward in their thinking, enabling them to continually improve their practice.

Researchers should remember that they bear some responsibility for the teachers and students they are working with because of the political nature of critical literacy. If teacher educators are going to introduce preservice teachers to critical literacy practices, they need to understand that it is a complex process. As a researcher and supporter to preservice teachers, I was constantly reflecting on my own practice to be sure that I was building confidence rather than mandating particular strategies. I purposefully did not require preservice teachers to use the strategies they were learning until they were inclined to do so. Gradually, many took on critical literacy in different forms in their field placements.

It should not be assumed that all preservice teachers will embrace, feel comfortable with, or understand this approach during their preservice year or beyond. It is important to be mindful of the premise of transformative education, which entails reflecting in order to take action for social change. Taking action can start small within the classroom or school, but at some point should move toward the community to teach students about their role in the larger society. In general, critical literacy should be explored in preservice programs, where students feel safe to question and reflect. Once preservice teachers have their own classrooms, the support needs to continue. Perhaps professional development can take on a new perspective and help teachers look at the social implications surrounding their schools and what that means for instruction.

NOTE

1.   A pseudonym.

REFERENCES

Broemmel, A. D., Meller, W. B., & Allington, R. L. (2008). Preparing expert teachers of reading for urban schools: Models and variations in the literature. In L. Wilkinson, L. M. Morrow & V. Chou (Eds.), *Improving literacy achievement in urban schools: Critical elements in teacher preparation* (pp. 83-104). Newark, DE: International Reading Assocation.

Creswell, J. W. (1998). *Qualitative inquiry and research design: Choosing among five traditions.* Thousand Oaks, CA: Sage.

Davis, K. L., Brown, B. G., Liedel-Rice, A., & Soeder, P. (2005). Experiencing diversity through children's multicultural literature. *Kappa Delta Pi Record, 41*(4), 176-197.

Douglas-Hall, A., Chau, M., & Koball, H. (2006). *National Center for Children in Poverty; Basic facts about low-income children: Birth to age 6.* Retrieved from http://nccp.org/publications/pub_680.html

Dozier, C., Johnston, P., & Rogers, R. (2006). *Critical literacy/critical teaching.* New York, NY: Teachers College Press.

Dyson, A. H. (2004). Writing and the sea of voices: Oral language in, around, and about writing. In R. B. Rudell & N. J. Unrau (Eds.), *Theoretical models and processes in reading* (5th ed., pp. 146-162). Newark: DE: International Reading Association.

Freire, P. (2005). *Pedagogy of the oppressed, 30th anniversary edition.* New York, NY: Continuum International. (Original work published 1970)

Giroux, H. A. (1987). Introduction. In P. Freire & D. Macedo (Eds.), *Literacy: Reading the word and the world* (pp. 1-27). South Hadley, MA: Bergin & Garvey.

Hatch, J. A. (2002). *Doing qualitative research in education settings.* Albany, NY: State University of New York Press.

Knobel, M. (2007). Foreword. In L. P. Stevens & T. W. Bean (Eds.), *Critical literacy: Context, research, and practice in the K-12 classroom* (pp. vii-x). Thousand Oaks, CA: Sage.

LeCompte, M. D., & Preissle, J. (1993). *Ethnographic and qualitative design in education research* (2nd ed.). New York, NY: Academic Press.

Luke, A., & Freebody, P. (1997a). Critical literacy and the question of normativity: An introduction. In S. Muspratt, A. Luke & P. Freebody (Eds.), *Constructing critical literacies: Teaching and learning textual practice* (pp. 1-18). Cresskill, NJ: Hampton Press.

Luke, A. & Freebody, P. (1997b). Shaping the social practices of reading. In S. Muspratt, A. Luke & P. Freebody (Eds.), *Constructing critical literacies: Teaching and learning textual practice* (pp. 185-225). Cresskill, NJ: Hampton Press.

McDaniel, C. A. (2006). *Critical literacy: A way of thinking, a way of life.* New York, NY: Peter Lang.

Patton, M. Q. (2002). *Qualitative research and evaluation methods* (3rd ed.) Thousand Oaks, CA: Sage.

Rosenblatt, L. M. (1978). *The reader the text the poem.* Carbondale, IL: Southern Illinois University Press.

Serafini, F. (2003). Informing our practice: Modernist, transactional, and critical perspectives on children's literature and reading instruction. *Reading Online, 6*(6). Retrieved from http://www.readingonline.org/articles/art_index.asp?HREF=serafini/index.html

Stevens, L. P., & Bean, T. W. (2007) *Critical literacy: Context, research, and practice in the K-12 classroom.* Thousand Oaks, CA: Sage.

Strauss, A., & Corbin, J. (1990). *Basics of qualitative research: Grounded theory procedures and techniques.* Newbury Park, CA: Sage.

Strizek, G. A., Pittsonberger, J. L., Riordan, K. E., Lyter, D. M., & Orlofsky, G. F. (2006/2007). *Characteristics of schools, districts, teachers, principals, and school libraries in the United States: 2003-2004 Schools and Staffing Survey (NCES 2006-313 Revised).* Retrieved from http://nces.ed.gov

U.S. Census Bureau. (2006). *Tennessee quick facts.* Retrieved from http://quickfacts.census.gov/qfd/states/47000.html

ukpokodu, O. N. (2004). The impact of shadowing culturally different students on preservice teachers' disposition toward diversity. *Multicultural Education, 12*(2),19-28.

Woodson, J. (2001). *The other side.* New York, NY: Putnam.

Woodson, J. (2002). *Visiting day.* New York, NY: Schlastic Press.

Wooten, D. (2000). *Valued voices: An interdisciplinary approach to teaching and learning.* Newark, NJ: International Reading Association.

Wyeth, S. D. (1995). *Always my dad.* New York, NY: Knopf.

CHAPTER 9

"PREPARING STUDENTS FOR THE TEST IS NOT NECESSARILY PREPARING THEM TO BE GOOD WRITERS"

A Beginning Urban Teacher's Dilemma

Laura Pardo

Learning to teach is a complex, lengthy undertaking because teachers need to have sound knowledge of subject matter, curriculum, children, and pedagogy. No Child Left Behind (NCLB) has made it imperative for teacher candidates to understand school reform, standards, and high-stakes testing. Teacher candidates often encounter conflicting stories from their professors and school-based mentors about what is important to know to be well-prepared for classroom teaching. Urban teachers are also confronted with students whose racial, social, linguistic, and cultural backgrounds are unlike their own. For some urban teachers these struggles can be the impetus for leaving the classroom (Anyon, 1997). Although not all beginning teachers leave teaching, most are faced with numerous problems ranging from classroom management to motivating students to

Research on Urban Teacher Learning: Examining Contextual Factors Over Time
pp. 133–146
Copyright © 2010 by Information Age Publishing

understanding and acknowledging issues of diversity (Roehrig, Pressley, & Talotta, 2002).

This study examined one beginning teacher as she learned to teach writing to her urban fourth-grade students. Not only did Bethany[1] face the typical struggles of beginning teachers, but the realities of urban school teaching caused her to confront a tenuous context where her own pedagogical choices were constrained. The school's focus on test preparation permeated not only the support Bethany received from her colleagues, but also her decisions for writing instruction. Bethany's case illustrates both the complexities of learning to teach in an urban school and the necessity of understanding and navigating one's context when learning to teach.

THEORETICAL FRAMEWORK

Learning to teach is a gradual process and beginning teachers move into their first years of teaching with underdeveloped or pseudo-conceptual understandings of pedagogical models (Smagorinsky, Cook, & Johnson, 2003). Smagorinsky and his colleagues claim that teachers set out with these immature concepts, and what and whom they encounter along this twisting pathway determines how quickly and effectively they learn to teach. Additionally, they see social practice and learning as inseparable and posit that "practice contributes to learning and thus to concept development, working in dialectical relationships with the principles that bring order and unity to concepts" (p. 10). If beginning teachers are not able to teach in ways that agree with or build upon these conceptual understandings, they confront conflict which may lead to compromise or abandonment of initial concepts. Vygotsky (1987) wrote that ways of thinking are internalized through cultural practice and in relation to conflicting contexts; therefore, concepts move forward in fits and starts (i.e., the twisting path). Vygotsky's twisting path referred to the path that children traverse as they transition from concepts to concrete complex thinking. He described children as moving back and forth between concepts as they tried to understand the complexity of each. Smagorinsky et al. (2003) applied this metaphor to learning to teach and suggested that novice teachers, with their ill-formed pedagogical understandings, travel this same twisting path.

On this path beginning teachers engage in legitimate peripheral participation (Lave & Wenger, 2001). Lave and Wenger explained that learning is situated in communities of practice and that learning is not individual but rather mediated by others in the learning community. Learning is distributed among the members in the community and those with experience may participate more, making the participation by novices peripheral. In schools, these communities of practice include not only people, but also policies, curricula, and resources (Grossman, Thompson, & Valencia, 2001). What might begin as peripheral participation is legitimized by others in the community, and gradually the participation increases in complexity and the conceptual development of the novice deepens. Schools and teaching act as mediational contexts and promote activity, thinking, and concept development (Smagorinsky et al., 2003): "We see the environments themselves and their conflicting goals and demands as contributing to teachers' decisions and the conceptions that inform them" (p. 25). The school context, then, is mediational because it both contributes to teachers' thinking and knowledge formation and also serves to legitimatize participation in the school's community of practice.

This research suggests that teachers develop practices and solidify concepts based on immersion in practice. Grossman et al. (2001) added to this understanding when they stated, "The different policies that districts implement and that new teachers face actually provide the 'lens' through which they learn to teach" (p. 15). Conceptual development is essentially shaped by both the communities of practices as well as the policies that frame the curriculum. How teachers react to both of these factors determines the number of twists on the learning to teach path. Some beginning teachers acquiesce, others accommodate, and some resist (Grossman et al., 2001). Acquiescence might make the pathway more linear and less hilly, but it probably won't lead to more defined conceptual understandings of particular pedagogy. Resistance might indicate that teachers possess fairly concrete concepts; however, resisting may make the path an uphill climb, particularly if the practices are in opposition to the practices of the school community. Accommodation may be the safest route to a navigable path, but it involves compromise of conceptual development and the journey may take longer.

The complexities of learning to teach as defined by this set of research served as the framework for the current study. Bethany was immersed in a community of practice that put her conceptual understandings under scrutiny and caused her to embark on a twisting, turning, and often uphill path.

METHOD

I developed a case study of second-year teacher Bethany across an entire school year. The research question for this study was, "What factors influenced Bethany as she learned to teach writing in her urban fourth-grade classroom?"

Bethany's Context

At the time of this study, Bethany was a 24-year-old, White woman, teaching in the same urban district where she had student taught. During Bethany's first year of teaching she had been placed in three different schools and grade levels because of changing enrollment and teacher instability. These kinds of problems are prevalent in urban settings (Mirel, 1999) and Bethany's situation, while unfortunate, was not unique. During her second year of teaching, Bethany taught fourth grade at Parkside, a magnet school for the fine and performing arts.

Parkside was also a failing school. Primarily because of low test scores, Parkside had failed to meet adequate yearly progress (AYP) in the preceding school year and was awarded a *Reading First* grant. Because *Reading First* focused on improving the performance of kindergarten through third-grade students, the policy affected Bethany tangentially. As part of Parkside's magnet grant, Wednesdays were set aside as early release days for students and as work days for teachers. During the year of this study, Wednesdays were used as professional development for teachers in K-3 and focused on *Reading First*. That left the Grades 4-6 teachers without a specific purpose during schoolwide planning time.

Prompted by the principal and school improvement team, Parkside's reading teacher, Suzy, met with Bethany and a third/fourth grade teacher, Amanda, on Wednesday afternoons to help them prepare students for the fourth-grade state writing assessment. Because AYP is, in large part, determined by these test scores, the fourth-grade students needed to do well on the upcoming writing test. The goal was that students would sufficiently increase their scores so that Parkside would no longer be considered a failing school.

Data Collection and Analysis

I interviewed Bethany at the beginning and end of the school year. I observed Bethany's writing instruction once each month beginning in October, for a total of eight observations, taking fieldnotes and collecting artifacts of practice each time. At five points throughout the year, I videotaped Bethany's writing instruction and then viewed these videotapes with Bethany. During the audiotaped viewing sessions Bethany thought aloud to illuminate her instructional moves and interactions with students. She also provided me with copies of curriculum and assessment documents, her writing templates and rubrics, long and short-term plans, demographic data on each of her students, and the names of additional resources that supported her thinking and planning for teaching writing.

The data were analyzed both deductively and inductively. First, audio-tapes from the interviews and the viewing sessions were transcribed and all data was indexed. Then, each transcript was read and coded per five categories that Roehrig et al. (2002) identified as common challenges for beginning urban teachers. Fieldnotes were also coded using the same five categories. Those categories were:

- Self—teacher's knowledge, background, expectations
- Student—behaviors, language, diversity
- Professional responsibility—curriculum, classroom management
- Adults within the school setting—parents, colleagues, mentors, the principal, the larger school community
- Outside the school—isolation, bureaucracy

Within these five codes, the researchers identified 22 challenges of beginning teachers. I began with this framework because I wanted to see in what ways Bethany typified beginning teachers. I hypothesized that she would share some of the same challenge areas but that there would also be factors that influenced her due to the policy mandates and reforms that emerged with NCLB. Roehrig et al.'s work was published in 2002, the year NCLB emerged, suggesting to me that the literature they reviewed was conducted with teachers who were teaching prior to NCLB. I expected to find that Bethany's areas of challenge would include factors directly connected to NCLB.

Once the data had been coded into these five areas, the research question was revisited and the categories were revised to answer the question. After rereading and recoding the data in terms of the factors that influenced instructional decisions for writing, I ended up with seven factors. They included policy environment, colleagues, school community, students, teacher's identity, resources, and teaching tools. These factors were then ranked from most influential to least influential and specific examples were identified within each factor. Finally, I quantified the number of times each factor was identified across the data. Factors that occurred in more than 25% of the total coded items were considered to have a strong effect on Bethany's writing decisions, those that occurred between 15-25% were considered to have a moderate effect, and those that occurred less than 15% were considered as only slightly influential.

FINDINGS

Of the seven factors influencing Bethany's writing instruction, two exhibited a great deal of influence, two had moderate influence and three were not very influential. First, the policy environment exhibited the most influence on Bethany's instructional decisions. Second was collaboration with two of her colleagues. Third and fourth were the school and larger community and Bethany's teaching identity. The fifth, sixth, and final factors were Bethany's teaching tools, the materials she was provided to support her writing instruction, and her students.

The Policy Environment and Colleagues

Bethany's policy environment and her colleagues influenced her instructional decisions a great deal. At times these two factors had much overlap and it was difficult to separate whether certain decisions were made because of a policy expectation or because her colleagues were reacting in a certain way because of a particular policy. For that reason, these two factors will be discussed together.

Because the results of the fourth-grade state test would determine if Parkside made AYP, all instructional efforts at grade four were placed on preparation for the writing test. The principal, reading teacher, and school improvement team decided that the way to prepare the fourth-grade students was to engage them in deadline writing, using various organizational templates for pre-writing. Suzy, Amanda, and Bethany met every Wednesday afternoon to discuss and plan the topics and templates for these lessons. Then, every Monday, Suzy would introduce a new topic and template with the fourth-grade students and Bethany and Amanda would bring students through the writing process. Students would complete the writing piece by Friday so that they could begin the process again the next Monday.

I witnessed this kind of writing during my first three observations in Bethany's classroom, but on my fourth visit the students were creating quilt squares for a collaborative quilt. It became apparent during the lesson that students were designing the squares based on a piece of writing about determination. In the viewing session of this lesson, I asked Bethany how this lesson evolved.

> This time, we read two Faith Ringgold stories. Then [Suzy] explained the story quilt and how we were going to create it. Instead of them all doing a whole paper on determination, we took, I drew the template up on the board and I explained that they were going to do, just number two box. And that this whole story on the quilt is going to be longer than four paragraphs. It's going to have an opening paragraph, a closing paragraph, and then it's going to have 20 ... there's 22 of my regular ed students so it's going to have 22 squares in the middle.

As we continued to talk about this project, Bethany revealed that she had not really understood what Suzy wanted her to do.

> I messed up at the beginning of the project. I should have done the shared writing together [the introduction] and then sent them off to their one paragraphs, and then come back and do the closing at the end. But, I don't know what happened; we went through and talked about what it meant to be determined and then I just sent them off and they started. The next day, we were already revising and some of the kids thought they were done. I did it backwards. They'd already done the middle paragraphs and I should have done the introduction first.

Because Bethany was enacting writing pedagogy that was designed by Suzy and discussed at a Wednesday meeting, she did not take ownership of the instruction and therefore was uncomfortable with its implementation. Bethany made very few instructional decisions for writing; rather, she enacted what she understood from the weekly meetings with Suzy and Amanda. And, as the monologue above illustrates, sometimes she did not understand exactly what she was to do, and she muddled through, delivering the instruction she thought would prepare her students for the standardized writing test.

Across the year, Bethany tried to do exactly what Suzy modeled on Monday and she attempted to follow through the expectations outlined in the Wednesday meetings. Because the principal and school improvement team had sanctioned these meetings, and they all had more experience with teaching than she did, Bethany felt that they would know how to prepare students for the state writing test. In talking about Suzy, Bethany said,

> she's really, I mean that's her thing, reading and writing. I think she, that's who I rely on the most and what, not what she says goes, but what she says, because she's been teaching for so much longer than I have. I respect how she thinks and how or what approach I should take. But it's not like when we're meeting, the three of us, it's Suzy talking and me and Amanda taking notes about what we should do—it's always talking together.

When I pushed Bethany by asking what contributions she had made that the group implemented, she responded, "It's just like, the three of us, like, thinking together and we've all had the [professional development] training, which helps." While Bethany felt that the Wednesday meetings were a collaborative effort, and in many regards they likely were (I never attended a Wednesday meeting), the result remained the same—Bethany made instructional decisions for writing based on the conversations and ideas that emerged from these conversations with her colleagues.

School Community and Bethany's Identity

The contextual factors of community and personal identity exerted moderate influence over Bethany's writing instruction. While the first two factors, policy environment and colleagues, were interwoven; these two factors were not. The nature of Bethany's school community, its magnet status in particular, limited her instructional decisions. First, in order to implement the school's focus on the fine and performing arts, students and teachers in Grades 4-6 engaged in Arts Academy three mornings a week for an hour and a half each morning. During this time students took elective courses such as choir, keyboarding, or dance with each teacher and support staff member teaching a course. Because Arts Academy took up a large chunk of instructional time, Bethany felt conflicted about how to implement her writing (and reading) instruction so that it fit within the constrained parameters of the Arts Academy. She expressed that if she had more time she might implement Writing Workshop "like Fountas and Pinnell talk about" in addition to the writing that prepared students for the writing test.

A second way the magnet focus of the school impacted Bethany's writing instruction emerged during the second semester. The school had recently entered into an agreement with a prestigious art institute and students were learning to appreciate and analyze various genres of art. The fourth through sixth-grade teachers decided to use paintings in their language arts classes and they asked students to "read" the texts and then to write both critically and descriptively about the art work. During the second semester, when Bethany might have made her own instructional decisions because Suzy began working with the third-grade teachers (in preparation for their taking the fourth-grade writing tests), she focused her students on responding to artwork during writing time. Bethany had less say about the way she implemented writing instruction because of a school decision to use artwork during writing time.

The fourth factor that influenced Bethany's writing instruction was her own identity which included her values, background experiences, and beliefs. While Bethany claimed that she wanted to enact Writing Workshop, her background experiences supported a more traditional approach to writing. As an elementary student Bethany reported that she struggled with reading: "I was a Title One student, so I would always go out of the room for ... extra help with reading and writing." In reflecting upon her own writing in high school and community college she stated,

> Writing was really easy. I could do a 50-page paper on the computer the day before it was due. I would just sit down at the computer and type it out. I wouldn't do all the drafts you were required to do.

Although her teacher education program and the professional development class advocated using process approaches to teach writing, Bethany claimed that since she "never needed to go through all those steps, [she] didn't pay that much attention to the process model." Her implementation of writing instruction mirrored her personal experiences. She taught her students to use templates and to work quickly so they could finish a piece in one week. Her past experiences were affecting her decisions, albeit at a subconscious level.

Bethany had recently emerged from a teacher preparation program where she learned about Writing Workshop and process writing approaches to teaching writing. The theory behind Writing Workshop recognizes that teaching writing is difficult, but suggests that if students write daily, have ample time and choice, and if the teacher presents students with models of good writing, they can gain the skills and confidence needed to become writers. When interviewed in the fall, Bethany claimed to embrace this model, and she described her ideal Writing Workshop:

> The kids feel comfortable writing on their own and everyone is working on different things, at their own pace. I'm doing a short mini-lesson, whether it's on changing words into more expensive words or more parts of a sentence, something like that, or voice.

Bethany hoped to establish a Writing Workshop by drawing on ideas from her teacher preparation and from a district required professional development class that focused on balanced literacy.

Teaching Tools, Materials, and Students

The three factors that exhibited the least amount of influence over Bethany's instructional decisions included her teaching tools, the materials her district had provided her to support her writing instruction, and her students.

Bethany's teaching tools for writing included her conceptual understandings of process writing, Writing Workshop, balanced literacy, six plus one traits of writing (a published program), and rubrics. Bethany called her writing time Writing Workshop all year even though it did not look like the process approaches found in the literature. The evidence supports that she was enacting her underdeveloped understanding of Writing Workshop. The framework she used for teaching writing skills came from the six plus one traits (a published program). After the state test in January, Bethany created and maintained a word wall, which she had learned about her in undergraduate program, but had not been able to "get to" in the first semester because of the looming state test and the template writing.

The materials she had to use for writing instruction were various books from the professional development course she was enrolled in and handouts, templates, and rubrics that she got from Suzy or the state's department of education website. There was little evidence in the data set to support that Bethany drew from these tools or materials in any more than a cursory way. She utilized these ideas and materials if they were raised in the Wednesday meetings with Suzy and Amanda, but she was not seen to access them on her own. Even though she mentioned several books from her professional development class, I never witnessed her using them nor were they ever visible in the classroom.

It was not until our final interview in late May that Bethany named the dilemma that she was struggling with when she said, "Preparing students for the test is not necessarily preparing them to be good writers." Bethany had acquiesced to the school's goal of preparing students for the state test rather than asserting her own ideas of how to prepare her students to be good writers. In addition, because Bethany was in her second year of teaching, and both Amanda and Suzy had been teaching for much longer (Amanda for eight years, and Suzy for over thirty), Bethany felt that they were more knowledgeable about teaching writing in this school, and she followed their lead, partially out of respect.

> I think Suzy influences me the most. The only bad thing, well not bad thing, well it is a bad thing. She is so driven by the [state assessment], that it's like what she's saying is to prepare them for the [state assessment], not necessarily to prepare them to be good writers.

As we concluded this interview, I asked Bethany what her goals were for writing for the next school year. She stated:

> We're going to jump right in with senses template. [Suzy], the one that prepares them for the [state test], that's like her thing. She worked a lot with our kids on the four box template, so that's what we'll use. She's working on the structure of a paragraph and having a main idea, three details, and a conclusion. I believe she's using the same template next year.

I followed up by asking her about the templates. She did not yet know her placement for next year, and I wondered if she would use the templates if she were not at Parkside.

> The one that I'm going to change over the summer a little bit, I really like that one, the one with the different senses. I liked that one and I would use that wherever I was at. Um, the first template with the four boxes, I don't

know if I'd use it. I mean, I will if I'm here, but it's like … you know what I mean, it's not like Wow! It's just four boxes.

Bethany enacted a test preparation writing pedagogy and labeled it Writing Workshop most of the year. Additionally, she planned to implement a similar pedagogy—one that used templates, rubrics, and deadlines—in the next school year. Even though she verbalized that this kind of writing was not necessarily teaching her students to be good writers, she had internalized the pedagogy that she thought would prepare students to do well on the state test.

Surprisingly, Bethany's students exerted little influence on her instructional decisions. Rarely in our conversations, viewing sessions, or formal interviews did Bethany bring up issues related to students and instructional decisions. In the fall interview, I asked Bethany if she had specifically chosen to work in this district because it was an urban setting. She replied,

Yeah, that's the type of kids I wanted to work with because I think I can make a bigger difference. They're not getting much support at home. If I can give them as much support as I can in class [then I'll be making a difference].

However, the data did not suggest that Bethany made any of her instructional decisions because of her students and the urban setting of their school. During interviews and informal conversations Bethany rarely spoke of individual children; instead she referred to "low writers," "slow writers," and "Title One" students. While I initially wondered about what I interpreted as lack of passion, as the year unfolded my classroom observations revealed that Bethany knew the abilities of her students and she provided differentiated instruction on a one-to-one basis. For example, during an individual conference one of her students was writing about how it might feel to be adrift on a boat. The student had never been on a boat, so Bethany proceeded to help her connect to a personal experience of riding in a car with the windows down. She explained to the student that she could use that experience to describe what it might feel like to be on a boat. I came to believe that Bethany cared deeply about her students and that the relationships she had with them were important; however, I have no data to suggest that she used who her students were, or what their needs or interests were, to organize her writing instruction or to plan specific whole group mini-lessons.

DISCUSSION

Recent research has pointed to emerging tensions that high-stakes tests and accountability measures are creating for many teachers. Standardized testing has changed over the years, and the new purposes of accountability were not the ones originally intended. Nevertheless, teachers and schools are being forced to make instructional decisions based on the high-stakes nature of standardized tests. Bethany, sadly, exemplified these unintended consequences. Her decisions for teaching writing were mainly focused on preparing students to pass the state test.

In this case, assessment policy served as curriculum. In particular, because Bethany was a beginning teacher, the high-stakes testing, standards-driven curriculum, and district-level mandates influenced her instructional decisions. She never questioned, but rather she enacted the assumptions that Suzy put forth and the building administrator, school improvement team, and Amanda supported. Her assumption was that the methods they were suggesting to teach writing would prepare her students for the state writing test. She simply acquiesced to their knowledge and experience. It is likely that her conceptual understandings of process writing and Writing Workshop were underdeveloped and because the path she traveled twisted around these concepts, she eventually abandoned them and began to implement writing pedagogy that did not match her stated goals for writing. Because her background experiences matched more closely with the test prep writing pedagogy, subconsciously, she may have abandoned these concepts more easily.

Learning to teach is complicated and paying attention to conflicting factors of her teaching context was too much for Bethany to handle. The community of practice that she was immersed in—test prep writing instruction—provided her with a way to legitimatize her peripheral participation. As she learned more about the use of templates, rubrics, the six plus one traits, and deadline writing, she abandoned notions of process writing. It was easier for her to listen to Suzy and Amanda and implement a test preparation writing program than to consider her teacher education, her students' needs, or the materials she had at her disposal. And, while she mentioned that test prep writing was not the same as good writing, she maintained that she would do test prep writing during the next school year.

The seven factors that influenced Bethany's writing instruction were interwoven. It was, at times, difficult to separate certain aspects of each factor. Because most of the research on beginning teachers occurred prior to NCLB, this work revealed complexities in learning to teach that have only emerged recently. Therefore, understanding the interconnectedness of one's teaching context is something that needs more research. It seems likely that other novice teachers who are currently navigating our schools are struggling with these same set of challenges. The interplay of these factors within and upon the others appears to complicate the already difficult journey of learning to teach.

IMPLICATIONS

Implications from this study fall into three categories: those for beginning teachers, who, like Bethany are seeking support and validation; mentors, whether officially assigned like Suzy, or rather those who evolve naturally like Amanda; and teacher educators, who prepare beginning teachers like Bethany.

Beginning teachers might find comfort in this work because it affirms that learning to teach is difficult. Beginning teachers might learn valuable lessons from Bethany, in particular, that the context one is placed in strongly influences and shapes instructional decisions. While Bethany acquiesced to many of the policy demands and expectations of her colleagues, beginning teachers might be challenged to think about other ways of responding to policies—particularly accommodation or resistance. Bethany felt she had no real choice in how she implemented writing instruction; if she had known how other beginning teachers have reacted, it might have given her more courage and/or options for responding.

This study also illuminates the influence that school administrators and mentors have over beginning teachers. Administrators should consider what message they want beginning teachers to learn from mentors and make decisions carefully so that a building and district's goals are clearly represented to beginning teachers. Mentor teachers might receive regular and consistent training so that they discuss the challenges they see in the beginning teachers they work with and collaboratively work together to find the most effective ways to support them. Given the amount of influence Suzy exerted over Bethany, it seems this is something that cannot be ignored.

Teacher educators are reminded that students are not likely to maintain the passion they had for content during methods courses, particularly when they are confronted with conflicting goals and alternate pedagogies. Paying attention to national policies and the specific contexts of schools is crucial. It might be helpful to add scenarios or share case studies where teacher candidates are asked to think about decision making amidst conflicting tensions and competing goals. Additionally, teacher educators might help teacher candidates develop deeper conceptual understandings of what it means to enact certain pedagogies. Teacher candidates might benefit from being immersed in these models, not just reading or talking about them. Habits of practice including decision making, inquiry-based teaching, reflection, and connecting student learning to pedagogy are topics that warrant attention in teacher education.

CONCLUSION

This case highlights how context and the realities of urban school teaching influenced one beginning teacher's pedagogical choices. In Bethany's case, the test prep atmosphere of the school—heavily influenced by not making AYP, being labeled a failing school, *Reading First*, and a strong administration—worked to overwhelm Bethany and caused her to enact pedagogies that were not consistent with her stated goals. It was only at the end of the school year that Bethany began to realize that her instructional goals were in conflict with the pedagogy she was implementing. I was left with a feeling of dismay that Bethany's second year at Parkside might be exactly the same as her first. I am hopeful, however, that by sharing Bethany's story, teacher educators and researchers alike will continue the conversation and work of preparing teachers for urban classrooms.

NOTE

1.   Pseudonyms are used throughout.

REFERENCES

Anyon, J. (1997). *Ghetto Schooling: A political economy of urban educational reform*. New York, NY: Teachers College Press.

Grossman, P., Thompson, C., & Valencia, S. (2001). *District policy and beginning teachers: Where the twain shall meet*. A research report co-sponsored by Center for the Study of Teaching and Center on English Learning and Achievement (CELA) at the University of Albany.

Lave, J. & Wenger, E. (2001). *Situated learning: Legitimate peripheral participation*. Cambridge, England: Cambridge University Press.

Mirel, J. (1999). *The rise and fall of an urban school system: Detroit, 1907-1981, second edition*. Ann Arbor, MI: The University of Michigan Press.

Roehrig, A.D., Pressley, M., & Talotta, D.A. (Eds.). (2002). *Stories of beginning teachers: First year challenges and beyond*. South Bend, IN: University of Notre Dame Press.

Smagorinsky, P., Cook, L.S., & Johnson, T.S. (2003). *The twisting path of concept development in learning to teach*. Albany, NY: The National Research Center on English Learning and Achievement.

Vygotsky, L.S. (1987). *The collected works of L.S. Vygotsky: Problems of general psychology*. New York, NY: Plenum.

CHAPTER 10

A GROUNDED THEORY OF THE CONDITIONS AND RESOURCES IN LEARNING ABOUT URBAN TEACHING

Kelly A. Donnell

Researchers report that schools and teachers with the same resources do different things, with different results for students' learning. Resources are not self-enacting, and differences in their effects depend on differences in their use. That makes school improvement a difficult enterprise, one that depends as much on what is done with resources as what resources are available. (Cohen, Raudenbush, & Loewenberg Ball, 2002, pp. 80-81)

This chapter presents one key aspect of a grounded theory of urban teacher learning that resulted from a longitudinal, qualitative study. The study asked: How do beginning urban teachers experience the process of learning to teach? A critical finding indicated that the conditions and resources associated with teachers' learning experiences shaped beginning urban teachers' practice. In concert with the teacher's individual agency, particular contexts and conditions influenced the way in which the problem of learning to teach is continually reframed and resolved by

Research on Urban Teacher Learning: Examining Contextual Factors Over Time
pp. 147–165
Copyright © 2010 by Information Age Publishing

the beginning urban teacher. Specifically, the presence or absence of different aspects of culture, support and community, and time strongly influenced the type of teaching practice beginning urban teachers developed. Context and conditions are one aspect of a larger theory of learning to teach in urban settings. While some beginning teachers developed a transformative practice, others had difficulty "getting to we," that is, the ability to envision and enact transformative teaching practice, in which bidirectional learning between teacher and pupils is central (Donnell, 2007). Educative conditions, and the teacher's ability to mediate them, are critical to transformative urban teaching.

The urban context in which teachers work certainly influences how beginners learn to teach. However, as important and directly related to context are the conditions associated with teachers' learning experiences that support or subvert their growth. Conditions, which include resources such as time and support, organizational features such as school and classroom cultures, and teachers' roles and responsibilities contribute to either educative and miseducative learning experiences. In other words, given certain conditions, teachers are more likely to learn and grow successfully, while given other conditions, they are not. Furthermore, some aspects of the urban milieu make positive, educative conditions more difficult to come by. Within urban schools the very abilities and sensibilities beginning teachers have been struggling to learn are often discouraged or inhibited by bureaucratic, authoritarian, underresourced systems. The conditions that could support and develop teachers' learning about urban teaching are frequently absent. This chapter presents a grounded theory study that addresses the question: What are the conditions and resources that support or hinder beginners' learning about urban teaching?

METHOD

This chapter is based on a larger grounded theory study (Donnell, 2007) of the process of learning to teach in urban schools as teachers move from teacher education into the first year on the job. Because the purpose of this study was to develop a theoretical framework to understand how beginning teachers learn to teach, a constructivist grounded theory methodology was used. The study explored the following questions: How do beginning teachers experience the complex process of learning to teach in an urban setting? In other words, what is it like to learn to teach in an urban setting? What are the variables that account for similarities and differences in the learning-to-teach experiences of beginning teachers in urban settings? What is the relationship between these variables and the conditions and contexts of urban schooling? These questions are different from asking how teachers teach in urban schools in that they focus on the perceptions and lived experiences of beginners as they navigate the *learning* process. These questions explore whether and how the learning about teaching that takes place at one time is similar to, different from, or bears upon subsequent learning. They determine *how* and *why* beginning teachers learn what they do from a given learning opportunity.

Research Sites and Participants

In order to generate as much variation among participants as possible, I chose two very different urban teacher education programs. University A is a large research university in a major urban city in the northeastern United States. It is student-centered, practice-oriented, and urban. All beginning teachers at University A are assumed to be preparing to teach in urban schools. Four beginning teachers from University A were interviewed longitudinally.

College B is a large, private, coeducational college situated on the edge of the same urban city as University A. A large school of education grants undergraduate and graduate degrees, as well as teaching certification. Members of the college's Urban Teaching Scholars Program participate in an intensive 1-year master's degree program designed to address urban issues. Five beginning teachers from College B were interviewed longitudinally.

The range of variation among participants is presented in Table 10.1. In addition to the 9 longitudinal participants, 18 beginning teachers, both in teacher education programs and currently teaching in urban schools, were theoretically sampled and interviewed. As a result, this study is based on 57 interviews with 26 participants.

Data Collection and Analysis

In-depth interviews were chosen as the primary data source because of my emphasis on beginning teachers' perceptions of the lived experience of learning to teach. With constructivist grounded theory, the researcher strives to develop the dimensions of experience from the viewpoint of those who live it (Charmaz, 2000). Three to five 60-90 minute semi-structured interviews were conducted with each of the 9 participants who were followed longitudinally. These interviews were carried out over an eleven-month period. Each participant was interviewed at least once during their preservice teacher education program, the following summer, and the fall/winter of the first year on the job.

Data analysis was an ongoing process that was guided by emerging hypotheses, a process known as the constant comparative method (Glaser & Strauss, 1992). Charmaz (2000) outlines five specific strategies in the

Table 10.1.   Range of Variation Among 9 Primary Participants

Name	Age	Race	Teacher Education College	Number of Interviews	Previous Years of Teaching	Level
Karen, f	23	White	A	5	1	Elem.
Tia, f	22	Latina	A	5	0	Middle
Jules, f	23	White	A	4	0	Elem.
Tom, m	43	White	A	4	0	High
Mayva, f	23	African American	A	4	0	Elem.
Sarah, f	27	White	B	5	2	Middle
Peter, m	25	Other	B	5	0	High
Dorrie, f	23	Other	B	3	0	High
Sheila, f	25	White	B	5	0	Elem.

analytic process in constructivist grounded theory that I utilized in this study:

1. Simultaneous collection and analysis of data;
2. Two-step coding process—line-by-line coding followed by selective coding;
3. Memo writing to explore codes and define leads;
4. Theoretical sampling to refine ideas and concepts; and
5. Developing analytic framework.

Using the constant comparative method I made the following comparisons: comparing different participants, comparing different experiences/ideas from the same participant, comparing data with emerging concepts and categories, and comparing categories with other categories (Charmaz, 2000; Glaser & Strauss, 1992). Using the relationships between these categories I developed a theory of learning to teach in an urban setting for these participants that is grounded in the data of these teachers' perceptions and experiences of learning to teach. In this chapter I explore the category of conditions and resources.

THE CONDITIONS OF URBAN TEACHERS' LEARNING EXPERIENCES

The conditions of teachers' learning experiences played an important role in how beginning teachers developed their teaching practice and thought of themselves as teachers. Three conditions were particularly influential in teachers' learning. When teachers' school and classroom cultures were collaborative and supported high standards, when teachers received high-quality support, and when teachers had adequate time to focus on their practice and their learning, significant growth for the teacher was more likely. When these conditions were absent, teachers were more likely to struggle. In other words, some circumstances were more likely than others to create or support meaningful learning opportunities.

The conditions of teacher education programs, field placements, and school experiences can be educative or miseducative, depending on the form they take. When these conditions were educative, such as being provided with consistent, personalized support, teachers were more likely to use their experiences as an opportunity for learning. Conversely, when these conditions were miseducative, such as when school culture promoted compliance and isolation, learning to teach was hampered or misdirected. When conditions changed, the teacher's approach to the problems of learning to teach often changed as well.

School and Classroom Culture

A first condition of teachers' experiences that influences their learning is school and classroom culture. The cultures of the schools and classrooms in which beginning teachers find themselves strongly influence what and how they learn. The norms of school and classroom cultures can support or derail an effective urban teaching practice. In this study, participants' perceptions of their school and classroom cultures acted as both positive and negative conditions in beginners' learning processes, depending on the particular circumstances. Different ethos, norms, and characteristics of these cultures affected teachers in different ways. Not surprisingly, perceived norms of collegiality, high standards, consistency, empowerment, and sustained commitment to intellectual engagement tended to facilitate beginning teachers' and, therefore, pupils' learning. These cultures supported teachers' efforts at developing teaching practice that was responsive to pupils and adaptive to change. On the other hand, excessive transition in policies or turnover of staff, pretense, isolation, and dysfunction characterized school and classroom cultures that had a negative influence on teacher learning.

Urban systems and policies often reinforce unproductive school and classroom cultures (Fine, 1994). Urban school reforms are seen as either incidental to school life, on the one hand, or an imposition of lockstep procedures, on the other (Lebert, 2001). While not universal, many beginners worked in unsupportive and isolating school and classroom cultures that contributed to their sense of vulnerability and disempowerment. A few participants were fortunate to find themselves in or tenacious enough to locate for themselves schools and classrooms whose cultures focused on learning, support, and growth for both children and adults.

A simplistic list of educative and miseducative cultural norms belies the complexity of the reflexive interaction between participants' individual agency and the school and classroom culture. Through their individual agency, teachers interact with and both shape and are shaped by the cultures in which they teach. School and classroom cultures are not isolated variables; they are mediated by other conditions, by larger system and social policies, and by the individuals that are constituents within the given culture. Cobb (2001) warns that generalizations about school cultures may be misleading. It is difficult to define positive urban school climates because of the range and multifaceted nature of what constitutes "positive."

Cultural Conditions that Facilitate Teacher Learning

In school and classroom cultures that were collegial, committed to high standards, flexible, and responsive to people's needs rather than institutional concerns, beginning teachers' commitments were strengthened and they were able devote themselves to learning and teaching. Some schools respected teachers' professionalism and growth by implementing school policies and procedures that supported their work with children. For example, Marta chose a startup charter school for her first teaching position because she felt it would nurture and challenge her as a beginning urban teacher committed to social justice. She was not disappointed. She was hired in July and the school faculty spent the summer developing school mission, values, and curriculum, working to "be on the same page."

> Well a lot of the thing is we have a lot of ownership of things. If you look around the [staff] room we've come up with like core values or beliefs, what kind of culture we want our school to have. We do a lot of cultural building to get to know each other.... It's like I have a voice. We partake in those administrative decisions. And at times it gets dragged out because everybody comes up with different views and different personalities. But, you know, in the end it's nice to just even have your voice put out there. We are all kind of on the same page about a lot of things. (Marta, Summer 2003)

The culture of Marta's new school helped her develop ownership of her teaching. In addition, the faculty at Marta's school created a culture in which critical discourse was practiced. They engaged in mutual learning with one another by making conscious decisions to create a school culture that would support their vision of student and teacher learning. Being part of this process was empowering for Marta as a beginning teacher and helped her define and eventually enact her own transformative practice with her pupils.

Collegiality facilitated learning with and from both one's pupils and other adults. In fact, adult norms and expectations often set the stage for how teachers and pupils interacted with one another. In discussing how she capitalized on and tried to develop the norm of collegial respect in her startup charter school, Sarah, a resource room specialist, noted,

> It's ... the way that the teachers or the adults treat one another. You know, it sets an example for how the kids are going to treat one another. I made very clear at the beginning of the year that unless I need a little privacy, my policy is open door. If you need to come in, you come in, even if I have a class. And a lot of the teachers have said, "Well, ok, we are going to do that too." (Sarah, Fall 2003)

In confirming and reinforcing an existing positive condition, that of mutual respect and openness, Sarah became increasingly empowered. Her growing success in working with other adults reinforced her commitment to this approach with her pupils as well. The cultural conditions of collegiality, intellectual engagement, and consistent and high standards for teachers and pupils encouraged beginning teachers to develop a more reciprocal, transformative practice with their pupils.

Cultural Conditions That Undermine Teacher Learning

In contrast to the positive school and classroom cultural conditions that facilitated the learning of a few beginning urban teachers, many participants struggled in school cultures that made meaningful learning more difficult or that misdirected learning. In keeping with much of the literature on urban school conditions (e.g., Kozol, 1991; Weiner, 1993; Yeo, 1997) some participants saw their schools as unstable, unsupportive, authoritarian, and accepting of low standards for all involved. As one beginner put it, "It just seems like education isn't a priority at the school I'm at. I don't really know what is, but I don't really think it's student learning and teacher development" (Student teacher, Spring 2003). Participants often had the impression that the school was set up to undermine rather than support their work with pupils. More than fear for their physical safety, teachers were afraid that their best efforts at working with children could easily be questioned or even publicly challenged and criticized without due process. This left teachers feeling vulnerable, unwilling to take risks, and more likely to resign themselves to teaching practice that was uncontroversial and easy to manage.

Given the frequency of negative conditions, participants struggled to differentiate between those things that were within their ability to address or change and those that were not. Where should they invest their time, energy, and resources? As one teacher noted, "I feel so powerless some-times. There are so many things that I have no control over. So I have to figure out the stuff I have no control over and focus on the stuff I do have control over" (Student teacher, Spring 2003). Without consistency and support from school leadership, beginning teachers necessarily had to turn their time and energy to navigating a treacherous culture on their own while feeling increasingly stressed and incompetent. Focus on students and learning was diverted.

When cultural conditions at their schools reinforced feelings of isolation and incompetence, teachers were at particular risk of giving up on trying to learn, and instead taking the path of least resistance or leaving teaching. For example, Jill was assigned an extremely challenging group of students during her first year, a common problem for beginning teachers (Fideler & Haselkorn, 1999). Her principal sent her the clear message that she was on her own with classroom management.

> I got a note [from the principal]: "Don't send [pupils] to the office." There was a whole speech in front of the school like, "If there's a problem with the kid, it's the teacher's issue. I'm not here to deal with behaviors and if kids are meaningfully engaged they won't have any behavior problems." That was announced to the whole school like within the first few weeks of school. I mean that was like how the tone was set. I mean I'm not making it up! It's true! That's what I mean about [feeling like I'm] in one of those [urban teaching] documentaries: like, oh well it's *really* like this and people *really* can feel this incompetent and crazed. (Jill, Fall 2003)

Jill described her struggle with the frightening impulse to accept these negative cultural norms as givens and use them a lens for questioning the futility and personal costs of her best efforts at change. She was concerned that the overwhelming stress she was feeling would cause her to accept increasingly lower standards.

> And we'll forget, you know, as the norm gets pushed back so far. I think that's kind of where I'm at, stuck in back a little bit. Like "Wow, this is a job and I'm killing myself." I'm physically getting ill, I can't sleep a lot. And it shouldn't be this way and it wasn't this way in other settings at all. (Jill, Fall 2003)

While Jill was aware of the impact that the school culture was having on her own expectations and resolutions, other teachers were not. Without critical reflection and awareness of the gradual erosion of their ideals, principles, interactions, and decisions by negative school cultures it was unlikely that they could recover and move back to a place of confident growth.

Learning to teach is difficult under the best of circumstances. The cultures of schools and classrooms can serve to support or undermine beginners' learning about urban teaching. Teachers who learn to teach in negative, dysfunctional school cultures face an enormously challenging task. When asked what her school was like, one participant responded: "What's it like? This school is the most unorganized, dysfunctional place I've ever been in my life." (Student teacher, Spring 2003). If we are to expect success from beginning urban teachers

> it is crucial that research on learning to teach focus on the conditions of schools as well as on the individuals entering them. If schools operate in ways that are unresponsive to the needs of the students, it is unreasonable to expect novice teachers to learn to operate effectively in them. (Huling-Austin, 1992, p. 179)

This could be accomplished in part, by providing beginning teachers with a second condition of teaching and learning, the support and community necessary to navigate challenging contexts and unproductive school cultures.

Support and Community as a Condition of Learning

The amount, type, and quality of support available to beginning teachers are a second salient condition of teachers' learning experiences. It is considered a given in the field of teacher education that appropriate support will facilitate the process of learning to teach, while inappropriate support acts as a deterrent to meaningful learning (see for example, Feinman-Nemser, 2001; Quartz, 2003). However, how this support actually does (or does not) get played out in the learning process varied widely for participants in this study.

Support

While it is easy to assume that support of beginning teachers is, or at least should be, a necessity for learning, many participants in this study did not receive the support they needed. In this section I argue that although different kinds of support functioned as an educative condition of learning, general lack of support was a disturbingly frequent miseducative condition. For those who did receive support, individualized and context-specific support was seen as most useful by participants.

The teachers in this study indicated that support that was individualized to their specific needs, questions, and difficulties was particularly helpful. Individualized support helped beginners feel that their unique situation, for example as a new teacher, as a teacher of color, or as an uncertified beginning teacher, was recognized and incorporated into the learning process. For example, the principal at Jules' first teaching job was also new in his position. His empathy with this aspect of her teaching helped Jules feel that her role was valued and her needs were recognized:

> He's paying attention to me because he knows how he feels as a new principal. So he checks in with me a lot. And he schedules times and we sit down and he just asks how things are going. For every little thing that comes up in my classroom that I feel I need to communicate with him about, he says, "Let's keep talking about this." And he says, "I'm glad you came to me about it." So his support has been great. (Jules, Fall 2003)

An individualized approach to support helped participants pose and explore problems in their practice and develop practical knowledge about teaching.

Support that recognized individuals' particular needs, strengths, weaknesses, and experiences was seen as particularly valuable. As I discuss later in this section, however, without a community for teacher learning (Cochran-Smith & Lytle, 1999), an individualized approach to support reinforced the individualistic quality of teaching. If support confirmed for the beginner that the problem of learning to teach is an individually determined rather than a socially negotiated problem, teachers were at risk of an overly narrow view that they alone were fully responsible for what happened in the classroom (Britzman, 1991).

In a similar vein, participants also benefited when the support they received was contextualized. Generic advice or platitudes were plentiful but deemed meaningless by most participants. In particular, knowledge of and experience in urban schools was seen as a prerequisite for those offering support to the beginner. Supervisors, faculty, and others who lacked urban teaching experience were discounted. Their support was considered too generalized and irrelevant to the specific challenges and needs of urban teaching. In contrast, support that helped the beginning teacher explore and better understand the context of urban teaching was seen as especially helpful. In particular, experienced urban teachers were seen by many participants as having "all the smack," or key insights, on learning to teach in an urban setting:

> I had a great supervisor who is in the [city] Public Schools for 35 years, and then all of a sudden I get someone who's completely new to everything. I feel like my second semester - that's when I needed that other supervisor there. And that's when I feel like because I know that there were things that...she would tell people about different opportunities that were going on. And she would tell them about her experience. (Student teacher, Spring 2003)

Experienced urban teachers were viewed as the most authentic support in explaining how others have developed effective teaching practices. However, some participants tended to accept advice from experienced teachers carte blanche, without questioning or critically analyzing the reasoning behind the support. Uncritical acceptance of other teachers' suggestions based solely on their experience precluded participants from contextualizing or problematizing for themselves. When beginning teachers unthinkingly adopted the advice of more senior teachers they reinforced the myth of "experience as the best teacher" (Feiman-Nemser & Buchmann, 1983)

Types of Support

In addition to the individualized and contextual quality of support, participants benefited from having several different types of support as they learned to teach. Different types of support were beneficial in different circumstances. Under the right circumstances, emotional, logistical, instructional, and conceptual support served as conditions that facilitated resolution of the problem of learning to teach.

Consistent with the literature (e.g., Wang & Odell, 2002), the beginners interviewed for this study needed emotional support. The challenges and stress of urban teaching and the newness of their experiences were alleviated when participants had opportunities to "vent" negative emotions. Beginners appreciated talking to others who would simply listen, without necessarily attempting to solve problems: "The [teachers] I go to are very supportive. I mean, they may not have all the answers, but they are willing to listen. I just need to vent" (Student teacher, Spring 2003).

In addition to emotional support, participants benefited from logistical support. Because of the bureaucratic, institutional nature of urban schooling, participants looked for help in navigating unfamiliar and complicated territory. Beginners needed help in knowing how to negotiate the "red tape" inherent in daily life in urban schools. This type of support included help in locating materials, learning how get copies made, and filling out paperwork. However, neither urban teacher education programs nor urban schools were very forthcoming in providing this kind of practical support; it was provided by design in a few urban schools but by happenstance or not at all in most:

> I feel like you just find out things as you go along. There's really no one to sit you down and say, "This is what we do and this is how it's done." With some things I have to mess up first to find out no, that's not how it was supposed to be done.... So that's been really tough. (Beginning teacher, Fall 2003)

Without this practical support, time and energy was spent solving the logistical exigencies of daily classroom life that had little to do with learning about teaching.

A third type of support was instructional. Beginning teachers are often criticized for wanting only bunches of instructional strategies or a "bag of tricks" divorced from theory or critical reflection (Bullough & Gitlin, 2001). Instructional support is potentially very problematic if it reinforces a narrow and technical, rather than a transformative, problem-posing teaching practice. If teachers view instructional support and suggestions as immediate solutions to narrowly framed questions, they are unlikely to further explore their learning as the imminent instructional problem was seen as "solved."

However, instructional support can serve a variety of important purposes. One of these is helping beginners develop a foundation in pedagogical options from which teachers can draw as they respond to the particular needs and interests of pupils in specific contexts. For example, Dorrie was videotaped by her headmaster who helped her conduct a frame-by-frame analysis of her teaching. This exploration of her teaching decisions in combination with the specific and strategic alternatives he provided was extremely helpful to Dorrie.

> [The headmaster] was like, "Did you see that? You see what you did?" He did like a play by play. And he's like, "You stood still. You looked like you were ready. That's why the kids came in and took their seats. Instead of you know, fooling around." And all this stuff. So, I had a lot of support, left and right. (Dorrie, Summer 2003)

Support that identified and offered specific instructional techniques and strategies in light of the teacher's actual practice could be very helpful. This was particularly true when the teacher was able to develop and use this repertoire in critically choosing appropriate strategies in response to pupils' specific needs and interests, rather than as a predetermined, routine decision. Instructional support, therefore, was especially helpful when it engaged beginners in critiquing pedagogical ideas in light of their potential as tools to generate mutual and responsive learning with pupils.

A fourth type of support was conceptual in that it focused particularly on the concepts the teacher was or was not learning. Some teachers benefited significantly from support in critiquing their own learning about teaching. This type of support often took the form of questions about, challenges to, or alternative suggestions regarding the relationship between educational concepts and participants' teaching practice:

A lot of what [my supervisor] was talking about is trying to pick up on how much I was able to figure those things out for myself. But also when she thought a particular tangent that I had gone off on - was it helpful or appropriate? Did going that far confuse students? Or did it help students? (Student teacher, Spring 2003)

Context and individualization came together in a meaningful way when the individual offering the conceptual support knew about the participant's background, experiences, and short and long-tem goals. However, few practitioners engaged participants in the reflective critical discourse necessary for conceptual support.

In sum, four different types of support—emotional, logistical, instructional, and conceptual—formed a rich and necessary foundation for developing transformative practice and successfully resolving the problem of learning to teach. Quality support, which is quite different from evaluation, gave beginners opportunities to engage in critical discourse around a variety of aspects of their practice. With support, beginning teachers were better able to explore their perceptions, decisions, questions, and actions. This was particularly important in urban systems that often worked against continued learning and growth. As I discuss in the next section, the characteristics and functions of the specific communities within urban schools and teacher education programs often made support for beginners complicated.

Community

The term "teacher learning communities" (Cochran-Smith & Lytle, 1999) carries a particular emphasis on consciously engaging teachers in multiple viewpoints as they construct knowledge collaboratively. Teacher learning communities are often intended to provide interaction with others who share context, circumstances, or ways of thinking about teaching. While all participants in this study were part of de facto communities in the sense that they worked with groups of people in schools, very few had opportunities to participate in learning communities.

Cohorts. Many of the participants in this study were part of a university-based urban cohort during their student or initial teaching. Cohort groups can afford beginners with opportunities to develop a shared sense of membership and supportive networks (Carter, 1990; Stairs, 2006). Many participants in this study thought their urban cohort group was beneficial in learning to teach as a result of contact with like-minded others who shared their sensibilities, goals, and challenges.

The most helpful thing I thought was that [the cohort] provided 30 other people that were in the same similar situation, and that they were teaching in the same places, and had the same type of kids, and the same interests, and the same dedication to urban education as compared to just regular education. (Student teacher, Spring 2002)

A cohort often provided a safe place to experience morale boosting and emotional support without the concerns of being evaluated or conforming to cultural norms.

Supportive colleagues sometimes served as an informal cohort or team when participants moved to their first year of teaching. A White preservice teacher noted that the African American teachers at her school included and valued her as a member of a team.

> My coworkers realize how much I care about those kids. And that I'm in it just as much as they are, trying to make it right. So I mean, that helps. A lot of the books that I'm reading, a lot of the articles that I'm reading about this type of education are really disheartening because they kind of, what I said before, they make it seem as though I [as a White teacher] don't have any right to be doing this. So, my coworkers definitely challenge that idea. (Student teacher, Fall 2003)

While cohorts may not be the most powerful intervention in learning to teach (Su, 1990) they can provide safe, supportive, emotional outlets with like-minded others that were potentially meaningful to beginning teachers.

Teaching Learning Communities. Teacher learning communities are considered to have great potential to develop teachers' learning through interactions with others (Cochran-Smith & Lytle, 1999). Participants noted that some of their student teaching experiences were designed to incorporate teacher learning communities through coursework, meetings, and cohort activities. Despite the often forced nature of these situations, participants found them helpful in exploring teaching practice with others. This approach to working through teaching dilemmas was an important aspect of developing a transformative practice. Karen outlined the type of community many participants expressed an interest in:

> We do these "quality conversations" for our practicum ... like the last time we had to think of a problem or an issue. And it was very formal. It was very systematic. Like, "Ok, what is going on. Why is this happening? What can I do about it?" But then you don't have to strain by yourself. You are talking aloud with a few other people. That helps. Like when it is that kind of focused and systematic on how to go about some of the things that you are facing. (Karen, Spring 2003)

This type of teacher learning community was helpful for beginning teachers as it provided opportunities to work through the knowledge they were gaining and the dilemmas they were experiencing.

For the few teachers who did experience learning communities, these communities were not limited to school settings. Several participants spent time in local community organizations and found the support they received there more authentic than their teaching sites. These experiences helped them in understanding the families and communities they were serving from a different perspective:

> And in the prepracticum experiences it seems like you have more support actually than in the practicum student teaching. So you have constant feedback. Like it's usually in community organizations, they have like closer ties to the students and their families. I mean that's a resource too. It's just realer. (Student teacher, Spring 2003)

Extending the learning community outside of the school (Murrell, 2000) helped participants develop new, authentic understandings of teaching and schooling from the perspective of different constituents.

Effective support for beginning teachers and the development of learning communities required time, communication, and education of support personnel. However, as will be shown in the following section, adequate time for learning was in short supply for participants. As one preservice teacher concluded, despite enthusiastic and meaningful support from her cooperating teacher, "it's not like she has that much free time to talk to me after my allotted time is up" (Student teacher, Spring 2003).

Time

In addition to school and classroom culture, and support and community, a third condition that facilitated or impeded learning about urban teaching was time. As many teachers will attest, there simply are not enough hours in the day to meet all the demands of the job. One participant noted at the beginning of the school year: "Well, I think, you know, people have been saying that all day: 'Oh, I wish I had more time.'" (Beginning teacher, Summer 2003).

While many may agree that time is a necessary condition for teacher learning, teachers' roles and responsibilities become more demanding and infused with a restrictive notion of accountability. The demands of juggling a range of responsibilities and activities as beginning urban teachers left little time to reflect or otherwise meaningfully engage in their learning. However, without adequate time to focus on their learning, participants were propelled through their busy days in ways that became routine and unthinking, rather than deliberate and thoughtful. Quality learning simply was unlikely without adequate time.

Participants universally and emphatically bemoaned the egregious absence of time to do the daily work of teaching, let alone focus on learning. Participants also noted that those people who had the potential to influence their learning, from peers to colleagues to cooperating teachers to university supervisors and faculty, were also taxed for time. Stephanie's wish for additional time to problem-solve with her university supervisor was typical:

> But like maybe if [the teacher education program] built an additional hour in [for weekly discussion]. You know what I mean? Because I just feel like everybody who is involved in this process is so overextended, that like, our supervisor has to get back to [the university] to teach or get back for her office hours or has things to do. If it was almost like mandatory that there be time built in for site-specific sort of seminar feedback and problem solving, that might be useful. (Stephanie, Spring 2003)

While teacher education programs may espouse critical reflection, a mixed message is sent to participants about the value of these activities when actual time to engage in them is extremely limited or nonexistent.

Traditional student teaching placements only offered limited time in the classroom. This created several problems for beginning teachers. For example, some participants believed their role as a student required them to be successful in the classroom immediately (Britzman, 1991). Like many participants, Karen felt pressure to "get it right" quickly. If a new lesson or innovative approach did not work out right away, she abandoned it and reverted to interactions that ensured control and compliance from students.

> We don't have a lot of time I guess is the other thing. So you feel like, if it doesn't work right away, you have to give up on it. You have to move on right away. If it didn't go well right away, that then that's not working obviously. You need to go back to what kept them quiet and in their seats and have them doing their work. (Karen, Spring 2003)

A perceived lack of time to consider, try out, and evaluate different ways of teaching and interacting with pupils served to limit the development of transformative practice. When a sense of immediacy and time pressure became a condition of learning, beginners were apt to resort to safety of the status quo.

An authentic and productive focus on learning required time. Many teachers longed for uninterrupted stretches of time to focus on their teaching and believed that outcomes could be quite different if they could take the time to reflect, take stock, and catch up. In short, they needed time in order to become learners that were thoughtful, reflective, and deliberate. Compounding this, the conditions and cultural norms within both teacher education and urban schools discussed earlier in this chapter often exacerbated rather than relieved time pressure by insisting on policies and practices, such as extensive paperwork, that undercut opportunities for discussion, reflection, and thoughtful evaluation.

Participants had to make difficult decisions based on lack of adequate time. Urban school districts' prescriptive teaching practices often required teachers to follow the curriculum at a particular pace, frequently in preparation for standardized testing. More engaging or meaningful lessons were abandoned in order to "cover" the prescribed curriculum.

> I just feel I can't get it all together. I mean I'm behind. There's a certain point I need to be at by the mid year and since I'm already behind now.... I'm behind so it's just hard 'cause everything takes so long. And we only have 45-minute periods and any kind of fun, interesting activity is going to take two or three periods to get through. (Beginning teacher, Fall 2003)

Time is an elusive yet critical condition of learning to teach. Without adequate time, beginning teachers cannot be expected to engage in the intellectual, emotional, moral, and practical work required to successfully learn about teaching.

CONCLUSION

Throughout this chapter I have argued that the conditions of teachers' experiences in schools, teacher education programs, and professional development had a significant influence on teachers' learning and practice. These conditions could serve to facilitate or impede participants' learning about urban teaching. This study suggests that the critical component of learning experiences for teachers have to do with the conditions of culture, support and community, and time. When conditions were educative, such as meaningful support and adequate time to reflect, teachers were able to grow in their learning. Under miseducative conditions, such as school cultures that accepted low standards or a role of subordination, teachers' learning and growth were more likely to be frustrated. The nature of urban schools as bureaucracies and rigid institutional systems often do not support the conditions of learning that would help beginning teachers grow and become successful.

Every environment that is intended to support teacher learning, from teacher education programs to professional development opportunities to urban schools themselves, must work in concert to ensure that the positive forms of these conditions are in place. This requires building in adequate time for teachers to focus on their learning. It also necessitates ensuring that teachers have a range of support, appropriate and meaningful roles and responsibilities, and school and classroom cultures that are collegial and committed to the centrality of learning. Without these conditions, even the most promising new practices to promote teacher learning may fall short. Ensuring these conditions should lead the overall reconceptualization of teacher education programs and professional development for urban school teachers.

REFERENCES

Britzman, D. (1991). *Practice makes practice*. Albany, NY: State University of New York Press.

Bullough, R. V., & Gitlin, A. (2001). *Becoming a student of teaching: Linking knowledge production and practice* (2nd ed.). New York, NY: Routledge.

Carter, K. (1990). Teachers' knowledge and learning to teach. In W. R. Houston (Ed.), *Handbook of research on teacher education: A project of the Association of Teacher Educators* (pp. 212-233). New York, NY: Macmillan.

Charmaz, K. (2000). Grounded theory: Objectivist and constructivist methods. In N. Denzin & Y. Lincoln (Eds.), *Handbook of qualitative research* (2nd ed.). Thousand Oaks, CA: Sage.

Cobb, J. (2001). Graduates of professional development school programs: Perceptions of the teacher as change agent. *Teacher Education Quarterly, 28*(4), 89-107.

Cochran-Smith, M., & Lytle, S. (1999). Relationship of knowledge and practice: Teacher learning in communities. In A. Iran-Nejad & C. D. Pearson (Eds.), *Review of research in education* (Vol. 24, pp. 249-306). Washington, DC: American Educational Research Association.

Cohen, D., Raudenbush, S., & Loewenberg Ball, D. (2002). Resources, instruction, and research. In F. Mosteller & R. Boruch (Eds.), *Evidence matters: Randomized trials in education research* (pp. 80-119). Washington, DC: Brookings Institute Press.

Donnell, K. (2007). Getting to we: Developing a transformative teaching practice. *Urban Education, 42*(3), 223-249.

Feiman-Nemser, S. (2001). From preparation to practice: Designing a continuum to strengthen and sustain teaching. *Teachers College Record, 103*(6), 1013-1055.

Feiman-Nemser, S., & Buchmann, M. (1983). When is student teaching teacher education? *Teacher and Teacher Education, 3*(4), 255-273.

Fideler, E., & Haselkorn, D. (1999). *Learning the ropes: Urban teacher induction programs and practices in the United States*. Belmont, MA: Recruiting New Teachers, Inc.

Fine, M. (Ed.). (1994). Chartering urban school reform. In *Chartering urban school reform: Reflections on public high schools in the midst of change* (pp. 5-30). New York, NY: Teachers College Press.

Glaser, B., & Strauss, A. (1992). *The discovery of grounded theory: Strategies for qualitative research*. New York, NY: Aldine de Gruyter.

Huling-Austin, L. (1992). Research on learning to teach: Implications for teacher induction and mentoring programs. *Journal of Teacher Education, 43*(3), 173-180.

Kozol, J. (1991). *Savage inequalities: Children in America's schools.* New York, NY: Harper & Row.

Lebert, L. L. (2001). Urban schools: Challenges for the new millennium. In G. Duhon (Ed.), *Problems and solutions in urban schools* (pp. 265-273). Lampeter, Wales: The Edwin Mellen Press.

Murrell, P. (2000). Community teachers: A conceptual framework for preparing exemplary urban teachers. *Journal of Negro Education, 69*(4), 338-348.

Quartz, K. H. (2003). "Too angry to leave": Supporting new teachers' commitment to transform urban schools. *Journal of Teacher Education, 54*(2), 99-111.

Stairs, A. J. (2006). *Preservice teacher learning in an urban school-university partnership.* Unpublished doctoral disseration, Boston College, Chestnut Hill, MA.

Su, Z. (1990). The function of peer group in teacher socialization. *Phi Delta Kappan, 71*(9), 723-727.

Wang, J., & Odell, S. (2002). Mentored learning to teach according to standards-based reform: A critical review. *Review of Educational Research, 72*(3), 481-546.

Weiner, L. (1993). *Preparing teachers for urban schools, lessons from 30 years of school reform.* New York, NY: Teachers College Press.

Yeo, F. (1997). *Inner-city schools, multiculturalism, and teacher education: A professional journey.* New York, NY: Garland.

PART III

IMPACT OF POLICY ON URBAN TEACHER LEARNING

CHAPTER 11

PROFESSIONALISM > POLITICS + POLICY + PEDAGOGY

The Power of Professionalism

Audrey A. Friedman and Frank Daniello

If you think back to algebra class, you may recall the Axiom of "Equals," and more specifically, the Transitivity Rule. One of three rules that govern the use of the "=" (equal) sign, the Transitivity Rule states:

$$\text{If } a = b, \text{ and } b = c, \text{ then } a = c$$

As this is indeed one of the simpler axioms in mathematics, it is no wonder that the *politics* of the federal government have applied this rule in enacting the most recent *policy*, The No Child Left Behind Act of 2001 (NCLB), that dictates *pedagogy*: how and what pupils must learn and how they must be assessed; how schools must operate; and what, how, and when teachers must teach, especially in the context of urban schools. Compensatory in nature, current educational policy rewards schools and teachers for successful pupil performance on high-stakes tests, simply moving the deficiency for poor performance from the pupil to the school

Research on Urban Teacher Learning: Examining Contextual Factors Over Time
pp. 169–189

and subsequently, the teacher. In essence, politics and policy have extended the deficit model of pupil achievement to include schools and teachers, rather than placing the blame where it squarely belongs: on "the array of savage economic and social problems that undercut children's school success, problems created and abetted by government polices" (Weiner, 2007, p. 5). Therefore, applying the Transitivity Rule to the urban context (u = urban).

$$\text{If } pfu = sfu, \text{ and } sfu = tfu, \text{ then } pfu = tfu.$$

If urban pupil failure (pfu) = urban school failure (sfu), and urban school failure (sfu) = urban teacher failure (tfu), then urban pupil failure (pfu) = urban teacher failure (tfu).

Although seemingly altruistic, adopting national standards as a panacea for diminishing the achievement gap has established "uniform expectations for the academic performance of all students [but] offer[ed] a limited strategy of educational reform and improvement" (Sandholtz, Ogawa, & Scribner, 2004, p. 1198). This is especially prevalent in urban districts where, historically, pupil performance on standardized tests has been low due to under-funding of human and material resources; increasing pupil enrollment and diminishing space; rundown buildings; low teacher recruitment and retention rates; poor working conditions; lower percentages of teachers licensed in specific subject-matter areas, particularly mathematics, science, foreign language and special needs; lack of collaborative preparation time; safety; and numerous other variables indigenous to the urban context (Allen, 2008). Furthermore, education policies under the Clinton Administration and subsequent iterations, such as NCLB, not only diverted attention away from the more significant economic and social issues that plague metropolitan areas but also "intensified race and class stratification" (Weiner, 2007, p. 2). Additionally, NCLB's unspecific regulatory guidelines have led some states and districts (usually large, underresourced urban and rural districts) to adopt lower standards, create less rigorous assessments, or use local criterion-referenced tests to measure more "realistic," lower standards (Sandholtz et al., 2004).

Urban schools, pupils, and teachers also suffer from the Matthew Effect: the rich get richer and the poor get poorer. More affluent districts are not riddled with the social ills that plague urban districts and can devote capital to all aspects of education that increase pupil performance on high-stakes assessments and attainment of Adequate Yearly Progress (AYP) and as a result, acquire more resources from the state and federal governments. Poor districts, already underresourced and influenced by multiple factors (Weiner, 2005) that do not impact their more affluent suburban peers, cannot devote as much capital to enhancing pupil performance and thus fall farther behind. Others even argue that high-stakes accountability measures subsumed under current policy are particularly detrimental to urban schools and teachers:

> [While] high-stakes accountability gets teachers' attention, provides them with objective information, and increases their focus on issues of instruction, the nature of incentives and teacher motivation, the use of testing data, and the targeted nature of instructional focus in probation schools marginalizes low-performing students, increases gate-keeping processes, and works against the spirit of the policy. (Diamond & Spillane, 2004, p. 1169-1170)

Furthermore, McNeil (2000) asserts that "educational standardization harms teaching and learning and, over the long term, restratifies by race and class" (p. xxvii).

Regardless of resources, working conditions, or high-stakes testing, most research identifies the teacher as a critical variable in pupil achievement. Some researchers have gone as far as to create a Teacher Quality Index (Stronge & Hindman, 2006), which provides administrators a protocol for hiring the most highly qualified teacher. And although the authors state that, "pinning down teacher effectiveness is a bit like defining beauty, 'because it is often in the eyes of the beholder'" (Allen, 2008, p. 6), their text *Qualities of Effective Teachers* is in its second edition (2007). Apparently, the authors have discovered the magic formula for predicting teacher effectiveness. Their premise, however, "Unless we do, in fact, hire quality teachers, we all lose as our schools fail and children suffer" (Allen, 2008, p. 6), echoes the same equation posed earlier in this discussion. Pupils and schools fail because teachers fail.

$$\text{If } pfu = sfu, \text{ and } sfu = tfu, \text{ then } pfu = tfu.$$

In the following discussion, we explore the impact of four critical variables on urban teachers and urban teaching: politics, policy, pedagogy, and professionalism. First we define each of these variables and the power each has historically held and currently wields in the present state of urban teaching. We then explain the interrelationship among these variables with respect to power. Finally, we demonstrate that the most positive, critical, and powerful variable in this relationship is professionalism. This is not because of the deficit status, negative value, or predictive validity policy and pedagogy have assigned to teacher professionalism but because of the professionalism and commitment that the majority of urban teachers continue to demonstrate despite "the powerful political mythology touted consistently in the media that schooling is the most effective way to overcome social inequality" (Weiner, 2007, p. 5). Weiner

(2007) argues that there is "evidence that our educational system repro-
duces existing social relations a great deal more efficiently than it dis-
rupts them" (p. 5) and that urban pupil success is singularly the
responsibility of the urban teacher.

POLITICS, POLICY, PEDAGOGY AND PROFESSIONALISM: DEFINED AND DESCRIBED

Politics (P1) and Policy (P2)

Politics and policy are inextricably linked. Politics (*pŏlĭ-tĭks*) derived
from the Greek *politikos*, is the (1) art or science of government or governing, especially the governing of a political entity, such as a nation, and the
administration and control of its internal and external affairs;
(2) methods or tactics involved in managing a state or government;
(3) intrigue or maneuvering within a political unit or group in order to
gain control or power; and (4) the often internally conflicting interrela-
tionships among people in a society.[1] In this discussion, politics is defined
as the art of governing a nation through activities, methods, or tactics
involved in maneuvering to gain power and control over the educational
system and the resulting conflicts among related stakeholders in society,
specifically urban teachers. Historically, from Plato to the Puritans, from
charity to charter schools, from post-Civil War legislation to *Plessy vs. Fer-
guson*, politics have maneuvered local, state, and national education to
serve an agenda, seemingly to serve democracy and equity. Yet, politics
have consistently dictated inequitable funding and policies for urban
schools: "Children in one set of schools are educated to be governors;
children in the other set of schools are trained for being governed"
(Kozol, 1991, p.176). Although political decisions around schooling are
complex and multidimensional, these decisions for the most part have
been and continue to be driven by hegemonic principles established to
maintain the status quo.

Policy (pŏlĭ-sē) derived from Middle English *policie* and from the Old
French *police* is (1) a plan or course of action, as of a government, political
party, or business, intended to influence and determine decisions,
actions, and other matters; (2) a course of action, guiding principle, or
procedure considered expedient, prudent, or advantageous[2]; and (3) reg-
ulation and control the affairs of a community, especially with respect to
maintenance of order, law, health, morals, safety, and other matters
affecting the public welfare.[3] In this discussion, policy is a political course
of action that determines decisions, actions, procedures related to education designed to regulate and control the affairs of a community, to main-

tain order, law, health, morals, safety, and other matters affecting the public welfare. Policy manifests itself in the specter of educational reform. We use the term "specter" because like an apparition, it represents something that it is not, much like *Macbeth's* witches' paradoxical prophecy "fair is foul and foul is fair" (1.1.10). All appear "fair" and good intentioned, as they attempt to pass down the cultures, identities, and values of civilizations, serve democratic ideals (except in the case of national identity reforms), improve literacy, close achievement gaps, and level the playing field for all pupils, but run "foul" as transactions that exclude critical stakeholders from policy-making decisions (Friedman, 2004, Friedman, Galligan, Albano, & O'Connor, in press), serve business (O'Brien, 2003), foster individualistic, competitive, and hierarchical approaches to education, and marginalize further already disenfranchised pupils and teachers, specifically those in urban schools (Garth-McCullough, 2007; Nichols & Berliner, 2007; Payne & Kaba, 2007; Settlage & Meadows, 2002; Weiner, 2005). These top-down, bureaucratic reforms achieve limited success because they do not emerge from the very institutions they wish to reform (Cuban, 1993; Rowan, 1990; Stritikus & García, 2000; Tyack & Cuban, 1995;) as in the case of standardized curricula (pedagogy) and more recent, high-stakes testing (Nichols & Berliner, 2007; Weiner, 2005), and rhetoric that "pretends that schools can compensate for the array of savage economic and social problems that undercut children's school success, problems created and abetted by government policies" (Weiner, 2005, p. 5). This specter looms especially large in urban schools.

ESEA, ECIA, IASA, or NCLB: A Policy by Any Other Name?

Over the past five decades, the federal government has legislated several iterations of a major law resulting in significant policies designed to improve education for all students. In 1965, the Elementary and Secondary Education Act (ESEA) was the first federal law to fund K-12 public education. ESEA targeted disadvantaged schools based on pupils' socioeconomic status and established the beginning of Title I funding, to address the needs of low-income students. In 1978, ESEA was amended to allow schools with over 75% low-income pupils to use funds in schoolwide programs. In 1981, ESEA became the Education Consolidation and Improvement Act of 1981 (ECIA). Reenacted under Reagan's New Federalism, this law increased the role of state departments of education in allocating and redistributing funds away from urban areas and low-income students and eliminated parent advisory councils, specific accountability measures, and compliance standards in regulating earmarked funds for desegregation and educational research (Darling-Hammond & Marks, 1983). In 1994 under the Clinton administration, ECIA reinvented itself as the Improving America's Schools Act (IASA), whose purposes were to promote school-wide reform, ensure high standards for all children, align efforts of states, local educational agencies, and schools to enhance pupil achievement, coordinate health and social programs with education services, redirect more funding to high-poverty schools, require accountability measures (high-stakes testing) for both teachers and pupils, and barter increased decision-making authority to schools and teachers in exchange for improved pupil performance. This Act opened the door for school choice and charter schools and required that all students, including special needs and English language learners, pass high-stakes assessments in order receive an academic diploma. Funding to high-poverty schools increased from 43% to 50% under this act.

The current form of ESEA, embedded into No Child Left Behind (NCLB) bipartisan legislation, is designed to diminish the achievement gap and provide quality education with significant emphasis on high-stakes accountability measures. Signed into law in January of 2002, NCLB links "federal dollars to draconian penalties for schools that cannot meet a series of one-size-fits-all standards. These penalties especially hurt schools that take on the greatest educational challenges" (see http://www.nea.org/home/NoChildLeftBehindAct.html). NCLB, a top-down accountability movement, controls schools and assumes that only "tests, school report cards, rewards and sanctions" (Moe, 2003, p. 82), "political strategies designed to bring 'market reform' to public education" (Kapp, 2004, p. 55) will improve student achievement. Funded at $12.7 billion, NCLB reclassified schoolwide fund use from 75% of socioeconomically disadvantaged students to 40% of the student body being classified as poor (Stullich, Eisner, McCrary, & Roney, 2006, p.1). This mandate created an elaborate system of testing "with as many as forty different test score targets for each school" (p. 53) with arbitrary cut-off scores, that if not attained, resulted in school take-over, privatization or closure.

Informed by free market capitalism, NCLB assumes that schools should compensate for the "social problems that undercut children's school success, problems created and abetted by government policies" (Weiner, 2005, p. 5) and "wipe out inequalities while the factors that help produce them remain in place" (Kapp, 2004, p. 54). Furthermore, Adequate Yearly Progress (AYP), NCLB's formula for evaluating school performance, targets and further marginalizes special needs students, English language learners, pupils of color, and economically disadvantaged populations. Thus, while the government funds programs to develop high-stakes assessments and additional programs to help students pass tests, it refuses to support bilingual education measures, under-funds the Individuals with Disabilities Act (IDEA), and closes Head Start and other early childhood intervention programs that potentially improve the life chances of all children.

Pedagogy (*P3*)

Pedagogy (pĕdə-gŏjē, -gŏjē) derived from Old French *pédagogie* and from Greek *paidagōgiā*, from *paidagōgo*, slaves who took children to and from school, is (1) the art or profession of teaching; (2) preparatory training or instruction;[4] (3) the function or work of a teacher; teaching; (4) the art or method of teaching; pedagogics; and (5) the activities of educating or instructing; activities that impart knowledge or skill.[5] In this discussion, pedagogy refers to the activities of educating or instructing that impart knowledge or skill determined by politics, which are enacted in policy. Historically, politics and policy have dictated pedagogy. Although the purposes of school have varied somewhat, the underlying mission of curriculum and instruction has been to assimilate and acculturate citizens into prevailing and dominant cultural values, beliefs, and mores.

In *A Treatise on Pedagogy for Young Teachers*, (1884) Edwin C. Hewett, the President of Illinois State Normal University, defined pedagogy as "mean[ing not only] the science and art of teaching; but [also] the taking of young children, and, by means of both skillful teaching and wise training, leading them up to worthy manhood and womanhood" (see http://www.nimbus.org/ElectronicTexts/Hewett.Pedagogy.html). To accomplish this goal, a teacher must possess three distinct fields of knowledge:

> A knowledge of the being who is to be taught and trained, a knowledge of those branches ... by which his mental growth is to be promoted, and a knowledge of the proper methods by which the matter to be taught, and the being to be taught, shall be brought into the most healthful and fruitful relations to each other. (p. 1)

Hewett elaborates on what is to be taught, how it is to be taught, to what end it is to be taught, and what function the "pedagogue" is to play in this process. He concludes with 17 General and 12 Special Principles which essentially state that the purpose of education is to "perfect the individual" for a socially efficient society.

A Pedagogy of Testing

Despite ardent efforts to instantiate critical pedagogy as essential to education for critical citizenry in a global society (Folsom, 2007), not much has changed since Hewett's "Treatise." In fact, policy has legislated even more prescriptive pedagogies in efforts to assimilate, acculturate, and perfect the individual for participation in a socially efficient society. Since the enactment of Improving America's Schools Act (IASA), pedagogy has returned to the Stanford-Binet era of high-stakes testing, becoming a pedagogy unto itself. High-stakes testing links performance to pupils, schools, and teachers and uses resulting data to make decisions about pupil retention, assignment to remedial programs, high school graduation, and entry into postsecondary education. The impact on teachers includes performance evaluations; bonus pay; school, grade-level, and subject matter assignments; and professional status. Proponents argue that increased test scores evidence intended results, while critics contend that changes in test scores are subject to testing artifacts, shifts in the tested populations, and other factors. Critics also identify other effects, including pupil disengagement, dropping out, cheating; teacher stress and cheating; and focus on test preparation. Concerns also identify threats to privacy, individual rights, and freedoms posed by the collection and maintenance of data on individual performance by government institutions. Of particular note is that high-stakes testing encourages teaching to the test (McNeil, 2000). Proponents view this practice as a positive as it focuses teachers' and students' efforts toward higher achievement. Opponents assert that teaching to the test narrows curricula, constrains innovation and creativity among students, limits the view of student capabilities, and assails teacher autonomy and professionalism. In one example, Virginia Beach, Virignia parents became irate because schools had taken away their children's recess to focus more time on teaching to the test; recess was restored, but this demonstrates that school boards will go to irrational and developmentally inappropriate lengths to assure that pupils meet state and federal standards (Sinha, 2000). Reville (2007) suggests that a reformed NCLB should "right-size" school days to meet the needs of today's students, which include educating not only in core subjects, but also in the arts.

In order to assure that NCLB reform policies are being implemented, the federal government (politics) established a set of 24 policy indicators that characterize trends in standards-based policymaking in all 50 states, which have been tracked since 1997 (Swanson, 2006). In essence, the government has developed pedagogy to measure the measurement of the measures. These indicators address four core areas: standards, assessments, accountability, and teacher quality. Each state receives a point for each year it implements standards-based policies in these four core areas. Since 1997, Massachusetts initially placed and has remained at the top with 10 points, while Montana has earned only 3 points, with states averaging approximately 8 points. Swanson (2006) also cites evidence derived from refined regression analyses that there has been a

> consistently positive [and significant, $p < .10$] relationship between achievement gains and the implementation of standards-based policies related to academic-content standards, aligned assessments, and accountability [three of the four core areas] measures ... [with more] robust achievement in mathematics compared to reading [as measured by National Assessment of Educational Progress]. (p. 9)

It is important to note that this level of significance is hardly significant in light of urban pupil performance. Grade 4 students in large urban districts score 17 percentage points lower in reading and 15 percentage points lower in mathematics than peers across the nation, while Grade 8 students in metropolitan districts score 15 percentage points lower in reading and 21 percentage points lower in mathematics (see Table 11.1).

Despite policies and pedagogies designed to improve pupil learning, urban pupil achievement in reading and mathematics is still below the national average, suggesting that perhaps high-stakes testing and subsequent pedagogies are punishing our pupils. More critical to urban school pupil achievement is the fact that money, publicity, and essential resources have shifted away from schools to the testing industry, further exacerbating the education of poor and minority children (McNeil, 2000, 2001, 2004).

Another serious outcome of high-stakes testing and educational reform is what Hargreaves (2000) calls "intensification" or mandated, sometimes ineffective, prescriptive pedagogies designed "neither [to] address the inadequate conditions present [in schools] or [to] assist new teachers in finding a personally meaningful teaching style" (p. 119). Many of these approaches conflict with pupil-centered methodologies and best practices advocated by professional organizations, such as the National Council of Teachers of Mathematics, National Council of Teachers of English, and International Reading Association (Costigan, 2004). New teachers' prac-

Table 11.1.   Reading and Mathematics Performance in Public Schools by Urbanicity (Districts That Enroll at Least 2.5 Million Pupils)

	Average % Below Basic Skills in Reading Central City Schools	Average % Below Basic Skills in Reading All Public Schools	Average % Below Basic Skills in Mathematics Central City Schools	Average % Below Basic Skills in Mathematics All Public Schools
Grade 4	55	38	43	28
Grade 8	43	28	44	13

tices are imposed rather than "organically developed understandings" (Costigan, 2008, p. 86). Furthermore, imposed practices often contradict more constructivist methodologies learned in teacher education coursework (Weiner et al., 2001) and more significantly "do nothing to enhance understandings of students, their lives or their home communities, which, in turn, do a frank injustice to students from poor urban communities" (p. 98). As Bracey (2000) argues, "Under the gun of the tests, teachers are abandoning their usual curricula and modes of teaching to lecture about test-oriented material" (p. 1). High-stakes tests also dilute the curriculum especially in high-poverty schools where teaching to and preparing for the test have replaced important curriculum (Orfield & Wald, 2001, p.1).

The Reading First initiative, one of the largest programs created under NCLB, designed to establish "research-based" reading programs for K-3 students, replaced widely used reading programs because its stronger "focus on improving classroom teachers' instruction skills with emphasis on consistent and coherent reading instruction for all children" (Kauerz, 2002, p.4) would improve pupils' reading achievement. Restricting teachers' pedagogical autonomy, Reading First's curriculum incorporates direct instruction with scripted lessons, an "approach that should not be used all of the time, for all educational objectives, or for all students" (Joyce & Weil, 2003, p. 313), and ineffectively addresses the academic learning needs of disadvantaged students (Dudley-Marling & Paugh, 2005). In the meantime, suburban school students are exposed to meaningful, quality instruction devoted to interacting with language-rich texts. Despite $900 million spent annually (Barone, Hardman, &Taylor, 2006) assessment data indicate that Reading First has not diminished the achievement gap as the "national average remains flat in reading" (Lee, 2006, p. 10). Hargreaves and Shirley (in press) suggest that government should invest in living conditions and medical care: "Years of research in school effectiveness still show that most of the explanation for differences in student outcomes exists *outside* the school" (p. 171). Investment in broader social services would potentially lead to more students having access to a quality education.

Prescribed pedagogy portray teachers as passive recipients of external knowledge (Fullan & Hargreaves, 1996). When change venues deemphasize or ignore teacher knowledge and expertise and view teaching as a technocratic cadre of skills, they deprofessionalize teachers, devalue their expertise, and cast them in a deficit light. One teacher observed:

> The demands and requirements placed on our young learners have multiplied and both the students and teachers are wearing out under the pressure.... A well-planned, scripted lesson might be the most perfect lesson,

but if it isn't something that is right for the kids and you, then the lesson will more than likely be ineffective. (Friedman et al., in press)

Craig (2004) recounts elementary urban teachers' observations that being forced to implement mandated prescriptive curricula was "like being visited by the plague" or "[being] under siege" (p. 1252). Bullough, Burbank, Gess-Newsome, Kauchak, and Kennedy (1998) concluded that in Utah and Florida, linking classroom teaching more closely to higher standards has led to "translated [teaching practice] into trivial performance-based behaviors" (Weiner et al., 2001, p. 645). Ironically, mandated initiatives have forced many teachers to become slaves to pedagogy, a bizarre twist to the Greek derivation, *paidagōgos*, (slaves who took children to and from school), posed earlier in this section. Instead of developing artful practice in service of developing critical citizens, teachers have been relegated to implementing dictates of national, state, and local policies legislated by market-driven politics, practices that, more often than not, contradict teachers' philosophical beliefs.

Professionalism (P4)

Professionalism (prə-fĕshə-nə-lĭzəm) derived from Middle English *professen*, to take vows, from Old French *profes*, that has taken a religious vow (from Medieval Latin *professus*, avowed), and from Medieval Latin *professāre*, to administer a vow, and from Latin, *professus* to acknowledge, is (1) professional status, methods, character, or standards; (2) the use of professional performers, as in athletics or in the arts;[6] (3) the expertness (skillfulness by virtue of possessing special knowledge) characteristic of a professional person; and (4) the standards, views, and behavior of one who engages in an activity.[7] In this discussion, professionalism is the status, methods, character, views, expertness, and behavior of urban teachers that implement pedagogy in a manner that is conducive to learning and committed to the highest standards of educational practice.

That states enact plans to assure that all teachers are highly qualified, especially those serving minority and children in high-poverty schools, is at the heart of NCLB. In 2006, the federal government mandated that all states submit plans that outlined metrics for identifying districts that lacked highly qualified teachers and actions to assure that 100% of teachers would be highly qualified. Desiring highly qualified teachers seems logical given that scholars have observed that teacher effectiveness is critical to pupil achievement (Darling-Hammond, 2000; Darling-Hammond, Berry, & Thoreson 2001; Darling-Hammond & Youngs, 2002; Wayne & Youngs, 2003). Yet, in a study using general hierarchical linear modeling, findings indicated that education, years of experience, and race had little impact on student achievement (Muñoz & Chang, 2007, p. 157). Still others note that the complexity of teaching (Cochran-Smith & Zeichner, 2005) and teacher effectiveness depend on a variety of variables such as teacher achievement level, pedagogical content knowledge, and context, (Marzano, Pickering, & Pollock, 2001; Stronge & Hindman, 2006), with school-level factors impacting pupil achievement above and beyond that of individual teacher-level characteristics. Defining and measuring highly qualified teachers has become as critical as measuring pupil performance via high-stakes testing (Stairs, 2003). As mentioned earlier, some researchers have gone as far to create a Teacher Quality Index (Stronge & Hindman, 2006), which provides administrators a protocol for hiring the most highly qualified teacher.

Kennedy (2008) argues, "The problem is that *teacher quality* has become such a ubiquitous term that it lacks a clear meaning" (p. 59). Definitions of teacher quality vary according to stakeholders. Those who hire look for credentials, test scores, and education. Administrators define teacher quality as the quality of classroom practice. Politicians and policymakers view a quality teacher as one who effectively raises pupil achievement via test scores or who "subscribe[s] to [politicians' and policymakers'] particular beliefs and values" (p. 59). Kennedy offers a taxonomy, which includes personal resources (beliefs, attitudes, values, personality traits, education), performance (daily practice), and effectiveness (impact on pupils). Her bottom line, however, is that we need "a coherent strategy for orchestrating our assessments into coherent systems that ultimately enhance the qualities we value most" (p. 63) especially if the goal is to hire high-quality teachers to serve pupils in high-poverty schools. Thus, if federal, state, and local institutions can operationalize the variable of teacher quality, they will be able to measure "it," use "it" to sort out existing and/or hire/fire effective/ineffective teachers, and voilà, raise pupil tests scores on high-stakes assessments, ultimately improving the life chances of marginalized pupils. Underlying this research is the premise that pupil failure = teacher failure.

What is ironic is that the most critical variable in pupil achievement, the teacher, is repeatedly excluded from the very democratic process designed by politicians and enacted in policy that evaluates their personal traits, measures their performance, and determines their effectiveness. Teachers are not "actors" in the process, but rather "objects" of the process. Despite disparaging media critique, legislated deprofessionalization, and repeated exclusion from the ideals they are charged to serve and uphold, many continue to work in places where "democracy is subverted, domination takes place, and human relations are manipulated" (Kincheloe, 1999, p. 71). Although schools have moved far from "visions of civic education that emphasize uniquely democratic forms of participation, debate, and action" (Kahne & Westheimer, 2003, p. 40), many teachers continue to champion integration, rather than annihilation or absorption of differences, live democratic values, accomplish democratic goals in daily life, and view the relationship between education and democracy as inextricable, with democracy being a moral way of living realized through continued and deep inquiry and collaboration.

Friedman et al. (in press) in a case study of 9 urban and 10 suburban/urban teachers identified four teacher subcultures of democratic practice amidst the turbulence of educational reform: subculture of compliance, subculture of noncompliance, subculture of subversion, and subculture of democratic inquiry and practice. Most prevalent among teachers were subcultures of subversion and democratic inquiry and practice. In a subculture of subversion, although teachers perceive that mandated pedagogies do not effectively and justly address the needs of the diverse learners they serve, they ostensibly comply, but within the confines of the classroom, modify prescriptive pedagogy to accommodate the needs of their learners, thus creating a subculture of subversion. Although seemingly democratic as this approach best serves pupils in the classroom, it does not serve the school community, profession, and society writ large. Potentially best practices remain in the teachers' classrooms, not subject to rigorous inquiry and examination that may lead to enhancement and proliferation, increased pupil achievement, and improved teacher efficacy. Additionally, such behavior, when discovered, exposes the teacher to critique and reprisal from administrators who are pressured to enact local, district, and state mandates within the context of transactional leadership (Friedman, 2004).

In the subculture of democratic inquiry and practice, teachers practice democracy by conducting systematic and comparative inquiry into mandated and personal pedagogy. They systematically inquire into practice to compare a variety of constructs and conceptualizations of pupil learning and achievement. Based on evidence, they either implement the new initiative, refuse to implement the new initiative, or modify the initiative to serve their pupils most effectively. Such teachers collaborate with others and subject personal practice to scrutiny. This reflective and systematic approach allows for teachers to practice democracy in a way that teaches for, participates in, acts for, and models democracy for pupils, colleagues, and the greater community. It lives democratic ideas of collaboration, contributes to unity and serves the greater mission of acting for social justice by improving instruction and the success of urban pupils. These teachers are "socially and politically critical and responsible, professionally competent and in touch with contemporary developments" (Hargreaves, 2003, p. 55). Furthermore, such teachers have significant impact on the success of reform initiatives (Coburn, 2004; Datnow, Hubbard, & Mehan, 2002; Fullan, 1993; Fullan & Hargreaves, 1996; Hargreaves, 2003; Olson, 2002; Spillane, 1999) and are the most critical agents of practice reform and ultimate power brokers in policy enactment (McLaughlin, 1990; Schwille et al., 1983).

Although teachers are often not part of policy and pedagogy brokering, they demonstrate a strong sense of professionalism based on a commitment to personal beliefs about teaching and learning. This professionalism appears in communities of inquiry and practice, instructional leadership teams and transformative action (Friedman, 2004), and personalized environments that enhance education for "disenfranchised students in large urban districts" (Garth-McCullough, 2007, p. 268). As a result of a local university and urban high school collaboration, seven teachers have become National Board Certified (Friedman et al., in press). Their motivation was to demonstrate that despite consistent attacks against their professional identity and competence, they indeed met the nation's highest professional standards for teaching and deserved to be among those who served urban pupils.

Professionalism also takes the form of teacher-leadership. Recognizing the competence of teachers and innovative schools, Boston Public School leaders have established grants for "Discovery Schools," which allow faculty to have autonomy in making decisions about pedagogy based on data comprised of multiple formative and summative assessments that truly show what pupils know and are able to do. Teachers, who have a role in pedagogical decision-making and feel supported in their school contexts, are more likely to impact pupil achievement on multiple measures more positively (Rex & Nelson, 2004). Assessment systems that involve the day-to-day input of professionals as opposed to those identified as high-stakes can serve as more useful, credible, and dependable monitors of pupil learning and achievement Linn (2000).

PROFESSIONALISM (P4) > POLITICS (P1) + POLICY (P2) + PEDAGOGY (P3): THE POWER OF PROFESSIONALISM (P4)

During a recent conversation with an assistant headmaster at a local urban, public high school (personal communication, January 15, 2009), she explained the series of "budget cuts in human and material resources being implemented" noting that "many of our teachers received 'pink slips'" and continued, "we are being hit hard, losing new teachers and more experienced ones, good teachers who really care about the students and their success." When asked how the teachers were handling the cuts, she replied: "These teachers are professionals. They will continue to work hard and serve our students, regardless of what is happening. That is why we hate to lose any one of them!"

Current research in complexity theory best describes urban teachers as a complex adaptive system. In complexity theory, systems are constructed by control parameters that are both external and internal. For example, urban school systems are constructed and constrained by external forces such as politics, policy, and pedagogy. These systems are further impacted by internal factors, teacher-shared beliefs and values, such as "all students can learn" or "these pedagogies need modification to address the needs of diverse learners." All factors function as control parameters but to no truly predictable end as complex systems are non-linear and unexplained by simple causality (Buell & Cassidy, 2001; Phelps & Hase, 2002). Chaos (unpredictability), which is always present in a system, is not a negative term but rather describes the complexity, connectedness, and contiguousness of the relationships and forces that exist within a system, especially in urban schools. Complexity theory further assumes that feedback such as reciprocity, recursion, and reiteration is always occurring among agents within the system; this permits systems "to [re]frame themselves, and thus continue to develop, progress, and emerge" (Smitherman, 2004, p. 11). Urban teachers working together in a professional learning community are more effective at educating students collectively than when working in isolation. As collaborative professionals, they form a complex adaptive system, which is synergistic, creating a whole that is greater than the sum of its parts. These systems are not hierarchical as "[t]here seems to be no evidence that self-adapting, complex systems have a governing leadership" (McVey, 2004, p. 6). All teachers function in some capacity as leaders in the system; transformational or distributed leadership is present throughout and among all agents. Teachers are not only educating pupils, but are also directing professional development, solving dilemmas of practice, and modifying policy and pedagogy.

For a complex adaptive system to survive, its agents must have enough in common to interact and "compensate for one another's lapses" (Davis & Sumara, 2005, p. 316). We argue that it is urban teacher professionalism that has accommodated and compensated for the lapses of politics, policy, and pedagogy and the various "fractals" or patterns of ineffective behavior that appear at different system levels (Davis & Sumara, 2000). Politics and NCLB policy have legislated pedagogy of high-stakes assessment, which in most cases, has punished urban pupils and urban schools (Adams, 1995; Darling-Hammond, 2000; Dunne, 2000; Kapp, 2004; McNeil, 2001, 2004; Payne & Kaba, 2007). In many instances, it is urban teachers who have modified pedagogy either through a subculture of subversion or a subculture of democratic inquiry and practice to ensure that they as professionals implement the best and most culturally relevant practices of the profession to provide pupils with access to effective curriculum and instruction. When faced with new policies or educational challenges, urban teachers use holistic, specific, local, diverse knowledge of pupils, context, community, content, pedagogy, and the profession— knowledge that politicians who legislate policy do not possess—to resolve issues: "When a complex system [urban teachers] is faced with a problem, an adequate solution [is] found in these pools of diversity" (Davis & Sumara, 2005, p. 316).

Previous discussion has explained the historically pervasive and powerful role politics has played in forming educational policy and the widespread pedagogical initiatives policy has enacted. In terms of power, it might be hypothesized that politics and policy hold greater value; yet, it is professionalism—the status, methods, character, views, expertness, and behavior of urban teachers who implement pedagogy in a manner that is conducive to learning and committed to the highest standards of educational practice—that exerts the most significant influence on pupil learning and achievement. Einstein observed that doing the same thing over and over again, knowing that the results will be the same, is *insanity*. For centuries, politics and policy have dictated educational insanity, moving the quintessential pendulum to and fro maintaining a status quo, but it is teacher professionalism, the ability of urban teachers to adapt to roller coasters of initiatives, mandates, media critique, and public bashing, that leads to pupil learning. Although politics, policy, and pedagogy have failed, it is a powerful sense of professionalism that informs teachers to do the right thing, implying that:

Professionalism *(P4)* > Politics *(P1)* + Policy *(P2)* + Pedagogy *(P3)*.

NOTES

1. For source of definition see http://www.ask.com/web?q=dictionary%3A +politics&content=ahdict%7C45767&o=0&l=dir
2. For source of definition see http://www.ask.com/web?q=dictionary%3A +policy&content=ahdict%7C40407&o=0&l=dir
3. For source of definition see http://www.merriam-webster.com/dictionary/ police
4. For source of definition see http://www.ask.com/web?q=dictionary%3A +pedagogy&content=ahdict%7C27907&o=0&l=dir
5. For source of definitions (3), (4), and (5) see http://www.thefreedictionary .com/pedagogy
6. For source of definition see http://www.ask.com/web?q=dictionary%3A +professionalism&content=ahdict%7C20375&o=0&l=dir

7. For source of definitions (3) and (4) see http://www.thefreedictionary.com/
    professionalism

REFERENCES

Adams, D. W. (1995). *Education for extinction.* Lawrence, KS: University Press.

Allen, R. (2008). Giving all students high quality teachers. *Education Update, 50*(3), 4-6.

Barone, D., Hardman, D., & Taylor, J. (2006). *Reading First in the classroom.* Boston, MA: Pearson.

Bracey, G. (2000). *High stakes testing.* Retrieved from http://epicpolicy.org/files/cerai-00-32.html

Buell, M. J., & Cassidy, D. J. (2001). The complex and dynamic nature of quality in early care and educational programs: A case for chaos. *Journal of Research in Childhood Education, 15*(2), 209-221.

Bullough, R. V., Burbank, M., Gess-Newsome, J., Kauchak, D., & Kennedy, C. (1998). What matters most: Teaching for America's future? A faculty response to the report of the National Commission on Teaching and America's Future. *Journal of Education of Teaching, 24*(1), 7-33.

Coburn, C. E. (2004). Beyond decoupling: Rethinking the relationship between the institutional environment and the classroom. *Sociology of Education, 77,* 211-244.

Cochran-Smith, M., & Zeichner, K. M. (2005). *Studying teacher education: The report of the AERA panel on research and teacher education.* Mahwah, NJ: Erlbaum.

Costigan, A. (2004). Finding a name for what they want: A study of New York City's teaching fellows. *Teaching and Teacher Education: An International Journal of Research and Studies, 20*(2), 129-143.

Costigan, A. T. (2008). Canaries in the coal mine: Urban rookies learning to teach language arts in "high priority" schools. *Teacher Education Quarterly, 35*(2), 85-103.

Craig, C. J. (2004). The dragon in school backyards: The influence of mandated testing on school contexts and educators' narrative knowing. *Teachers College Record, 106*(6), 1229-1257.

Cuban, L. (1993). *How teachers taught: Change and constancy in American classrooms.* New York, NY: Teachers College Press.

Darling-Hammond, L. (2000). Teacher quality and student achievement: A review of state policy evidence. *Education Policy Analysis Archives, 8*(1). Retrieved from http://epaa.asu.edu/epaa/v8n1

Darling-Hammond, L., Berry, B., & Thoreson, A. (2001). Does teacher certification matter? Evaluating the evidence. *Educational Evaluation and Policy Analysis, 23,* 57-77.

Darling-Hammond, L., & Marks, E. L. (1983). *The new federalism in education: State responses to the 1981 Education Consolidation and Improvement Act.* Report prepared for the U.S. Department of Education. CA: Rand. 1-107.

Darling-Hammond, L., & Youngs, P. (2002). Defining "high qualified teachers": What does "scientifically-based research" actually tell us? *Educational Researcher, 31*(9), 13-25.

Datnow, A., Hubbard, L., & Mehan, H. (2002). *Extending educational reform: From one school to many.* New York, NY: Routledge.

Davis, B., and Sumara, D. (2000). Curriculum forms: On the assumed shapes of knowing and knowledge. *Journal of Curriculum Studies, 32*(6), 821-46.

Davis, B., & Sumara, D. (2005). Challenging images of knowing: Complexity science and educational research. *International Journal of Qualitative Studies in Education, 18*(3), 305-321.

Diamond, J. B., & Spillane, J. P. (2004). High-stakes accountability in urban elementary schools: Challenging or reproducing inequality? *Teachers College Record, 106*(6), 1145-1176.

Dudley-Marling, C. & Paugh, P. (2005). The rich get richer; the poor get direct instruction. In B. Altwerger (Ed.), *Reading for profit* (pp. 156-171). Portsmouth, NH: Heinemann.

Dunne, D. W. (2000, June 29). Are high-stakes tests punishing some students? *Education World.* Retrieved from http://www.educationworld.com/a_issues/issues093.shtml

Folsom, C. (2007). Moving teacher education forward: A model for a new pedagogy. *Teacher Education and Practice, 20*(3), 320-333.

Friedman, A. A. (2004). Beyond mediocrity: Transformational leadership within a transactional framework. *International Journal of Leadership in Education: Theory and Practice, 7*(3), 203-224.

Friedman, A. A., Galligan, H.T., Albano, C.M., & O'Connor, K. (in press). Teacher subcultures of democratic practice amidst the oppression of educational reform. *Journal of Educational Change.*

Fullan, M. (1993). *Change forces: Probing the depths of educational reform.* Levittown, PA: Taylor and Francis.

Fullan, M., & Hargreaves, A. (1996). *What's worth fighting for in your school?* New York, NY: Teachers College Press.

Garth-McCullough, R. (2007). More with less: Urban teacher experiences in a new small school. *Negro Educational Review, 58*(3-4). 253-271.

Hargreaves, A. (2000). *Changing teachers, changing times: Teachers' work and culture in the postmodern age.* New York, NY: Teachers College Press.

Hargreaves, A. (2003). *Teaching in a knowledge society: Education in the age of insecurity.* New York, NY: Teachers College Press.

Hargreaves, A., & Shirley, D. (in press). *The fourth way: The long-awaited end of standardization and the inspiring future of educational change.*

Joyce, B., & Weil, M. (2003) *Models of teaching* (7th ed.). Boston, MA: Allyn & Bacon.

Kahne, J., & Westheimer, J. (2003). Democracy and civic engagement—what schools need to do. *Phi Delta Kappan, 85*(1), 34-44.

Kapp, S. (2004). NCLB's selective vision of equality: Some gaps count more than others. In D. Meier & G. Wood (Eds.), *Many children left behind: How the No Child Left Behind Act is damaging our children and our schools* (pp. 53-65). New York, NY: Beacon.

Kauerz, K. (2002). *Literacy No Child Left Behind policy brief.* Denver, CO: Education Commission of the States.

Kennedy, M. M. (2008). Sorting out teacher quality. *Phi Delta Kappan, 90*(1), 59-63.

Kincheloe, J. L. (1999). Critical democracy and education. In J.G. Henderson & K. R. Heeson (Eds.), *Understanding democratic curriculum leadership* (pp. 70-83). New York, NY: Teachers College Press.

Kozol, J. (1991). *Savage inequalities: Children in America's schools.* New York, NY: Crown.

Lee, J. (2006). *Tracking achievement gaps and assessing the impact of NCLB on the gaps: An in-depth look into national and state reading and math outcome trends.* Cambridge, MA: The Civil Rights Projects at Harvard University.

Linn, R. (2000). Assessments and accountability. *Educational Researcher, 29*(2), 4-16.

Marzano, R. J., Pickering, D. J., & Pollock, J. E. (2001). *Classroom instruction that works: Research-based strategies for every teacher.* Alexandria, VA: ASCD.

McLaughlin, M. W. (1990). The Rand Change Agent study revisited: Macro perspectives and microrealities. *Educational Researcher, 19*(9), 171-178.

McNeil, L. M. (2000). Contradictions of school reform: Education costs of standardized testing. New York, NY: Routledge.

McNeil, L. M. (2001). Contradictions of school reform: Educational costs of standardized testing. *Journal of Educational Change, 2*(1), 75-88.

McNeil, L. (2004) Faking equity: High-stakes testing and the education of Latino youth. In A. Valenzuela (Ed.), *Leaving children behind: Why Texas-style accountability fails Latino youth* (pp.57-111). Albany, NY: SUNY Press.

McVey, R.S. (2004, April). Classroom teams in the context of self-organizing, complex systems. Paper presented at the meeting of the American Educational Research Association, San Diego, CA.

Moe, T. (2003). Politics, control, and the future of school accountability. In P. E. Petersen & M. R. West (Eds.), *No Child Left Behind: The politics and practice of school accountability* (pp. 80-106). New York, NY: Brookings Institution.

Muñoz, M. A., & Chang, F. C. (2007). The elusive relationship between teacher characteristics and student academic growth: A longitudinal multilevel model for change. *Journal of Personnel Evaluation in Education, 20*, 147-164.

Nichols, S. L., & Berliner, D. C. (2007). *Collateral damage: How high stakes testing corrupts America's schools.* Cambridge, MA: Harvard Education Press.

O'Brien, L.M. (2003). Teacher education for a democratic society. *Childhood Education, 79*(6), 376-379.

Olson, J. (2002). Systematic change/teacher tradition: Legends of reform continue. *Journal of Curriculum Studies, 34*(2), 129-137.

Orfield, G., & Wald, J. (2001, April). High-stakes testing. *Motion Magazine.* 1-2.

Payne, C., & Kaba, M. (2007). So much reform, so little change: Building-level obstacles to urban school reform. *Social Policy, 37*(3/4), 30-37.

Phelps, R., & Hase, S. (2002). Complexity and action research: Exploring the methodological and theoretical connections. *Educational Action Research, 10*(3), 507-522.

Reville, P. (2007). Stop the narrowing of the curriculum by 'right-sizing' school time. *Education Week, 27*(9), 30-36.

Rex, L. A., & Nelson, M. C. (2004). How teachers' professional identities position high-stakes test preparation in their classrooms. *Teachers College Record, 106*(6), 1288-1331.

Rowan, B. (1990). Commitment and control: Alternative strategies for the organizational design of schools. *Review of Research in Education, 16*, 353-389.

Sandholtz, J. H., Ogawa, R. T., & Scribner, S. R. (2004). Standards gaps: Unintended consequences of standards-based reform. *Teachers College Record, 106*(6), 1177-1202.

Schwille, J., Porter, A., Floden, R., Freeman, D., Knappen, L., Kuhs, T., & Schmidt, W. (1983). Teachers as policy brokers in the content of elementary school mathematics. In L. Shulman & G. Sykes (Eds.), *Handbook of teaching and policy* (pp. 370-371). New York, NY: Longman.

Settlage, J., & Meadows, L. (2002). Standards-based reform and its unintended consequences: Implications for science education within America's urban schools. *Journal of Research in Science Teaching, 39*, 114-127.

Sinha, V. (2000, March 21). Give kids recess, Virginia Beach parents urge. *Norfolk (VA) Virginia-Pilot*, B1.

Smitherman, S. (2004, April). *Chaos and complexity theories: A conversation.* Paper presented at the meeting of the American Educational Research Association San Diego, CA.

Spillane, J. P. (1999). External reform initiatives and teachers' efforts to reconstruct their practice: The mediating role of teachers' zones of enactment. *Journal of Curriculum Studies 31*(2), 143-175.

Stairs, A. J. (2003). The controversy around defining "highly qualified" teachers and one university's definition in practice. *Teacher Education and Practice, 16*(4), 384-398.

Stronge, J. H., & Hindman, J. L. (2006). *The teacher quality index: A protocol for teacher selection.* Alexandria, VA: Association for Supervision and Curriculum Development.

Stritikus, T., & García, E. E. (2000). Education of limited English proficient students in California schools: An assessment of the influence of Proposition 227 on selected teachers and classrooms. *Bilingual Research Journal, 24*(1 & 2), 1-11.

Stullich, S., Eisner, E., McCrary, J., & Roney, C. (2006). *National assessment of Title I interim report to Congress: Volume 1: Implementation of Title I.* Washington, DC: U.S. Department of Education, Institute of Education Sciences.

Swanson, C.B. (2006, January). *Making the connection: A decade of standards-based reform and achievement.* Retrieved from http://www.centerforpubliceducation .org/site/c.kjJXJ5MPIwE/b.1536671/k.9B6A/Research_review_Effects_ of_highstakes_testing_on_instruction.html

Tyack, D., & Cuban, L. (1995). *Tinkering toward utopia: A century of public school reform.* Cambridge, MA: Harvard University Press.

Wayne, A. J., & Youngs, P. (2003). Teacher characteristics and student achievement gains: A review. *Educational Research, 73*, 89-122.

Weiner, L. (2005). Neoliberalism, teacher unionism, and the future of public education. *New Politics, 10*(38). Retrieved from http://www.wpunj.edu/~newpol/issue38/weiner38.html

Weiner, L. (2007). Neoliberalism, teacher unionism, and the future of public education. *New Politics, 10*(2). Retrieved from http://www.wpunj.edu/newpol/issue38/weiner38.html

Weiner, L., Rand, M., Pagano, A., Obi, R., Hall, A., & Bloom, A. (2001). Illuminating the impact of state educational policy promoting school reform on curriculum and instruction in programs of urban teacher preparation. *Educational Policy, 15*(5), 644-673.

CHAPTER 12

CONCLUSION

Developing Synergy
Between Learning and Context

Kelly A. Donnell and Andrea J. Stairs

Our purpose in editing this book has been to highlight research on urban teacher learning over time in a way that recognizes the often complicated and always complex nature of the topic. We hope that readers have been informed and inspired to continue the difficult work of theorizing, studying, and supporting urban teacher learning, always keeping in mind the pressing need to retain qualified, committed urban teachers. We believe the future of urban education depends on all of us moving forward with this agenda. Reflecting upon the major themes of this volume has led us to hypothesize about a new way of understanding beginning teachers' learning in urban contexts. In particular, we are interested in the situated nature of learning, the synergistic interplay between learning and context, and strengthening the research agenda on urban teacher learning.

Research on Urban Teacher Learning: Examining Contextual Factors Over Time
pp. 191–197
Copyright © 2010 by Information Age Publishing

THE SITUATED NATURE OF LEARNING

The studies in this volume have reinforced the initial assumption of this text: that learning is situated in context. For several decades there have been differing assumptions about what it means to learn and know, high-lighted in scholarly debates about cognitive and situated theories of learning. Cobb and Bowers (1999) have suggested two core metaphors representing these debates: knowledge as an entity and knowing as an activity. We believe the empirical research shared in this text suggests that urban teacher learning is not represented by discrete pieces of knowledge but by teachers' grappling with professional decisions that take into account all of their knowledge, skills, commitments, and dispositions while situated within their social context. We agree with Putnam and Borko (2000) who posit that "the physical and social contexts in which an activity takes place are an integral part of the learning that takes place within it" (p. 4).

More recent work in cognitive science has recognized learning as an active, constructive process and situated theories as particularly useful in longitudinal studies of learning to teach because they focus on how teach-ers learn in various settings (Feiman-Nemser, 2008). The studies collected here have closely considered the how and why of situated urban teacher learning, suggesting a new, synergistic model for conceptualizing the situ-ated nature of learning.

THE SYNERGISTIC INTERPLAY BETWEEN LEARNING AND CONTEXT

Synergy (from the Greek syn-ergos, συνεργος meaning working together) is the term used to describe a situation where different entities cooperate advantageously for a final outcome. Simply defined, it means that the whole is greater than the individual parts.[1]

The scholarship on teacher learning concurs that teachers learn by undergoing some form of change or growth (Kagan, 1992; Richardson & Placier, 2001). As we stated in the introduction, how teachers *acquire* this change and *utilize* this growth is where the literature diverges. In this vol-ume of research, we have asserted that it is vital to determine what and how teachers learn about teaching within the conditions and contexts of urban education, an area which few scholars have examined. The studies in this volume illuminate the potential for what we believe is a more pow-erful synergistic relationship between the context of urban teaching and urban teacher learning.

A synergistic relationship assumes an iterative process in which the context and conditions have a dynamic influence on the learners (here assumed to be teachers), and what and how they learn. As an iterative process, the teachers can then also influence the context and conditions of the workplace. Quite simply, the resulting whole is greater than the individual parts (learning and context). A synergistic view of teacher learning in context recognizes the complexity of the issues—making each urban context, each individual classroom unique and highlighting the situated nature of learning. Learning more about the synergistic interplay between teachers and the contexts and conditions in which they teach and learn can provide insights into supporting their abilities and growth.

The recent focus on support for individual teacher learning over time, as exemplified in promising research on induction models (see, for example, Moir & Gless, 2001) is an exciting and critical next step, as is the growing body of literature on the role of working conditions (see, for example, Hirsch & Emerick, 2006; Ingersoll, 2004). Leithwood (2006) captures the recent directions in theory and research:

> There is good evidence to show that teachers' working conditions matter because they have a direct effect on teachers' thoughts and feelings — their sense of individual professional efficacy, of collective professional efficacy, of job satisfaction; their organizational commitment, levels of stress and burn-out, morale, engagement in the school or profession; and their pedagogical content knowledge. These internal states are an important factor in what teachers do and have a direct effect on what happens in the classroom, how well students achieve, and their experience of school. "Teachers' working conditions are students' learning conditions." Working conditions matter! (pp. 88-89)

One of the contributions of the emerging body of literature on supporting teacher learning is its active response to "our pervasive and long-standing failure to recognize and respond to variations in the effectiveness of our teachers" (Weisberg, Sexton, Mulhern & Kelling, 2009, p. 2). As these authors remind us, teachers are learners—thoughtful, individual professionals, not "widgets"—interchangeable parts of equal effectiveness. The research in this volume highlights the idea that focusing on both improved induction and working conditions, among other factors, has powerful potential to further our understanding of the iterative nature of synergistic learning and practice.

For example, Dunn illuminates this idea from her emic, urban teacher's perspective. Her learning was a highly individualized and transformative process, focusing on relationships with students, "managing" her classroom, and working within the bureaucratic system. The teachers in Tricarico and Yendol-Hoppey's study, second career candidates in high-needs areas, found the degree of satisfaction over setting and meeting their teaching goals required them to be self-directed learners. Self-efficacy and the degree of control over their own teaching and the barriers they faced were key to teacher learning. In Meller's chapter, one teacher learned that complex pedagogies such as critical literacy practices do not come with instructions, teachers' guides, or a checklist but that with time, support, and reflection beginning urban teachers can continually improve critical literacy practice even with small initial steps.

However, a cautionary note is in order: a synergistic relationship between teacher learning and context does not necessarily result in an educative, productive outcome. The teacher may mediate the conditions of his or her practice in a way that results in miseducative learning. In arguing for the situated, social processes of teacher learning, Rosaen and Florio-Ruane (2008) draw upon Dewey's concept of "educative experience" (p. 707). Dewey, as the first educational philosopher to stress the importance of situation in learning, recognized that the situation itself is not educative, but the way the learner cocreates meaning by linking language, experience, and the development of thought creates meaningful learning. We believe the same can be said for urban teachers who are in the midst of the synergistic, iterative process of learning to teach.

For example, as Pardo's chapter concludes, the pressure from colleagues influenced the teacher in her study to go against her own instructional goals, often in miseducative ways. Similar findings were reported by Meller as her participant struggled to implement critical literacy. However, several studies in this volume bear out the exciting and generative transformations that can result from positive synergy. We see in both Stairs' and Ross, Dodman, and Vescio's chapters that the synergistic learning that resulted from positive conditions in an urban professional development school and early experience in high-needs schools, respectively, were productive and educative.

The literature on the conditions and contexts of urban schools reinforces the notion that supportive workplace conditions can improve retention (Hirsch & Emerick, 2007). It also reminds us about the power dynamics involved:

> Schools are not simply victims of inexorable demographic trends, and there is a significant role for the management and organization of schools in both the genesis of, and the solution to, school staffing problems. In sum, the data suggest that improvements in the above aspects of the teaching job would contribute to lower rates of turnover, diminish school staffing problems and, hence, ultimately aid the performance of schools in high-poverty communities. (Ingersoll, 2004, p. 15)

People in positions of power make important decisions regarding contexts and conditions that directly affect teachers, as Friedman and Daniello point out in their chapter, and teacher education is one arena for addressing these decisions with beginning teachers. In Mueller's study, for example, as teachers became better able to address urban conditions they became advocates for student learning over time. Similarly, in Ross, Dodman, and Vescio's chapter, participants chose to teach in high-needs schools and were more successful as a result of prior experiences in congruent school contexts. Working in urban school contexts can provide opportunities for beginning teachers to become learners and professionals.

EDUCATIVE OR MISEDUCATIVE? STRENGTHENING THE RESEARCH AGENDA

As noted above, the new, synergistic view of learning we propose assumes that the context and learner cooperate advantageously, one influencing the other in positive ways to ultimately create more powerful learning and working conditions for teachers, students, and all school personnel. As was made evident in the studies shared in this text, each urban context presents some common and yet some unique challenges for teacher learning over time. The goal is for the dynamic learning process to encourage positive growth, which requires a determined focus on the educative nature of learning experiences over the miseducative. Donnell's conceptual framework outlined in this text reinforces the need to better understand how and when the synergistic relationship between teachers and their working conditions results in educative rather than miseducative learning about urban practice. A synergistic view of learning in the urban context affords teachers openings to apply their learning in ways that alter their conditions, and therefore, promote more educative learning opportunities in an ongoing, cyclical process.

In light of the authors' work included in this text, some implications for further research have become apparent. First, we suggest expanding smaller studies that view beginning teachers as both professionals and learners who are mediating the conditions and contexts of their learning. We do not mean to suggest that small studies such as many included here are not critical to moving the research agenda forward. Rather, we think studies of varying sizes will increase the complexity of the topic and provide further findings perhaps not captured in this collection. This is difficult with longitudinal work, and with a lack of funding in the area of urban teacher learning it is plausible that smaller studies will remain the trend for the foreseeable future. Nevertheless, studies of any size that follow teachers over time are most important for continuing to develop a richer picture of the phenomenon.

Second, and related to the first point, we suggest researchers explore avenues for establishing research teams and/or collaboratives on the topic of urban teacher learning over time. With a concerted, collective effort by contributors and readers of this book, the body of research in this area has the potential for limitless growth and resulting practice and policy implications. With the many recent technological advances, it is easier than ever before for people around the country and the world to connect in real time. Utilizing technologies to connect scholars who then collaboratively design and conduct research around common research questions explored in various contexts would contribute greatly to the research agenda.

Third, we suggest using a range of methodological approaches in future research. This text centered primarily on qualitative work, often in case study format. It may be possible for researchers to collaborate in ways that draw upon what may be learned from quantitative and mixed-methods studies, similar to Ross, Dodman, and Vescio's contribution in this text. Some questions we are left with that could be answered by employing a range of methodological approaches are, What is the impact of varying contexts of teacher preparation, induction, and professional development that effectively help teachers mediate their contexts in educative ways? What additional contexts and conditions are educative for urban teachers, and how can we assure their effective implementation and development? How are students impacted by teachers who experience a synergistic interplay between learning and context?

It is our hope that the findings from research in this volume will engender discussion and further research on new professional norms and the influence of contexts, conditions, and resources in urban schools. Consideration of context and conditions is increasingly seen as a critical aspect of enhanced teacher learning and improved teacher performance, increased student achievement, and success for traditionally underserved student populations. We believe that continued focus on the synergistic interplay between urban teacher learning and context will contribute to improved urban education for all.

NOTE

1. Definition obtained from http://en.wikipedia.org/wiki/Synergy.

REFERENCES

Cobb, P., & Bowers, J. (1999). Cognitive and situated learning perspectives in theory and practice. *Educational Researcher, 28*(2), 4-15.

Feiman-Nemser, S. (2008). Teacher learning: How do teachers learn to teach? In M. Cochran-Smith, S. Feiman-Nemser, D. J. McIntyre & K. E. Demers (Eds.), *Handbook of research on teacher education: Enduring questions in changing contexts* (3rd ed., pp. 697-705). New York, NY: Routledge, Taylor & Francis Group and the Association of Teacher Educators.

Hirsch, E., & Emerick, S. (2007). *Teacher working conditions are student learning conditions: A report on the 2006 North Carolina Working Conditions Survey.* Retrieved from www.teachingquality.org

Ingersoll, R. (2004). *Why do high-poverty schools have difficulty staffing their classrooms with qualified teachers?* Washington, DC: Center for American Progress and the Institute for America's Future.

Kagan, D. M. (1992). Professional growth among preservice and beginning teachers. *Review of Educational Research, 62*(2), 129-169.

Leithwood, K. (2006). *Teaching working conditions that matter: Evidence for change.* Toronto, Ontario, Canada: Elementary Teachers Federation of Ontario.

Moir, E., & Gless, J. (2001). Quality induction: An investment in teachers. *Teacher Education Quarterly, 28*(1), 109-114.

Putnam, R. T., & Borko, H. (2000). What do new views of knowledge and thinking have to say about research on teacher learning? *Educational Researcher, 29*(1), 4-15.

Richardson, V., & Placier, P. (2001). Teacher change. In V. Richardson (Ed.), *Handbook of research on teaching* (4th ed., pp. 905-947). Washington, DC: American Educational Research Association.

Rosaen, C., & Florio-Ruane, S. (2008). The metaphors by which we teacher: Experience, metaphor, and culture in teacher education. In M. Cochran-Smith, S. Feiman-Nemser, D. J. McIntyre & K. E. Demers (Eds.), *Handbook of research on teacher education: Enduring questions in changing contexts* (3rd ed., pp. 706-731). New York, NY: Routledge, Taylor & Francis Group and the Association of Teacher Educators.

Weisberg, D., Sexton, S., Mulhern, J., & Kelling, D. (2009). *The widget effect: Our national failure to acknowledge and act on differences in teacher effectiveness.* Brooklyn, NY: The New Teacher Project.

ABOUT THE CONTRIBUTORS

Frank Daniello is a doctoral student in curriculum and instruction at the Lynch School of Education at Boston College. His research and scholarly interests are in educational leadership, policy, school reform, and curriculum theory.

Stephanie L. Dodman is a doctoral student at the University of Florida in curriculum, teaching, and teacher education. Her research interests surround the preparation of preservice teachers for educational equity and the pedagogy and retention of teachers in high-poverty schools.

Kelly A. Donnell is an assistant professor of education at Roger Williams University. Her research interests include urban teacher learning, self-study, and mentors and cooperating teachers as teacher educators.

Alyssa Hadley Dunn is a doctoral student in educational studies at Emory University and a former high school English teacher in DeKalb County, Georgia. Her research interests include foreign teacher recruitment and preparation, multicultural education, and urban teacher education.

Nancy File is an associate professor and program director of early childhood education at the University of Wisconsin-Milwaukee. Her research examines teaching/learning processes in the classroom and teacher professional development.

Audrey A. Friedman is an associate professor of teacher education, special education, and curriculum and Instruction at the Lynch School of Education at Boston College. Her scholarship addresses teacher decision making about dilemmas of practice and curriculum reform.

Wendy B. Meller is an assistant professor in early childhood education at Rowan University. Her research and scholarly interests are in early literacy practices and urban education.

Jennifer Mueller is an assistant professor of teacher education at the University of Wisconsin–Milwaukee. Her research focuses on the role of teacher candidate identity in how candidates approach their teacher preparation and professional development, particularly in relationship to multicultural education.

Laura Pardo is an associate professor of education at Hope College where she teaches literacy methods and content area reading courses. Her research interests include beginning teachers, book club as an instructional model, and learning to teach in urban settings.

Dorene D. Ross is an Irving and Rose Fien Professor of Education in the College of Education at the University of Florida. Her research and practice are focused around the preservice and inservice preparation of teachers to work with children who are growing up in poverty.

Andrea J. Stairs is an assistant professor of literacy education in the College of Education and Human Development at the University of Southern Maine. Her research interests include urban teacher learning, teacher education in professional development schools, and teacher research in literacy.

Katie Tricarico is a doctoral fellow at the University of Florida. Her research interests include alternative teacher certification and issues involving equity in schools.

Vicki Vescio is a doctoral candidate at the University of Florida in curriculum, teaching, and teacher education. Her main areas of research interest are connected to working with preservice and inservice teachers in ways that help to support the learning of students across contexts of diversity.

Debora Wisneski is an assistant professor of early childhood education at the University of Wisconsin-Milwaukee. Her research interests include collaborative classroom research with teachers and children exploring the areas of classroom community building and play.

Diane Yendol-Hoppey is a professor of education and director of the Benedum Collaborative at West Virginia University. Her professional interests include practicing and prospective teacher inquiry-oriented professional development that strengthens both teacher leadership and school improvement.

INDEX

LaVergne, TN USA
03 May 2010

181375LV00002B/11/P